THE ACA FARMERS' HANDBOOK 2024

Agricultural Consultants
— **Association** —

Published for The Agricultural Consultants Association
by
TNS Training Projects Limited
Block 3, The Presbytery,
Castle Street,
Carrick-on-Suir,
Co. Tipperary.
Tel (051) 645705
Email: info@farmershandbook.ie
Web: www.farmershandbook.ie

Published 2023 by
TNS Training Projects Limited
Block 3, The Presbytery,
Castle Street,
Carrick-on-Suir
Co. Tipperary

© TNS Training Projects Ltd. 2023

ISBN
9781999-839550
ISSN 1649-6752

This book is intended as an aid to farmers and those involved in providing services to the farming community and is based on our understanding of current regulation and practice. While every effort has been made to ensure accuracy, the authors or publisher will not accept any liability for loss, distress or damage resulting from any errors or omissions.

2024
12–15 NOVEMBER
HANOVER, GERMANY

THE WORLD'S LEADING TRADE FAIR

SAVE THE DATE!

we innovate
animal farming

   www.eurotier.com

MADE BY

The Production Team

Principal Author

Martin O'Sullivan has been a practising agricultural consultant for over 40 years specialising in farm business and taxation. Along with his farm consultancy duties he is also a partner in O'Sullivan Malone, Accountants & Statutory Auditors based in Carrick on Suir and is a bi-weekly farm business columnist with the Farming Independent. He has been the principal author of the Farmers' Handbook since its inception thirty one years ago. He holds an honours degree in Agricultural Science (UCD), a Diploma in Forensic Accounting from Chartered Accountants Ireland and a diploma in Financial Services (UCD). He is a former president of the Agricultural Consultants Association (ACA) having held the office on two occasions.

Collaborators/Contributors

Diarmuid Foley B.Agr. Sc, Paddy Bruton B.Agr.Sc. (Forestry), Tadgh Dooley M.Agr. Sc., (Forestry), Dr. Tom Butler M.Agr.Sc. PhD, PJ Phelan B.Agr. Sc, Tom Ryan B.Agr. Sc, Barry Lonergan HCBS, BBS, ACA, CTC. Angela Casey Agricultural Consultants Association, John Butler, Kiely Gaule Financial Services Department of Social Protection, Teagasc & The Department of Agriculture, Forestry & the Marine, The entire team at O'Sullivan Malone & Co.

Advertising & Media Manager — Angela Casey

Design, Layout, Commercial & PR — IFP Media

The authors particularly wish to acknowledge the assistance given by the staff of Teagasc and the Department of Agriculture, Food & the Marine. Without their most willing co-operation the completion of this handbook would not have been possible.

Forestry Services Ltd.
Experienced Professionals

Forestry Services Ltd are the First Private Forestry Company in Ireland to achieve 'Dual Certification in Forest Management'.

Sustainable	Forest	Management

Biodiversity	Financial Return	Professionals

"We are now welcoming new members to our Group Certification Scheme"

Foreword by Minister Charlie McConalogue

Agri-food is Ireland's largest indigenous exporting sector and plays a vital role in Ireland's economy. Over the past number of years, the sector has faced several challenges, but the agri-food sector has demonstrated its resilience and continues to go from go from strength to strength.

The new CAP Strategic Plan will provide almost €10bn to our farming families over the next five years, supporting them to continue producing safe, nutritious and high-quality food to the best environmental standards. Budget 2024 demonstrates my unwavering commitment to our beef and sheep farmers. In this context I was pleased to announce that I have provided targeted supports of more than €118m for the livestock sectors. I will continue to provide the €200 per cow payment delivered in 2023. In addition, I intend to provide an additional payment for sheep farmers which, together with the current Sheep Welfare Scheme payments, will result in a payment equivalent to €20 per ewe in 2024. This will be the highest payment ever provided to our vitally important sheep sector. Total expenditure for my Department in 2024, including direct payments, will be some €3.1 billion.

It is important that we also make progress on longer term challenges. My Department remains focused on delivering the ambition of "Food Vision 2030 – A World Leader in Sustainable Food Systems". Food Vision charts a pathway to sustainability in all its dimensions – environmental, economic and social – and it places farm families right at its core.

I continue to work closely with my colleague the Minister for Finance on taxation issues relating to the agri- food sector. I am pleased with the renewal of the Consanguinity Relief for another five years. Generational renewal is a key policy objective for agriculture, nationally and in the EU. This measure encourages the lifetime transfer of farms, thereby enhancing generational renewal in the sector. The longer timeframe for its renewal will bring more certainty to farming families as they plan for their future. In this regard I should also mention the Succession Planning Advice Grant (SPAG), which supports those seeking succession planning advice.

I also welcome recent revisions to limits under the EU State aid regulations which provide additional support to young farmers. The aggregate lifetime amount of relief for the Young-Trained Farmers Stock Relief, Succession Farm Partnerships Tax Credit and the Young-Trained Farmers Stamp Duty Relief will be increased from €70,000 to €100,000.

I was pleased to secure the renewal of another important relief, the Acceleration of Capital Allowances for Farm Safety Equipment and changes to long-term leasing. I would also like to remind farmers that Accelerated Capital Allowances for Slurry Storage will be available for another two years. In addition, the extension by the Minister for Finance of the liability date for the Residential Zoned Land Tax provides an opportunity for people to engage with the process during 2024.

I would also like to mention that we have just launched the €500 million "Growth and Sustainability Loan Scheme" (GSLS), a long-term loan scheme that facilitates strategic investments by farmers, fishers, foresters and food businesses to assist with investment for growth and resilience, as well as for climate action and environmental sustainability.

I am delighted to again provide a foreword for the Farmers Handbook and Tax Guide and I look forward to working with all agri-food stakeholders in the coming year.

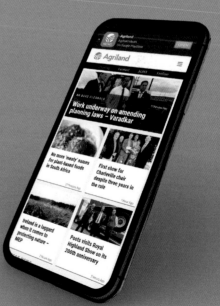

CONTENTS

Useful Tables & Charts ....

Chart 1 - Income Tax - Personal Tax Credits 18
Chart 2 - Income Tax Rate Bands 20
Chart 3 - Capital Acquisition Tax Thresholds 21
Chart 4 - Capital Gains Tax Payment Dates 21
Chart 5 - Welfare Rates & Benefits 22
Chart 6 - Conversion Factors 23
Chart 7 - Loan Repayment Amounts 24
Calendar 2024 26
ACA Member's Register 2023/24 29

Farm Subsidies, Supports & Incentives

CAP Reform Programme 2023-2027 – Main features 38
Basic Income Support for Sustainability (Biss) 39
Entitlements 40
Complementary Redistributive Income Support for Sustainability (CRISS) 43
Complementary Income Support Young Farmers (CIS-YF) 44
Agri-Climate Rural Environment Scheme (ACRES) 48
Organic Farming Scheme 52
On-Farm Capital Investment Scheme TAMS 3 53

Farm Enterprise Planning & Budgets

Effective Farm Planning 70
Dairying 72
Beef Production 78
Sheep Production 88
Tillage Crops 92

PART 1

PART 2

A national team of dedicated experts.

With over 30 offices across Ireland, our clients have access to a network of expertise across a broad range of sectors - from agribusiness and farming to renewable energy and food production. Our roots within each of our communities means we have deep local understanding and knowledge.

Speak with one of our team and see how we can help your business grow.

Contact us on **1800 334422** or visit **www.ifac.ie**

OUR OFFICES

Leinster

Bluebell, Dublin 12
Carlow, Co. Carlow
Drogheda, Co. Louth
Enniscorthy, Co. Wexford
Agri Practice, Danville, Co. Kilkenny
SME/Audit, Danville, Co. Kilkenny
Payroll Services, Danville, Co. Kilkenny
Mullingar, Co. Westmeath
Portlaoise, Co. Laois
Trim, Co. Meath
Tullamore, Co. Offaly
Wicklow, Co. Wicklow

Connacht

Athenry, Co. Galway
Balla, Co. Mayo
Collooney, Co. Sligo
Roscommon, Co. Roscommon

Munster

Bandon, Co. Cork
Blarney, Co. Cork
Cahir, Co. Tipperary
Farm Support, Cahir, Co. Tipperary
Dungarvan, Co. Waterford
Ennis, Co. Clare
Limerick City
Mallow, Co. Cork
Nenagh, Co. Tipperary
Skibbereen, Co. Cork
Templemore, Co. Tipperary
Tralee, Co. Kerry

Ulster

Cavan, Co. Cavan
Monaghan, Co. Monaghan
Raphoe, Co. Donegal

Stay in touch

ifac.ie   🐦 @ifac_Ireland   f @ifacIreland   in @ifac-Ireland   T 1800 334422

CONTENTS

PART 3

Farm Management Data
Agricultural Contractor Charges 106
Value of Slurries, Manure & Fertilisers 108
Feedstuffs & Forage Production Costs 109

PART 4

Farm Buildings
Crop & Forage Space Requirements 114
Animal Housing _ Space Requirements.. 115
Guide to Cost of Farm Buildings... 116
Planning Permission Requirements 117

PART 5

Farming and the Law
The Civil Court System... 121
Public Liability 122
Public Roads 124
Trees 124
Agricultural Vehicles 126
The Land 127

PART 6

Education: Third Level Courses & Grants
Third Level Grants.. 131
Assessment of Means 133
Student Holiday Earnings 133
Renewing Grants 133
Teagasc Course Charges 134

NATIVE TREE AREA SCHEME OPEN

It pays to plant trees. Plant one hectare of native trees and receive premiums of €22,060 over ten years subject to terms and conditions.

Also grants for planting costs and fencing. No afforestation licence required.

Explore your options at
www.gov.ie/forestry

Rialtas na hÉireann
Government of Ireland

CONTENTS

PART 7

Farming in Harmony with the Environment

Organic Farming 137
Advice, Training And Support 141
Protection of Water Regulations 142
Stocking & Fertiliser Restrictions 144
Measures to Prevent Pollution 146
Nitrates Derogation 148
Installation of Solar Panels 150

PART 8

Forestry

Ireland's Forest Industry 155
Afforestation (New Planting) 156
Native Tree Area Scheme (Nta) 158
Woodland Environmental Fund (WEF) 158
Environmental Report Grant (ERG) 158
Taxation of Forestry 162

PART 9

Farm Business Management

Trading & Collaborative Structures for Farmers 164
Employing Farm Labour 174
Employer's Obligations And Worker's Rights 176
Farm Relief Services 179
Farm Safety 180
Children on Farms 180
Older People on Farms 182

PART 10

Succession & Estate Planning

Planning for Succession 185
Banking Issues 189
Taxation Benefits for Timely Transfers 189
Retirement Relief (S598) 190
Gift Tax 190
Inheritance Tax Insurance (S72 Policy) 191
Valuing Farm Property 192
Income Tax Benefits and Consequences of Transferring 192

Get Training from Approved Trainers from Teagasc, ACA or Independent Advisors

- Develop your skills
- Protect yourself and your family
- Learn about safe slurry handling
- Understand the risks in farming
- Comply with safety legislation

Book Training with Teagasc or ACA.

Complete the electronic Risk Assessment Online at
www.farmsafely.com

An tÚdarás Sláinte agus Sábháilteachta
Health and Safety Authority

CONTENTS

PART 11

Wills and Estate Planning

Making Your Will 195
Entitlements Under a Will 199
Challenging a Will 201

PART 12

Pensions, Welfare & Health Benefits

State Benefits & Welfare Entitlements 204
State Health Benefits & Services 221
Acquiring Health Care Abroad 226
Benefits & Services for the Elderly 227

PART 13

Taxation

Income Tax 237
Taxation of Separated and Divorced Persons 239
Personal Tax Credits 2024 240
Personal Tax Reliefs 2024 242
Other Farm Tax Credits & Reliefs 245
Tax-Free or Tax Efficient Activities 252
Employing Family Members 255
Forming a Limited Company 259
Tax Relief Check List 264
Capital Acquisitions Tax 264
Capital Gains Tax 273
Some General Points on Capital Gains Tax 282
Stamp Duty 283
Stamp Duty - Points to Note 286
Self Employed PRSI 286
Value Added Tax 290
Universal Social Charge (USC) 291

Chart 1: Income Tax Credits.

	2020 €	2021 €	2022 €	2023 €	2024 €
Personal Tax Credits					
Single person	1,650	1,650	1,700	1,775	1,875
Married couple	3,300	3,300	3,400	3,550	3,750
Widowed person (year of bereavement)	3,300	3,300	3,400	3,400	3,600
Widowed person (subsequent years)	2,190	2,190	2,240	2,240	2,415
First year after bereavement	3,600	3,600	3,600	3,600	3,600
Second year after bereavement	3,150	3,150	3,150	3,150	3,150
Third year after bereavement	2,700	2,700	2,700	2,700	2,700
Fourth year after bereavement	2,250	2,250	2,250	2,250	2,250
Fifth year after bereavement	1,800	1,800	1,800	1,800	1,800
Single Person Child Carer	1,650	1,650	1,650	1,650	1,750
Other Allowances /Credits					
Dependent relative allowance	70	245	245	245	245
Incapacitated	3,300	3,300	3,300	3,300	3,500
Blind person	1,650	1,650	1,650	1,650	1,650
Both spouses blind	3,300	3,300	3,300	3,300	3,300
Age Allowance - Single / widowed	245	245	245	245	245
Married	490	490	490	490	490
Employee allowance	1,650	1,650	1,700	1,775	1,875
Home Carer	1,600	1,600	1,600	1,700	1,800
Earned Income Credit	1,500	1,650	1,700	1,775	1,875

Chart 2: Income Tax Rates & Bands.

2022	2023	2024
Single/Widow(er) €36,800 @ 20% Balance @ 40%	Single/Widow(er) €40,000 @ 20% Balance @ 40%	Single/Widow(er) €42,000 @ 20% Balance @ 40%
Married Couple (a)[1]€45,800 @ 20% (b)[2]€73,600 @ 20% Balanace @ 40%	Married Couple (a)[1]€49,000 @20% (b)[2] €80,000 @ 20% Balance @ 40%	Married Couple (a)[1]€51,000 @20% (b)[2] €82,000 @ 20% Balance @ 40%
Lone/Widowed/Parent €40,800 @ 20%	Lone/Widowed/Parent €44,000 @ 20%	Lone/Widowed/Parent €64,000 @ 20%

[1] (a) denotes single income couples [2] (b) denotes two income couples

Chart 3: Capital Acquisition Tax Thresholds.

Relationship to donor	Up to 9/10/2019	From 9/10/2019
Son, daughter or favourite niece or nephew	€320,000	€335,000
Brother, Sister, Niece, Nephew or Grandchild	€32,500	€32,500
Others	€16,250	€16,250

Chart 4: Capital Gains Tax - Payment Dates.

Disposal	Tax due by:
On or before 30 November in the tax year -Initial Period	15th December in that tax year.
From 1 December to 31 December in the tax year -Later Period	31st January in the following tax year

Chart 5: Pensions & Benefits.

Pension or Benefit	2023 €	2024€
Old Age Contributory Pension		
(i) Under 80:- Weekly Rate		
Personal rate	265.30	277.30
Qualified adult allowance (under 66)	176.70	184.70
Qualified adult allowance (66 or over)	237.00	248.60
(ii) 80 or over:- Weekly Rate		
Personal Rate	275.30	287.30
Person with qualified adult under 66	452.00	472.00
Person with qualified adult 66 or over	512.30	535.90
Widow's/Widower's Contributory Pension		
Under 66- Weekly Rate	225.50	237.50
66 and under 80	265.30	277.30
80 and over	275.30	287.30
Increase for a qualified child (under 12)	€42	€46
Increase for a qualified child (over 12)	€50	€54
Carer's Allowance		
Personal Rate (under age 60) - Weekly rate	236.00	248.00
Personal Rate (over age 60) - Weekly Rate	274.00	286.00
Maternity Benefit		
Personal Rate - Weekly	262.00	274.00
Farm Assist		
Personal Rate- Weekly Rates	220.00	232.00
Person with qualified adult	366.00	386.00
Qualified child increase (Under 12/over 12)	46/54	46/54
Child Benefit - Monthly Rates		
Per child	140 ea.	140 ea.

Chart 6: Conversion Factors.

To Convert	Multiply By	To Convert	Multiply By
inches to centimetres	2.54	cu. cm. to cu. inches	0.06102
centimetres to inches	0.3937	cu. feet to cu. metres	0.02831
feet to metres	0.3048	cu. metres to cu. feet	35.3147
metres to feet	3.2808	cu. yards to cu. metres	0.7646
yards to metres	0.9144	cu. metres to cu. yards	1.3079
metres to yards	1.09361	cu. inches to litres	0.1638
miles to kilometres	1.60934	litres to cu. inches	61.03
kilometres to miles	0.62317	gallons to litres	4.545
sq. in. to sq. centimetres	6.4516	litres to gallons	0.22
sq. cm. to sq. inch	0.15499	ounces to grams	28.3495
sq. metres to sq. feet	10. 7638	grams to ounces	0.03528
sq. feet to sq. metres	0.092903	pounds to grams	453.592
sq. yards to sq. metres	0.836103	grams to pounds	0.03528
sq. metres to sq. yards	1.19599	pounds to kilograms	0.4536
sq. miles to sq. km.	2.5899	kilograms to pounds	2.2046
sq. km. to sq. miles	0.386103	tons to kilograms	1,016.05
acres to hectares	0.40468	kilograms to tons	0.00098
hectares to acres	2.47105	acres to hectares	0.4046

Chart 7: Table of Half Yearly Repayments.

Six monthly loan repayments per €1,000 borrowed						
Years	3%	4%	5%	6%	7%	8%
2	258	263	268	272	276	281
3	174	179	183	187	190	194
4	133	137	141	142	145	148
5	107	111	115	116	122	124
6	92	95	98	100	103	106
7	81	83	86	88	92	95
8	71	74	77	79	82	86
9	63	67	71	75	76	80
10	57	61	64	66	70	74
11	54	57	60	63	66	70
12	50	53	56	59	62	65
13	46	50	53	57	60	63
14	44	47	51	54	57	60
15	42	45	48	52	55	59
16	40	43	47	50	53	56
20	34	37	40	43	46	50

FBA | LABORATORIES

Carrigeen Industrial Estate, Cappoquin, Co. Waterford
Tel. 058 52861, Fax. 058 52865
E- mail. fbaadmin@fba-labs.com www.fba-labs.com

Agricultural and Environmental Analysts

- Soil analysis packages for grassland and arable crop production.

- Comprehensive assessment of Soil Health includes determination of Carbon: Nitrogen ration, Base Saturation, Cation Exchange Capacity, Texture, Biological Activity tests for Carbon and Nitrogen.

- Soil mineral values, both required and antagonostic, for grassland and arable crop production.

- Silage tests for nutritive value with supplementary feed recommendations.

- Pre-ensilability test for grass silage.

- Drinking water, Soiled Water, Effluent and Slurry Testing.

Laboratory INAB accredited and
Department of Agriculture approved for soil analysis.
AHI designated for BVD and Johne's Disease testing.

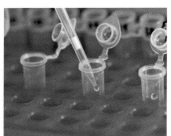

CALENDAR 2024

JANUARY						
S	M	T	W	T	F	S
	1	2	3	4	5	6
7	8	9	10	11	12	13
14	15	16	17	18	19	20
21	22	23	24	25	26	27
28	29	30	31			

FEBRUARY						
S	M	T	W	T	F	S
				1	2	3
4	5	6	7	8	9	10
11	12	13	14	15	16	17
18	19	20	21	22	23	24
25	26	27	28	29		

MARCH						
S	M	T	W	T	F	S
					1	2
3	4	5	6	7	8	9
10	11	12	13	14	15	16
17	18	19	20	21	22	23
24	25	26	27	28	29	30
31						

APRIL						
S	M	T	W	T	F	S
	1	2	3	4	5	6
7	8	9	10	11	12	13
14	15	16	17	18	19	20
21	22	23	24	25	26	27
28	29	30				

MAY						
S	M	T	W	T	F	S
			1	2	3	4
5	6	7	8	9	10	11
12	13	14	15	16	17	18
19	20	21	22	23	24	25
26	27	28	29	30	31	

JUNE						
S	M	T	W	T	F	S
						1
2	3	4	5	6	7	8
9	10	11	12	13	14	15
16	17	18	19	20	21	22
23	24	25	26	27	28	29
30						

JULY						
S	M	T	W	T	F	S
	1	2	3	4	5	6
7	8	9	10	11	12	13
14	15	16	17	18	19	20
21	22	23	24	25	26	27
28	29	30	31			

AUGUST						
S	M	T	W	T	F	S
				1	2	3
4	5	6	7	8	9	10
11	12	13	14	15	16	17
18	19	20	21	22	23	24
25	26	27	28	29	30	31

SEPTEMBER						
S	M	T	W	T	F	S
1	2	3	4	5	6	7
8	9	10	11	12	13	14
15	16	17	18	19	20	21
22	23	24	25	26	27	28
29	30					

OCTOBER						
S	M	T	W	T	F	S
		1	2	3	4	5
6	7	8	9	10	11	12
13	14	15	16	17	18	19
20	21	22	23	24	25	26
27	28	29	30	31		

NOVEMBER						
S	M	T	W	T	F	S
					1	2
3	4	5	6	7	8	9
10	11	12	13	14	15	16
17	18	19	20	21	22	23
24	25	26	27	28	29	30

DECEMBER						
S	M	T	W	T	F	S
1	2	3	4	5	6	7
8	9	10	11	12	13	14
15	16	17	18	19	20	21
22	23	24	25	26	27	28
29	30	31				

Connecting colleagues
and delegates from the
four corners of Ireland

MIDLANDS
PARK
HOTEL

Town Centre, Potlaoise, Co. Laois   www.midlandsparkhotel.com

Noel Feeney

President ACA

The Agricultural Consultants Association (A.C.A.) is the professional body representing the majority of private agricultural consultants operating in the Republic of Ireland. All members are required to hold a level 8 University Degree in an appropriate discipline, have at least two years relevant experience, hold professional indemnity insurance and observe a strict code of professional standards and behaviour and comply with the association's programme of Continuous Professional Development. Members provide advice, technical and administrative support to over 50,000 farmers in Ireland through a network of over 160 member firms employing in excess of 300 professional staff.

Services Provided

- Farm planning and technical advice in all areas of farming.
- Forestry consultancy, acquisitions, planting & management.
- Land valuations
- Farm buildings and yards, layout and planning.
- Laboratory analysis of agricultural products and inputs.
- Farm Accounts and Taxation Services
- Assisting and advising farmers on EU and Government funded schemes.
- Farm training courses & Knowledge Transfer Facilitation
- Compulsory acquisition orders (CPO's) – assessment and negotiation.
- Expert witness reporting and court attendance.
- Project management and new business set-up services.
- Environmental consultancy including preparation of environmental impact statements and integrated pollution control license applications.

Further information from the ACA Secretariat Office on 051- 645705 or email acaservices@aca.ie Website: www.aca.ie

AGRICULTURAL CONSULTANTS ASSOCIATION MEMBERS REGISTER

The following register includes full member whose membership is current as at the 1st November 2023. Members whose names appear on this list participate in the association's continuous professional development programme.

CARLOW
David Ashmore, Church Rd, Bagenalstown, Co. Carlow.	059-9721378
Brendan Reid, Leinster Co-op Mart,Killeshin Road, Co. Carlow.	087-1010455
Jane Peppard, Church Rd, Bagenalstown, Co. Carlow.	087-4523084

CAVAN
Oliver Crowe, CC Consultants Ltd., Killeshandra, Co. Cavan.	049-4334462
Pat Fitzpatrick, Aughacashel, Ballyjamesduff, Co. Cavan.	049-8544387
Kieran McCluskey, Carrickmacross Road, Shercock, Co. Cavan.	042-9691915
Tom Canning, Farranlady, Co. Cavan.	086-3825944
David Clarke, Kilcully, Ballyjamesduff, Co. Cavan.	086-8309698
Aidan Brady, Drumnagar House, Tullyco. Coothill, Co. Cavan.	087-6300480
John Callaghan, Main St., Kingscourt, Co. Cavan.	042-9668892
Jonathan Anderson, Corlisbrattan, Arva, Co. Cavan.	087-9787354
Helen Corcoran, CC Consultants Ltd, Kildallan, Co. Cavan.	086-0579992
Sinead Edwards, Killycrin, Bawnboy, Co. Cavan.	087-0565723
Annie Brady, Gallon, Carrickaboy, Cavan, Co. Cavan.	086-2481669

CLARE
Patrick Carrucan, Fanore, Craggagh, Co. Clare via Galway.	087-2894031
Pat McMahon, 54 Cathedral Court, Clare Road, Ennis, Co. Clare.	065-6823449
Denis Touhy, Market Square, Scariff, Co. Clare.	086-8925915
Niamh Grogan, Bealcragga, Connolly, Ennis, Co. Clare.	087-7424030
Siobhan Daly, Derrynavaha, Fanore, Co. Clare.	087-2083744
Michael Kelly, 54 Cathedral Court, Clare Road, Ennis, Co. Clare.	086-1693811
Ruairi O'Sullivan, 54 Cathedral Ct, Clare Road, Ennis, Co. Clare.	086-8181766

CORK
Michael Brady, Brady Group, The Lodge, Lee Road, Cork.	021-4545120
John Broderick, Ballymartin, Dungourney Co. Cork.	021-4668222
Patrick Fitzsimons, 32 Grand Parade, Cork.	087-2241106
Claire Greehy, Railway View, Macroom, Co. Cork.	087-2657089
William Martin, 16 St.Patrick's Hill, Cork.	021-4501338
Tony Murphy, Greengold Farm Advisors, Macroom, Co. Cork.	026- 23274
John O'Connell, Oatencake, Midleton, Co. Cork.	086-3067663

AGRICULTURAL CONSULTANTS ASSOCIATION MEMBERS REGISTER

CORK, contd.,

Owen O'Driscoll, 17 Bridge St, Skibbereen, Co. Cork.	028-23283
Valerie O'Neill, Skehanagh, Watergrasshill, Co. Cork.	086-3992537
Ricky Roycroft, Barleyfield, Kilbrittain, Co. Cork.	023-8849000
Fergus Blake,Charleville Busines Centre, Charleville, Co. Cork.	063-81188
Liam John Hennessy, FDC House, Kanturk, Co. Cork.	086-7742274
Patrick McCarthy, Glenangus, Adrigole, Skibbereen, Co. Cork.	087-2535690
Donal Corkery, Millstreet, Co. Cork.	087-0523601
Julie Roche, Brittas, Lombardstown, Mallow, Co. Cork.	086-2202475
Donal Corkery, Carrigaunroe, Shanballymore, Mallow, Co. Cork.	086-3363195
Sean O'Mahony, 7 Bayview, Clonakilty, Cork.	086-8118975
Adrian Buckley, Knockgorm, Drimoleague, Co. Cork.	086-8761864
Declan Dunne, Derreenataggert, Castletownbere, Co. Cork.	086-1655856
Brendan Crowley, Barrakilla, Ardgroom,Bearra, Co. Cork.	086-0386285
Tony Barry, Ahabeg, Waterfall, Castletownbere, Co. Cork.	086-1217324
Julia Drislane, Liss, Araglen, Fermoy, Co. Cork.	086-0676625

DONEGAL

Gary Grant, Gortanny, Quigley's Point, Co. Donegal.	074-9130772
Dale Hutchinson, Drumwell Ho., Gleneely, Carndonagh, Donegal.	087-9010774
Mark McConnell, TheGlebe, Stranorlar, Lifford, Co. Donegal.	074-9130772
Liam McKinney, Tievebane, Burnfoot, Co. Donegal.	074-9360060
Brian Dolan, Main Street, Creeslough, Letterkenny, Co.Donegal.	074-9138322
Edward Browne, Meeting House Street, Raphoe, Co. Donegal.	074-9145515
Wesley Carr, Moross, Tamney, Letterkenny, Co. Donegal.	087-7996206
Margaret Ann Reilly, Cashelmore. Creeslough, Donegal.	087-6207919
Eoin Gallagher, Killybegs Rd, Donegal Town, Co. Donegal.	087-9037884
Denis Faulkner, Leiter, Kilmacrennin, Co. Donegal.	074-9139679
Carol Conaghan, Fintra Rd, Killybegs, Co. Donegal.	087-6418605
Rita McLaughlin, Meeting House St, Raphoe. Co. Donegal.	087-1245608
Majella Bradley, Meeting House St, Raphoe, Co. Donegal.	086-2276395
Alicia Temple, Figart, Raphoe, Co. Donegal.	085-8391019
Diarmuid Coyle, Carrowcannon, Letterkenny, Co. Donegal.	085-8728678

DUBLIN

Philip Farrelly, Unit 5A, Balbriggan Business Park, Co. Dublin.	01-6906555
Richard Hackett, Knockcross, Balbriggan, Co. Dublin.	086-2703610
John Gallogly, Umit 5A, Fingal Business Park, Balbriggan.	01-6906555
Aoife Smith, Unit 5A, Balbriggan Business Park, Co. Dublin.	01- 6906555

AGRICULTURAL CONSULTANTS ASSOCIATION MEMBERS REGISTER

DUBLIN contd.,

Julian Pawlowski, 115 Merrion Grove, Booterstown, Co. Dublin.	087-6240811

GALWAY

Elaine Browne, Laraghmore, Ballyglunin, Tuam, Co. Galway.	087-2043098
Leo Keary, Dunkellin St., Loughrea, Co. Galway.	091-842698
John Bligh, Innovation Centre, GMIT, Dublin Road, Co. Galway.	086-8381530
Liam Walsh, Maam Cross, Connemara, Co. Galway.	087-2586147
Michael Finn, 4 Sycamore Grove, Gort, Co. Galway.	091-631033
Mairead Quinn, Ballyheragh, Cloghans Hill, Tuam, Co. Galway.	086-1229584
David Tarpey, Tarpey & Associates, Ardrahan, Co. Galway.	091-635555
Henry Lydon, Drumaveg, Moycullen, Co. Galway.	086-4077570
Shane Dolan, Kilquain, Craughwell, Co. Galway.	087-2310357
John O Connor, Hermitage Court, Dublin Rd, Galway.	086-2601384
Colin Fahy, Hermitage Court, Dublin Rd, Tuam, Co. Galway.	087-0537446
Mark Hanniffy, Ballinacourty, Clarinbridge, Co. Galway.	085-1461097
Colin Lyons, Menus, Dunmore, Co. Galway.	087-2997209
Liam Whyte, Cappanaughton, Kiltormer, Ballinasloe, Co. Galway.	087-0687702

KERRY

Kenneth Hayes, 2 Basin Road, Tralee, Co. Kerry.	066-7119533
James Kennedy, West Inch, Annascaul, Co. Kerry.	066-9157327
Philip O' Dwyer, Foxfort, Causeway, Co. Kerry.	066-7131952
Leonard Donnellan, Coolroe, Castlegregory, Co. Kerry.	066-7139837
Norma McKenna, 4 Park Business, Farranfore, Co. Kerry.	066-9763588
Eddie McQuinn, Oak View, Brewery Road, Tralee, Co. Kerry.	066-7129355
Diarmuid O'Sullivan, 93 New Street, Killarney, Co. Kerry.	064-6637414
Conor Lyons, Oakview, Brewery Rd, Tralee, Co. Kerry.	066-7129355
Deirdre Ward, Letterfinish, Sneem, Co. Kerry.	087-1228998
Margaret Mulvihill, Glin Road, Moyvane, Listowel, Co. Kerry.	087-9070231

KILDARE

John J. Mulhare, Tankardstown, Athy, Co. Kildare.	059-9145494

KILKENNY

Con Curtin, 12 The Paddocks, Kells Road, Kilkenny.	056-7752026
Seamus Brennan, Lisnafunchin, Castlecomer, Co. Kilkenny.	087-9451232

AGRICULTURAL CONSULTANTS ASSOCIATION MEMBERS REGISTER

KILKENNY contd.,

David Gahan, Cranrue, Paulstown, Co. Kilkenny.	086-1726213
Michael Kelly, Monteen, Thomastown, Co. Kilkenny.	056-7724655
Michael Tennyson, Cillin Hill Bus. Pk, Dublin Rd, Kilkenny.	056-7758532
Declan Dempsey, The Quay, Thomastown, Co. Kilkenny.	087-9051062
Fintan White, Boherkyle, Freshford, Co. Kilkenny.	087-9478954

LAOIS

Andy Dunne, 7 Kellyville Park, Portlaoise, Co. Laois.	057-8620157
Declan Phelan, Ballymullen, Abbeyleix, Co. Laois.	01-6906555
Andrew Mulhare, 7 Kellyville Park, Portlaoise, Co. Laois.	087-6509498
Susan Kavanagh, 7 Kellyville Park, Portlaoise, Co. Laois.	087-6615249
Mary Heavy, 7 Kellyville Park, Portlaoise, Co. Laois.	086-8760818
William Kelly, Leinster Co-Op Mart, Killeshin Road, Ballykillen, Carlow, Co. Laois.	087-1852170

LEITRIM

Enda Gilrane, Carrick on Shannon, Co. Leitrim.	071-9621920
Declan Oates, Tawley, Castlegal, Co. Leitrum.	071-9131014
Ray Gilmartin, Corlough, Drumshambo, Co. Leitrim.	087-8325519
Noelle Maguire, Gurteen, Garadice, Co. Leitrim.	083-0620885

LIMERICK

Martin Crowe, Carrigmore, Doon, Co. Limerick.	061-380948
William O'Regan, Dromrahnee, Ardagh, Co. Limerick.	069-76122
Michael Ryan, Gleneffy, Galbally, Co. Limerick.	087-9177302
David Walsh, Kilmacogue, Oola, Co. Limerick.	062-47657
John P O'Sullivan, Ballyine, Newcastle West, Co. Limerick.	086-8539297
Declan Murnane, Caherguillamore, Grange, Co. Limerick.	061-382801
Donal Gleeson, Unit 5 Deryknockane View, Raheen, Co. Limerick.	087 2989705
Gearoid Maher, Martin Crowe Ltd., Cappamore, Co. Limerick.	085-8536017
John Paul Julian, Unit 5 Ballycummin, Raheen, Co. Limerick.	087-2495552
Jim Barry, Broadford, Charleville, Co. Limerick.	087-8415617
Diarmaid Cummins, Carrigmore, Doon, Co. Limerick.	086-0630910
Michael O'Dwyer, Carrigmore, Doon, Co. Limerick.	086-2388284

LONGFORD

Andy Egan, Ferefad, Longford, Co. Longford.	043-3345720
Charles Byrnes, Robinstown, Granard, Co. Longford.	044-9396377
Paul Belton, Market St, Granard, Co. Longford.	087-6916822
John Enda Coyle, Cranley, Mostrim, Co. Longford.	087-9047617

AGRICULTURAL CONSULTANTS ASSOCIATION MEMBERS REGISTER

LONGFORD contd.,

Aisling Kiernan, Ballinalee, Co. Longford.	083-0706870
Thomas Quinn, Abbeylara, Co. Longford.	086-2215433
James Orohoe, St Albans, Battery Road, Longford.	086-1603358

MAYO

Liam Walsh, Well View, Killala Road, Ballina, Co. Mayo.	096-72791
Noel Walsh, Drum, Clogher, Ballina, Co. Mayo.	097-82991
Breian Carroll, Main St., Swinford, Co.Mayo.	094-9253742
Anne-Marie Clarke, 22 Ridgepool Village,.Ballina Co. Mayo.	086-2511012
Martin Heffernan,D-Mek Centre,Teeling St, Ballina, Co.Mayo.	096-73737
Patrick McIntyre, Riverside House, Newport Rd, Castlebar, Co. Mayo.	083-1451924
Brendan Kilkenny, Yew Tree Hse, Dalton St. Claremorris, Mayo.	087-6178189
Siobhán Ward, Doontas, Killasser, Swinford, Co. Mayo.	071-9181847
Michael Maloney, IPI Centre, Breaffy Rd., Castlebar, Co. Mayo.	094-9027300
John Mc Donagh, Rockfield, Westport, Co. Mayo.	098-35896
Oran Strong, Rathnanagh, Crossmolin, Co. Mayo.	087-1317412
Frances Burke, Well View, Killala Rd, Ballina, Co. Mayo.	096-72791
Andrew Kilduff, Main Street, Swinford, Co. Mayo.	086-3567331
Graham Cornish, Brownhall Demesne, Balla, Castlebar, Co. Mayo.	085-1344549
Gerard Connolly, Kilmaine, Claremorris, Co. Mayo.	087-7752602

MEATH

Peadar Moynihan, The Railings, Mullafin, Duleek, Co. Meath.	041-9825766
David O'Connell, Ballinderry Hse, Enfield, Co. Meath.	046-9555591
Ivan O'Neill, Lagore Little, Ratoath, Co. Meath.	087-4074907
Pat Smith, Lisgowan House, Derrockstown, Dunshaughlin.	01-8250263
Christopher Steenkamp, Rathroane Enfield, Co. Meath.	087-3418872

MONAGHAN

Niall Keenan, Main St., Ballybay, Co. Monaghan.	086-8044633
Ruairi Ward, The Square, Ballybay, Co. Monaghan.	042-9741195
Una Hanrahan, The Square, Ballybay, Co. Monaghan.	086-3864901

OFFALY

Ian Kenny, Ballyshane, Cloghan, Co. Offaly.	087-2501683
Eveline Gill, Killooley, Bluebell, Tullamore, Co. Offaly.	086-3824042
Liam Walsh. Unit 5, Courtyard Office Centre, Birr, Co. Offaly.	057-9125410
Ross Jackson, Woodview House, Lacka, Carrig, Birr, Co. Offaly.	086-8665030
James Kirwan, Clongowney, Banagher Co. Offaly.	087-2526543
Laura Johnston, Fortal, Birr, Co. Offaly.	087-2721213

AGRICULTURAL CONSULTANTS ASSOCIATION MEMBERS REGISTER

OFFALLY contd.,

Conor Camon, Kilburney, Cloughan, Birr, Co. Offaly.	087-7124174
ROSCOMMON	
Seamus Cusack, Cloonslanor, Strokestown, Co. Roscommon.	071-9633213
Noel Feeney, Lugnashammer, Cloghan, Boyle, Co. Roscommon.	071-9668088
Ian Tighe, Cloonfree, Strokestown, Co. Roscommon.	087-2757590
James Fitzgerald, Carrowberry, Castlerea, Co. Roscommon.	094-9880251
Seamus Feeney, Rooskey, Carrick on Shannon, Co. Roscommon.	071-9658931
SLIGO	
Fergal Boyle, Connaught Gold Mart, Ballymote, Co. Sligo.	087-3224684
Joseph Henry, Castlebaldwin, Co. Sligo.	087-1254100
Dermot Brennan, Drumartin, Tourlestrane, Co. Sligo.	087-3134408
Darren Leonard, Drimina, Tourlestrane, Co. Sligo.	085-8429918
TIPPERARY	
John G. Barlow, Gortavoher West, Glen of Aherlow, Co. Tipperary.	087-2523111
Tim Bourke, Killastafford, Cashel, Co. Tipperary.	062-63122
Anthony D. Cleary, Bantis House, Cloughjordan, Co. Tipperary.	087-2541691
Catherine O'Donoghue, Lisnernane, Aherlow, Co. Tipperary.	046-9555591
Pierce Ryan, Dempset St., Thurles Co. Tipperary.	086-3559797
Diarmuid Foley, Ballingarrane North, Clonmel, Co. Tipperary.	085-1595767
Martin O'Sullivan, Greenside, Carrick on Suir, Co. Tipperary.	051-640397
P.J. Phelan, Elmhurst, Barnane, Templemore, Co. Tipperary.	086-8046455
Victor Quinlan, Baptistgrange, Lisronagh, Clonmel. Tipperary.	052-6131498
Richard Rea, Martin & Rea Ltd. 8 Grattan St., Tipperary.	086-6070686
Willie Ryan, Roran, Borrisokane, Co. Tipperary.	087-2595864
Pat Walsh, The Presbytery, Castle St., Carrick on Suir, Co. Tipperary	087-9194880
Shane Hennessy, 8 Grattan Street, Tipperary Town.	086-2479182
Denis FitzGerald, FDC Hse, Church Street, Cahir, Co. Tipperary.	086-8602305
Mary Lynch, Bohercrowe, Limerick Rd, Tipperary.	087-2434365
John Ryan, Tinvoher, Loughmore, Templemore, Co. Tipperary.	086-8762510
Arnold O'Dwyer, Rossacrowe, Annacarty, Co. Tipperary.	086-3285575
WATERFORD	
Tom Rafter, 38 Kings Court, Maypark Lane, Waterford.	086-2798390
Tom Butler, F.B.A. Laboratory Ltd, Cappoquin, Co.Waterford.	058-52861
Terence Morrissey, Mweelnahorna, Ring, Co. Waterford.	058-44995
WESTMEATH	
James Carton, 4 Lough Owel Village, Mullingar, Co. Westmeath.	044-9396377

AGRICULTURAL CONSULTANTS ASSOCIATION MEMBERS REGISTER

WESTMEATH contd.,

Oliver Carroll, Reynella, Bracklyw, Mullingar, Co. Westmeath.	087-4190988
Thomas Dolan, Loughfield, Baltrasna, Moate, Co. Westmeath.	090-6481799
Padraig Fallon, Balrath South, Delvin, Co. Westmeath.	086-3033864
Jimmie Forbes, Meadowbrook, Turin, Mullingar, Co. Westmeath.	087-2111716
Gerry Langan, 1 Clonbrook Ct, Retreat, Athlone, Westmeath.	090-6472300
Michael Martyn, Kilbeg, Kilbeggan, Co. Westmeath.	057-9332882

WEXFORD

Laura Johnston, Clone Agri., Monamolin, Gorey, Co. Wexford.	087-2721213
Simon Byrne, Ballinavocran, Bunclody, Enniscorthy, Co. Wexford.	085-7260385

WICKLOW

Dr. N. Bielenberg, Stewarts Ltd., Woolgreen, Carnew, Co. Wicklow.	053-9426555
Michael Ryan, Grangebeg Park, Dunlavin, Co. Wicklow.	087-2618416
John Mallick, Garrymoe, Tinahely, Arklow, Co. Wicklow.	087-2997105
John Cullen, Kilmacanague, Bray, Co. Wicklow.	085-1503550

FORESTRY MANAGEMENT CONSULTANTS

Paddy Bruton, Forestry Services, Cillin Hill, Co. Kilkenny.	087-6579352
Padraig Dolan, 3 Tearmann Eala, REnmore, Co. Galway.	086-2457411
Paul Finnegan, Newline, Ballycrissane, Ballinasloe, Co. Galway.	090-9675287
Eamonn O Curraoin, Ballybroder, Loughrea, Co. Galway.	087-2472302
Marina Conway, Western Forestry Co-op, Finisklin Road, Sligo.	087-2234096
Kieran O Connell, Ard Na Veagh, Rathkeale, Co. Limerick.	087-2630234
Fionan Russell, Dunderry, Navan, Co. Meath.	087-2314138

ACA Secretariat
Block 3, The Presbytery, New Street, Carrick on Suir, Co Tipperary
Tel: 051-645705   Email: acaservices@aca.ie   Website: www.aca.ie

1

Farm Subsidies, Supports & Incentives

CAP Reform Programme 2023-2027 – Main features.................38
Pillar I Measures
Basic Income Support for Sustainability (BISS) 39
Entitlements 40
National Reserve - Young & New Farmer Categories 42
Complementary Redistributive Income Support for Sustainability (Criss) 43
Complementary Income Support Young Farmers (CIS-YF) 44
Coupled Income Support for Protein Aid................................45
Straw Incorporation Measure 45
Areas of Natural Constraint (ANC) 46
Pillar II Measures
Agri-Climate Rural Environment Scheme (ACRES) 48
Support For Collaborative Farming................................50
Suckler Carbon Efficiency Programme 51
Organic Farming Scheme 52
On-Farm Capital Investment Scheme Tams 3 53
Young Farmer Capital Investment Scheme 54
Dairy Equipment Scheme 55
Organic Capital Investment Scheme 56
Low Emission Slurry Spreading Equipment Scheme..........57
Pig & Poultry Investment Scheme 58
Animal Welfare and Nutrient Storage Scheme 58
Tillage Capital Investment Scheme................................59
Solar Capital Investment Scheme................................60
Farm Safety Capital Investment Scheme 60
Women Farmer Capital Investment Scheme....................62
Other Pillar II and Government Funded Schemes................64

CAP Reform Programme 2023-2027

The current CAP Strategic Plan, which commenced in 2023, aims to foster a sustainable and competitive agricultural sector that can support the livelihoods of farmers and provide healthy and sustainable food for society, as well as vibrant rural areas. The various measures contained in the programme define various eligible persons as follows:

Young Farmer:
A person of no more than 40 years of age at any time during the calendar year in which s/he, (i) first submits an application under Pillar I measures or (ii) submits an application under Pillar II measures, for young farmer support.

New Farmer:
For the application year 2024, new farmers are defined as farmers that have set up as head of a holding for the first time in their lives and within the past three years, started farming in 2021 or later, and must not have farmed previously. They must have finished a recognised course of education in agriculture, achieving an award at Level 6 on the National Framework of Qualifications 6 or its equivalent by 29th May 2024.

Active Farmer:
Active farmers are defined as those 'engaged in at least a minimum level of agricultural activity'. The farming activities can include meeting a minimum stocking rate (0.10 livestock unit per forage hectare), producing crops, cutting hay/silage, maintaining landscape features.

Woman Farmer:
A woman farmer is any individual farmer who is more than 18 and less than 67 years of age at the time of submitting a TAMS application and can demonstrate that they are a woman via one of the forms of personal identification listed in the terms and conditions for the On-farm Capital Investment Programme (to include at least Passport, Gender Recognition Certificate, and Birth Certificate); (ii) Meets the definition of an Active Farmer and, (iii) Is registered as a woman in the Department's Corporate Client System (CCS), is registered as 'female' on DAFM's Corporate Customer Management (CCM) system. She must also possess adequate occupational skills and competence and has control of and is managing an agricultural holding.

Pillar I Measures

Basic Income Support for Sustainability (BISS)

This measure is designed to provide a direct income support to Irish farmers to underpin their continued sustainability and viability. By supporting viable farm incomes, the measure supports farmers in the continuation of a secure food supply. This support builds on the similar support provided by its predecessor, the Basic Payment Scheme (BPS) and its predecessor the Single Farm Payment Scheme.

Elegibility

To receive a support under BISS, eligible applicants must:
- have an eligible hectare to accompany each payment entitlement.
- be a holder of a registered herd number or have applied for a herd number on or before 29 May 2024.
- meet the definition of an "active farmer".

The minimum payment is €100 and the maximum payment is €66,000 (excluding CRISS and Eco Scheme).

Eligibility for Other Schemes

The information declared in the BISS application will be necessary for inclusion in the following schemes:
- Hold one BISS payment entitlement for each eligible hectare claimed.
- Farmers may also apply through the BISS application for the following schemes: meet the definition of an "active farmer".
- Eco-Scheme (ECO).
- Complementary Redistributive Income Support for Sustainability (CRISS).
- Complementary Income Support for Young Farmers Scheme (CIS-YF).
- Protein Aid.
- Areas of Natural Constraints (ANC).
- Straw Incorporation Measure (SIM).
- Agri-climate Rural Environment Scheme (ACRES) – annual claim if already approved into the scheme.
- Organic Farming Scheme (OFS) – annual claim if already approved into the scheme.
- Suckler Carbon Efficiency Programme.
- Fodder Support Scheme, 2023.
- Tillage Incentive 7 Scheme.
- Multi-Species Swards Measure.
- Red Clover Silage Measure.
- National Liming Programme.

Convergence

The convergence mechanism aims to bring payment entitlement values towards a national average value. Entitlements may be subject to convergence, which will either increase or decrease their value over the first four years of the Scheme (2023-2026). In 2026 all entitlements will have a minimum value of 85% of the new national average entitlement value. Farmers who hold entitlements with an Initial Value between 90% and 100% of the new national average entitlement value will see no change in their entitlement value over the scheme through convergence. Farmers who hold entitlements with an Initial Value below 90% of the new national average entitlement value will have the value of their entitlements increased by one third of the difference between their Initial Value and 90% of the new national average value. This increase will take place in four equal steps over the first four years of the Scheme. Farmers who hold entitlements with an Initial Value over 100% of the new national average entitlement value will see their value decrease over the years 2023-2026. It is important to note that in 2026, no farmer will receive a payment greater than €285 per entitlement.

Land Availability Rule
To claim the direct payment under BISS, all of the hectares of land declared by the farmer to support his/her claim (owned, rented-in and leased-in) must be subject to an agricultural activity conducted by them for a period from the beginning of the year until after 31 May or for a period before 31 May to 31 December. In the case of the ANC scheme the land must be available to the applicant for the entire calendar year.

Leases/Letting Agreements
Where farmers enter into leases or letting agreements for any of the lands declared on their BISS application, the transferor and transferee are obliged to enter into a written lease or letting agreement, which includes the following information:
• Names, addresses and Herd Numbers of both transferor and transferee.
• LPIS Parcel Numbers for the lands subject to the agreement.
• Where part of a land parcel is involved, a map must be appended to the agreement to show the land involved.
• The period of the agreement (start date and end date).
• Details of the payments including the date payments are due and the sum(s) involved.
• The agreement must be signed and dated by both parties and the signatures witnessed by an independent person.
• The written rental/lease agreement must be in place prior to the start date of the agreement and available at inspection.

Entitlements

Payment under BISS is made to farmers who meet the active farmer requirements, hold payment entitlements and activate the payment entitlements by declaring an eligible hectare per entitlement.

Usage of Entitlements
All entitlements allocated under BISS and the National Reserve are subject to a two-year usage rule. If a farmer has unused entitlements for two consecutive years, the

lowest value entitlements held by that farmer revert to the National Reserve in the second year of non-usage.

Transfers of Entitlements

Applications to transfer entitlements can be made by farmers, or their farm advisor who has been authorised by the farmer. A change to the registration details of a herd-number (e.g. the addition or removal of an individual) requires the same change to the registration details of entitlements and a Transfer of Entitlements application is required. Transfers can arise in a variety of circumstances such as, inheritance, lease, sale, gift, change of legal entity (company or partnership) or a cessation of a partnership.

Inheritance of Entitlements

Entitlements will be transferred according to the will, where a will is in place, or the laws of intestacy if there is no will. In cases where a deceased person bequeaths land in a will but has not made any provision for their entitlements within the will, these entitlements or a share of these entitlements will transfer with the eligible land unless there is a legal impediment preventing the transfer.

Lease of Entitlements

Entitlements may be leased with or without land. Leasing with or without land does not incur any clawbacks.

Frequency of Transfer Entitlements

Entitlements may not be transferred more than once in a scheme year, unless by way of inheritance or anticipated inheritance.

Inspections

In submitting a BISS application, applicants agree to permit officials or agents of the Department to carry out on-farm inspections, with or without prior notice. When notified of an on-farm inspection, the applicant should arrange to be present for the inspection or have a representative nominated in his/ her place to assist the inspecting officer. If applicants are farming other land to that indicated on their current BISS application form, they must bring it to the attention of the inspecting officer on the day of the inspection. The number of farmers chosen for inspections will vary with the type of inspection as follows:

- Land eligibility inspections will apply to approximately 5% of applicants.
- Cross compliance inspections including ECO Systems, Complimentary Income Support for young farmers, Areas of Natural Constraint,ACRES scheme, Straw Incorporation Measure and Organic Farming Scheme.
- At least 5% of farmers must be inspected under the Animal Identification and Registration requirements for cattle and 3% for sheep/ goats as prescribed under the relevant Regulations.

National Reserve – Young & New Farmer Categories

The 2024 National Reserve will provide support to the two mandatory categories of Young Farmer and New Farmer. Successful applicants will receive an allocation of payment entitlements at the national average entitlement value on eligible land on which they hold no entitlements; and/or a top up to the national average entitlement value on existing entitlements held by them where such entitlements are below the national average value, subject to a maximum allocation of 50 payment entitlements.

Young Farmers

A Young Farmer applying to the 2024 National Reserve is defined as follows:
- Aged no more than 40 years of age at any time during the calendar year in which s/he first submits an application under the National Reserve.
- Is setting up a holding as head of the holding, solely or jointly, for the first time or has set up such a holding during the five years preceding the first submission of an application under the National Reserve.
- Has successfully completed a recognised course of education in agriculture giving rise to an award at Level 6 or equivalent on the National Framework of Qualifications.
- Submits a valid 2024 Basic Income Support for Sustainability (BISS) application under a herd number on which the applicant is included.

New Farmers

A New Farmer applying to the 2024 National Reserve is defined as follows:
- Set up a holding for the first time or during the three years preceding the first submission of a National Reserve application.
- Has successfully completed a recognised course of education in agriculture giving rise to an award at Level 6 or equivalent on the National Framework of Qualifications.
- Submits a valid 2024 Basic Income Support for Sustainability (BISS) application under a herd number on which the applicant is included. Applicants who benefitted from an allocation under the Basic Payment Scheme National Reserve from 2015-2022 will not be eligible for an allocation under the Basic Income Support for Sustainability National Reserve from 2024.

Eco-Scheme

This voluntary annual agri-environmental scheme for all farmers is aimed at maximising farmer participation in order to achieve climate and environmental improvements across all farmed lands. The list of eight agricultural practices proposed for the Eco-Scheme is set out below. A farmer will have to select at least two agricultural practices to receive the Eco-Scheme payment.

1. Space for Nature (Non-productive areas and landscape features).
2. Extensive livestock production - maximum overall stocking rate of 1.5LU / ha for the calendar year. Minimum stocking rate requirements similar to ANC.
3. Limiting Chemical Nitrogen Input.
4. Planting of Native Trees/Hedgerows - a minimum planting rate of three native trees or 1 metre of hedgerow per eligible hectare, or an enhanced option comprising six native trees or 2 metres of hedgerow per eligible hectare (counts as two actions).
5. Use of GPS Controlled spreader and/or sprayer - application of chemical fertiliser either compound or liquid and/or plant protection products to be applied with a GPS controlled spreader or sprayer.
6. Soil Sampling & Appropriate Liming - carry out soil sampling on all eligible hectares and apply lime in accordance with the soil test results where appropriate (only available as an Eco action every three years once selected).
7. Enhanced Crop Diversification - planting of a break crop (beans, peas, OSR or Oats) as part of enhanced crop diversification on 25% of the arable area.
8. Sowing a multi species sward - sowing of a multi species sward on at least 6% of eligible hectares in the year the action is selected.

Support Rates
Support is based on an annual payment for all eligible hectares covered by the commitments, i.e. farmers will receive payment on all eligible hectares on their holding. An expected 129,000 eligible farmers could participate in the scheme, and the payment per hectare will be impacted by the actual participation rate. As an indicative figure only, if 85% of the eligible hectares currently claimed by farmers participate in the scheme successfully and assuming all hectares receive the same payment rate, the payment rate would be approximately €74 per hectare.

Complementary Redistributive Income Support for Sustainability (CRISS)

This support is designed to redistribute CAP funds from larger farms to medium and smaller sized farms and is now a mandatory scheme within the EU Regulation governing the CAP Strategic Plan. The basic premise behind the measure is that support through CAP should go to those who need it the most, or those who are contributing most to the CAP objectives, and that redistribution of funds from larger farms to small and medium sized farms aids this objective.

Structure
It is proposed to pay the CRISS up to the first 30 hectares at a rate of approximately €43 per hectare, an arrangement which allows a greater number of farmers to benefit.

Eligibility
Eligible beneficiaries are required to:
• Submit a BISS application each year via the online application system, declaring

their farmland located within the jurisdiction of Ireland.
- Meet the minimum requirements to receive a direct payment.
- Meet the definition of a "active farmer".

Support Rates
It is proposed to ring-fence 10% of the direct payments ceiling for CRISS. It is expected that this will translate to an average payment rate of approximately €43.14 per hectare (up to 30 hectares), though exact rates will fluctuate based on participation.

Complementary Income Support Young Farmers (CIS-YF)

This scheme is designed to provide support to appropriately qualified young farmers entering the agriculture sector in the years immediately following the young farmer setting up as head of the holding, solely or jointly. This measure will also provide certainty in terms of the level of income support for eligible applicants for up to five years, which is an important factor in financial planning.

Eligibility
Eligible applicants must first be entitled to a payment under the Basic Income Support for Sustainability (BISS). Farmers meeting the eligibility conditions may apply to this support on an annual basis. All eligible hectares declared by the applicants up to a ceiling of 50 hectares per applicant can receive support. Support is not based on the number of entitlements held by the applicant.

Support Rates
A payment per eligible hectare subject to a maximum of 50 hectares per eligible applicant is proposed under the CIS-YF measure. It is expected that the average rate will be approximately €178 per hectare across the CAP period, though exact rates will fluctuate based on participation.

Qualifying Young Trained Farmers
To qualify for participation in the Young Farmers Scheme, a farmer must meet all of the following conditions. They must be:
- Aged no more than 40 years of age at any time during the calendar year in which s/he first submits an application under CIS-YF.
- Is setting up a holding as head of the holding, solely or jointly, for the first time or has set up such a holding during the five years preceding the first submission of an application under CIS-YF.
- Has successfully completed a recognised course of education in agriculture giving rise to an award at Level 6 or equivalent on the National Framework of Qualifications.
- Entitled to payment under the Basic Income Support for Sustainability (BISS).

Coupled Income Support for Protein Aid

The Protein aid Scheme is designed to provide a direct financial support for farmers growing eligible protein crops, thus providing greater certainty for growers of these crops, thereby improving the competitiveness of nationally grown legumes. A payment rate of circa. €583 per hectare is expected to be paid for beans, peas, lupins, and soya. The protein/cereal mix crop is expected to be paid at half the full protein crop rate i.e. €292 per hectare.

Eligibility

To receive support under Protein Aid, eligible applicants must meet the definition of an "active farmer" and submit a valid 2024 BISS application and have eligible crops declared on the BISS application, such as beans, peas, lupins, soyabean, protein/cereal mix crop. The crop must be grown to a commercial standard with the appropriate seeding rates.

Support Rates

The payment rate will be linked to the variation in the grown area. The payment will be made per hectare at a rate of circa €350 per hectare. It is proposed that a payment rate of €175 per hectare would be paid for mixed cropping. The annual indicative allocation for this intervention is proposed at €7m, amounting to a total indicative financial allocation of €35m for the period 2023-2027.

Straw Incorporation Measure

The purpose of the measure is to encourage tillage farmers to increase soil organic carbon levels by chopping and incorporating straw from cereal crops and oilseed rape. Once eligible crops on parcels which have been declared as participating in the scheme are combined, the straw is chopped, spread evenly and incorporated into the soil in the parcel. The measure will be a one-year contract with automatic renewal unless opt-out is triggered by the beneficiary or by the Department Agriculture, Food and the Marine. The maximum duration will be five years.

Eligibility

Application for this measure will be incorporated into the annual BISS application process. Where a tillage farmer declares eligible crops (wheat, oats, barley, rye, oilseed rape) they will have the option to then apply. They will be required to identify the relevant parcels on which they will chop straw and incorporate it into the soil. There will be a minimal eligible area of 5 hectares and a maximum area of 40 hectares.

Support

Support will be by way of an annual area-based payment per hectare. The support payment will compensate the farmer for the additional cost of the chopping, spreading and incorporation of straw into the soil. The indicative payment rate will be €250 per hectare for cereal crops (barley, wheat, oats, rye) and €150 per hectare for oilseed rape given the lower market value for oilseed rape straw.

Areas of Natural Constraint (ANC)

Incorporating Support for Island Farming

Those farming in designated areas face significant hardships from factors such as remoteness, difficult topography, climatic problems and poor soil conditions. These payments will, by encouraging continued use of agricultural land, contribute to maintaining the countryside as well as to maintaining and promoting sustainable farming systems.

Payment Rates

Table 1.1: Area of Natural Constraints Payments

Category	Area (ha)	Payment/ha (€)
Category 1	1st 12 ha	148.00
Category 1	13-34 ha	112.00
Category 2	1st 10 ha	111.00
Category 2	11-30 ha	104.00
Category 3	1st 8 ha	93.00
Category 3	9-30 ha	88.25
Island farmers additional:		
Area of Specific Constraints (Island Farming)	0-20 ha	250.00
	21-34 ha	170.00
	35-40 ha	70.00

It should be noted that, further to the re-designation of ANC lands, the previous designated land types of Mountain, More Severely and Less Severe have changed to Category 1, 2 and 3 respectively under the 2020 scheme e.g. if an applicant had 10 hectares of Mountain Lands in 2019 they now have 10 hectares of Category 1 lands.

Note - Applicants maintaining a combination of Category 1, 2 and 3 land, will be paid up to a maximum of 30 hectares except where the area of Category 1 land declared is between 30 and 34 hectares. In these cases, the payment will be based on the number of hectares of Category 1 land declared.

Conditions for Eligibility

Beneficiaries must:

- Be 18 years or over and comply with the description of 'active farmer'.
- Occupy and farm at own risk a minimum of three hectares of forage land, situated in a recognised ANC area.
- Undertake to actively farm and manage the land situated in an ANC area and applied on in the given year of application.
- Comply with Cross Compliance requirements.
- Have a holding that meets the minimum stocking levels.

Partners in a registered partnership can continue to benefit individually under the Scheme, based on the area of ANC land they contribute to the partnership.

Minimum Stocking Density Requirements

The minimum stocking requirement is 0.10 livestock units per forage hectare. This is down from 0.15 LU/ha in 2022 but still equivalent to 1 ewe per hectare, as the livestock unit values have been revised. The minimum stocking requirement will be based on an applicant's stocking profile in the previous calendar year, i.e. 2023. Where an applicant did not satisfy the minimum stocking requirement in 2023, they can choose to use their stocking profile in 2024 instead. The minimum stocking requirement retention period is 28 weeks.

Table 1.2: Livestock Unit Values for Area of Natural Constraints Scheme

Type of Animal	Livestock Unit Value	Proof which may be required
Dairy cows	1.0	Herd Register in order + CMMS compliant
Male Cattle over 2 years	1.0	Herd Register in order + CMMS compliant
Heifers 2 years and over	0.8	Herd Register in order + CMMS compliant
Other cows 2 years & over	0.8	Herd Register in order + CMMS compliant
Female or Male Cattle 2 years or under	0.6	Herd Register in order + CMMS compliant
Female or Male Sheep	0.1	Flock Register up to date Most recent sheep census completed
Female or Male Goats	0.1	Flock Register up to date Most recent sheep census completed
Horses	0.8	Breeding mares must have bred a foal in the previous 2 years
Female or male donkeys	0.8	Only 50% of the stocking requirement can be met using donkeys
Female or Male Deer	0.3	Proof of ownership

Eligible Land

In order for land to qualify for payment the following conditions apply:
- The land must have an agricultural activity carried out on it.
- The land must be used and farmed by the applicant and must be suitable for and compatible with the farming enterprise.
- Parcels, including commonage parcels, must be maintained in such a condition as to ensure the land is suitable for grazing or cultivation.
- In order to be eligible for payment, the land in question must be available to the applicant for the entire calendar year. Lands farmed by the applicant on the basis of an 11-month conacre agreement are also deemed eligible for payment under the ANC Scheme.
- There must be independent access for animals and/or machinery. Independent access means access by public or private roadway or by a defined right of way. Access over adjoining landowners land is not acceptable.
- There must be appropriate fencing for the farming enterprise which means stock-

proof fencing that will control the applicant's animals and also neighbouring farmer's animals. In mountain/hill areas this generally means sheep fencing.
- There must be defined external boundaries, except in the case of commonage.
- If at inspection an applicant claims to be farming land with animals, then the type of animal must be appropriate to the land and there must be handling facilities available to meet the animal welfare requirements.

Partnerships
Applicants registered under the Farm Partnership Registration process were required to submit one 2023 Basic Payment Scheme and other Area-based Schemes application form through the Departments online facility. In order to be considered under the ANC scheme at an individual level each partner should individually declare all land farmed by them within the partnership. The following rules obtain in regard to partnerships;
- All partners who declare designated ANC lands at individual level will be considered under the ANC scheme.
- Individual maximum land thresholds will be applicable to each individual partner in respect of designated ANC lands declared. Thereafter, scheme eligibility requirements in respect of the stock retention period and the annual average stocking density must be met at overall partnership level in respect of all forage hectares.
- Only one payment under ANC will issue to the Partnership. All Payments due to the individual partners will be combined into a single payment which will issue to the partnership.
- Where the overall partnership holding fails to meet scheme eligibility requirements in respect of either the seven-month stock retention period or the annual average stocking density no payment will be due to the partnership or any of the partners.

Note: Readers are reminded that the information as set out above is based on the 2023 scheme details. The 2024 scheme may have some variations in detail.

Pillar II Measures

Agri-Climate Rural Environment Scheme (ACRES)

ACRES (Agri-Climate Rural Environment Scheme) is Ireland's new Agri-environment climate scheme proposed as part of Ireland's CAP strategic plan. This new €1.5 billion agri-environment scheme will be a farmer-friendly scheme. ACRES aims to contribute significantly to achieving improved biodiversity, climate, air and water quality outcomes. It will be available in two formats, the first being a general scheme which will be available nationally and offers a range of actions for individual farmers, both targeted and general. The second option is the Co-operation approach and is available to farmers in defined high priority geographical areas and involves results-based payments as well as bespoke farm and landscape actions. Contracts have been awarded for the management of Co-operation Projects (CP), and farmers will be supported by new teams, who will develop local action plans for their zones.

Rea Group

This firm has been providing services to farmers & self employed for over 30 years

Agri-Business

- Expert Witness Reports in relation to accidents and loss assessment

- Compulsory Purchase Negotiations Oral Hearings and Compensation involving roads, greenway, wayleave

- Reports and Recommendations involving Family Law disputes

- Farm Succession, land transfers land leases, advise on wills

- Mediation of disputes

- E.U. Farm Schemes

- Farm Partnerships

- Bank Proposals

Taxation advise for
Farmers and Agri-Business, Ltd., Farming Ltd companies,
Farm and Business tranfers, CGT, CAT, accounts and income tax returns.

Richard J Rea - 086 6070686   Tom Dawson 086 - 8238283   Marion Ryan - 086 3838583

Munster/Leinster   Tom Dawson 086 8238283
Mayo/Galway   AnneMarie Clarke 086 2511012
Sligo/Roscommon/Leinster   Joe Henry 087 1254100
Nationwide   Richard J. Rea 086 6070686
                                Marion Ryan 086 3838583

CONSULTANTS IN AGRICULTURE, BUSINESS, VALUATIONS & MEDIATION
CONTACT
8 Grattan Street, Tipperary Town, Co. Tipperary
Tel: 062-52166 / 062 52361   Email: info@reagroup.ie
www.reagroup.ie

Eligibility
To be eligible to participate a farmer shall:
- Be aged 18 years or over on date of submission of the application for support.
- Be the holder of an active Business ID. Herd 'Owner' status is required as Herd Keeper is not acceptable.
- Have all lands farmed declared in the applicant's name on the Integrated Administration and Control System (IACS).
- Have submitted a BPS 2021 application.
- All lands brought into the scheme must be declared in the applicant's 2022 BPS and also declared on the applicant's BISS application for all subsequent years of participation.
- The ACRES General approach will be open to all categories of active farmers eligible in the defined mapped area for ACRES General.
- The ACRES Co-operation approach will be open to all categories of active farmers eligible in the defined mapped area for ACRES CP zones.
- Farmers participating in other environmental schemes may apply for ACRES, but if approved may have payments adjusted in either scheme to ensure no double funding takes place.

Payment & Duration
ACRES general offers a maximum of €7,311 per year. The level of payment a farmer may achieve will be determined by the payment rates for the actions selected and undertaken satisfactorily. ACRES co-operation offers a maximum of €10,500 per year with a maximum results-based payment of €7,000 with an extra non-productive investment and landscape maximum of €3,500. The level of payment will be determined by results-based scorecards, non-productive investments, and landscape actions, which will be designed for land-types and region. The duration of this scheme is five years.

Support For Collaborative Farming

This measure will continue to operate in the new CAP programme 2023-2027. This scheme aims to support farm partnerships and other proposed forms of collaborative farming being used or proposed to be used in Ireland. It is generally accepted that farmers working in partnerships with their spouse, partner or offspring on the family farm, or coming together with another farmer to work the two farms in a common structure, can help to overcome issues such as the lack of land mobility, the age profile of farmers, work/life balance, as well as bringing about an increase in competitiveness and assisting in developing the sector to take advantage of smart, green growth opportunities.

Support
This support scheme is available for the formation of registered farm partnerships only. All new farm partnerships meeting the entry requirements will be eligible to receive a contribution of 50% towards the vouched costs in legal, accounting and business planning expenditure involved in setting up the partnership up to a maximum of €1,500 per beneficiary.

Suckler Carbon Efficiency Programme

The aim of this programme is to provide support to beef farmers to improve the environmental sustainability of the national beef herd. The programme aims to build on the gains delivered thus far through the Beef Data and Genomics Programme (BDGP) and the Beef Environmental Efficiency Programme (BEEP) by improving the genetic merit of the Irish suckler herd and reducing the greenhouse gas intensity of Ireland's beef production.

Eligibility

In order to be eligible an applicant must:

- Have submitted a BISS application in a reference year and continue to submit BISS applications on which all their lands are declared for the duration of the Suckler Carbon Efficiency Programme.
- Have beef breed animals born in the herd in each scheme year of the measure.
- Be a member of the Bord Bia Sustainable Beef and Lamb Assurance Scheme.

Actions

1. **A Replacement Strategy:** The replacement strategy will cover both the Dams and the Sires. In years 1 and 2, 80% of the calves born on the holding must be sired by a 4-star or 5-star sire on the maternal or terminal index. In years 3 and 4, this will increase to 85% while in year 5, it will increase to 90%. On the Dam

side, in year 1, at least 50% must be at least 4-star on the replacement index on 31 October 2023. This increases to at least 65% by 31 October 2025 (year 3), and at least 75% by 31 October 2027 (year 5).

2. **A Genotyping Programme:** At least 70% of the reference number of animals on the holding must be genotyped each year of the scheme.
3. **A Weighing Measure:** The Suckler Cow and Calf pair are weighed prior to the calf being weaned and not before the calf is at least 100 days old. This targets the weaning efficiency of suckler cows and calves by measuring the liveweight of the calf at weaning as a percentage of the cow's liveweight.
4. **Data Recording:** Participants must provide a range of data through animal events records and surveys including:
    *   Calves – ease of calving, quality and docility, size, vigour/vitality, scour and pneumonia.
    *   Cows – milking ability and docility, culling reasons.
    *   Stock bulls – docility and functionality, culling reasons. A mandatory training course for participants in the Suckler Carbon Efficiency Programme must be undertaken in each of the first two years of the programme.

Support Rates

The number of Suckler Cows eligible per herd will be based on a specified historical reference period, which will provide a ceiling for payment but there will be scope to reduce numbers without penalty. It is proposed that a higher rate of payment of €150 per cow will issue for the first 10 suckler cows in a herd with a payment of €120/cow applying thereafter up to the budget limit.

Organic Farming Scheme

The overall objective of the Organic Farming Scheme is to deliver enhanced environmental and animal welfare benefits and to encourage producers to respond to the market demand for organically produced food.

Eligible Persons

As in the previous Organic Farming Scheme, a series of core requirements defines basic eligibility. Key conditions include:

*   Requirement of minimum farm area of 3 hectares for tillage holdings, 1 hectare for horticultural producers (provided that 50% of eligible area for organic payment is cropped each year) and 6 hectares for all others.
*   Registration with one of the Organic Control Bodies, possession of a valid organic license and registration with DAFM.
*   Requirement to meet the productivity objective, the minimum stocking levels must equal 0.5 LU per hectare.

- Table 1.3: Organic Farming Scheme Payments.

Horticulture	Area: 6 ha or less	Area: 6ha-60ha	Area: >60ha
In conversion	€300/ha	€220/ha	€60/ha
Full organic status	€200/ha	€170/ha	€30/ha
Tillage (min. 6ha)	Area: less than 20ha.	Area: 20ha-60ha.	Area: >60ha.
In conversion	€260/ha	€220/ha	€60/ha
Full organic status	€170/ha	€170/ha	€30/ha
All other holdings	Area: 3-60ha	Area: >60ha	
In conversion	€220/ha	€60/ha	
Full organic status	€170/ha	€30/ha	

In addition, a top-up of €30/ha. per annum for red clover is included up to a maximum of 10 hectares.

On-Farm Capital Investment Scheme TAMS 3

The aim of this scheme is to provide support to farmers looking to invest in capital projects on their farms. This scheme is a response for the need to increase environmental efficiency in the agricultural sector through on farm investment and the adoption of new technologies; the need to support young farmers in accessing finance so they are in a better position to invest in and develop their farm enterprise; and the need to improve animal health and welfare, and farm safety on farm. Grant aid will be provided for investment in the following categories:

- Young Farmer Capital Investment Scheme.
- Dairy Equipment Scheme.
- Organic Capital Investment Scheme.
- Low Emission Slurry Spreading Scheme.
- Pig and Poultry Investment Scheme.
- Animal Welfare and Nutrient Storage Scheme.
- Tillage Capital Investment Scheme.
- Solar Capital Investment Scheme.
- Farm Safety Capital Investment Scheme.
- Women Farmer Capital Investment Scheme.

Conditions

All applicants must:

- Must be an Active Farmer, aged 18 or over.
- Be the holder of an active Herd number/ flock/tillage or department identifier.
- Have declared a minimum of 5 HAs (1 HA for horticulture producers) of 'eligible land' owned and/or leased or rented which have been declared under the BISS in the year of application or preceding year.
- Must also comply with requirements on planning permission and tax clearance.

To qualify for enhanced grant rates and investment limits:
- Young farmers must be aged no more than 40 at any time during the calendar year in which s/he submits an application and meet the conditions for being 'head of the holding' and the requirements for the appropriate training and/or skills.
- Women farmers- aged between 18 and 66 at any time during the calendar year in which she submits an application for women farmer support. She must also meet the conditions for being 'head and of the holding' and meet the requirements for the appropriate training and/or skills required.

Farm Safety Training Requirement
It shall be mandatory that all applicants will have completed within the last five years prior to the submission of their claim for payment, the half day Farm Safety Code of Practice (given by Teagasc or other trained persons) or have completed the FETAC QQI Level 6 Advanced Certificate in Agriculture (Green Cert.). In the case of a Registered Farm Partnership or a Company the course must have been completed by the young farmer.

Tax Compliance
In the case of grant payments of less than €10,000 applicants will be required to indicate the tax district dealing with their tax affairs and also to declare that to the best of their knowledge that their tax affairs are in order. For grant payments of €10,000 or more in any 12-month period, applicants will be required to furnish a valid Tax Clearance Certificate or Tax Clearance Certificate Reference Number from the Revenue Commissioners before payment of grant-aid is made.

Investment Limits
The investment limits are €90,000 per holding or €160,000 in the case of a registered partnership with two or more eligible partners.

Young Farmer Capital Investment Scheme
The objective of the Scheme is to provide an incentive to young farmers to upgrade their agricultural buildings and equipment by providing them with an increased level of support to meet the considerable capital costs associated with the establishment of their enterprises.

Grant Aid
Grant aid will shall be paid at the rate of 60% up to the applicable maximum investment ceiling of €90,000 per holding. In the case of an application by two or more eligible partners in a partnership registered on the Department's Register of Farm Partnership, the maximum eligible investment ceiling shall be increased to €160,000. Where a registered farm partnership contains one qualifying young farmer, grant-aid will be paid at 60%, subject to all qualifying conditions being met, on the first €90,000 and 40% on the remaining balance. Under TAMS 3, grant aid per investment item is based on the lowest of;

- the Departments reference costs applicable at the date of approval,
- the total eligible paid invoices,
- the cost proposed by the applicant on their application.

Eligible Applicants
The Scheme is open to farmers who:
- are more than 18 years and not more than 40 years of age at the date of submitting the application form;
- meet the requirements of set-up for the first time within five years of the date of receipt of an application under this Scheme;
- own or have leasehold title to the site on which it is proposed to carry out the development;
- have a minimum of 5 hectares owned and /or leased which have been declared under the BISS Scheme in the year of application or preceding year or in the case of intensive enterprises;
- generate a minimum of 20 production units from farming;
- fulfil the necessary educational requirements on the date of application or within 36 months from the date of issue of Department approval to the applicant to commence works. If this criterion is not met the applicant will not be eligible for the 60% rate.

Eligible Investments
The scheme covers a very comprehensive range of farm investments such as dairy structures, milking and cooling equipment, animal housing, slurry storage, mobile slurry equipment, animal handling equipment, slat replacement, silage pit resurfacing, energy efficient pig and poultry housing upgrades along with various other farm investment supports. A detailed list of eligible investments can be found on the Department of Agriculture by searching under TAMS 3.

Applications & Further Information
Further information can be had from the www.agriculture.gov.ie. Intending applicants should contact their local ACA or Teagasc advisor.

Dairy Equipment Scheme
The objective of the Scheme is to encourage new entrants/young farmers in milk production by providing them with a level of support to meet the considerable capital costs associated with establishment of their enterprise and ensuring that they have the most up-to-date technology available to compete in the modern dairy sector.

Grant Aid
Grant aid is paid at the rate of 40% up to a maximum investment ceiling of €90,000 per holding. Applicants who receive approval to proceed with investment works at the maximum ceiling of €90,000 under this scheme are not eligible to apply for grants under any other TAMS 3 scheme with the exception of the Low Emission Slurry Spreading (LESS) Equipment Scheme. In the case of an application by two or more eligible partners in a registered partnership, the maximum increases to €160,000.

Eligible Applicants

The Scheme is open to farmers who:

- own or have leasehold title to the site on which it is proposed to carry out the development.
- have a minimum of 5 hectares owned and /or leased which have been declared under the Basic Payment Scheme in the year of application or preceding year or in the case of intensive enterprises.
- Must provide details that they are in compliance with farm waste and farm nutrient storage as set down in S.I.No.31 2104.

Eligible Investments

The scheme covers investment in new milking installations and upgrades, cooling equipment, in-parlour feeding systems, water heaters and auto washers. A detailed list of eligible investments can be found on the Department of Agriculture by searching under TAMS 3.

Applications & Further Information

Further information can be had from the www.agriculture.gov.ie. Intending applicants should contact their local ACA or Teagasc advisor.

Organic Capital Investment Scheme

The objective of the Scheme is to facilitate the development of the organic sector so as to ensure a regular supply of high quality organic produce to the market. Financial assistance will be directed towards projects which improve the organic sector and provide the producers of the basic product with an opportunity of enhancing income. It also aims to provide an incentive to young organic farmers to upgrade their agricultural buildings and equipment by providing them with an increased level of support to meet the considerable capital costs associated with the establishment of their enterprises.

Eligible Applicants

The Scheme is open to organic operators who are licensed organic operators registered with an approved certification body and own or have leasehold title to the site on which it is proposed to carry out the development.

Eligible Investments

A detailed list of eligible investments can be found on the Department of Agriculture by searching under TAMS 3.

Grant Aid

Grant aid is paid at the rate of 40% for licensed organic operators and 60% for farmers who are also current participants in the Organic Farming Scheme up to a maximum investment ceiling of €90,000 per holding. Applicants who receive approval to proceed with investment works at the maximum ceiling of €90,000 under this scheme are not eligible to apply for grants under any other TAMS 3 scheme with the exception of the Low Emission Slurry Spreading (LESS) Equipment Scheme. In the case of an application by two or more eligible partners in a registered partnership, the maximum increases to €160,000.

Applications & Further Information
Further information can be had from the www.agriculture.gov.ie. Intending applicants should contact their local ACA or Teagasc advisor.

Low Emission Slurry Spreading Equipment Scheme
The principal objective of the Scheme is to assist farmers purchase new equipment for the spreading of slurry which has distinct environmental advantages.

Eligible Applicants
The Scheme is open to farmers who:
• Hold a Department identifier.
• Have a minimum of 5 hectares which have been declared under the Basic Payment Scheme in the year of application or preceding year, or;
• Are engaged in the breeding, rearing or fattening of pigs and have a minimum of 60 production units at the time of application in accordance with Annex B of the Scheme.

Level of Grant Aid
Grant-aid at a rate of 60% up to the applicable maximum investment ceiling of €40,000 per applicant. However, in the case of a joint application by two or more eligible partners under a registered partnership, the maximum eligible investment ceilings referred to above shall be increased to €60,000. The investment ceiling under this scheme is NOT subject to the overall TAMS II investment ceiling of €90,000 per holding. Under TAMS 3 grant aid per investment item is based on the lowest of;
• The Departments reference costs applicable at the date of approval.
• The total eligible paid invoices.
• The cost proposed by the applicant on their application.

Eligible Investments
The following equipment types are eligible for aid provided they have one of the spreaders as specified:
• New tanker fitted with a Dribble bar spreader, Shallow injection spreader or Trailing shoe spreader.
• Umbilical slurry spreading system (base pump, hose reel, maximum of 500m Lay Flat Hose and all fittings) with Dribble bar spreader, Shallow injection spreader or Trailing shoe spreader.
• Retrofitting of existing tanker with Dribble bar spreader.
• A detailed list of eligible investments can be found on the Department of Agriculture by searching under TAMS 3.

Applications & Further Information
Further information can be had from the www.agriculture.gov.ie. Intending applicants should contact their local ACA or Teagasc advisor.

Pig & Poultry Investment Scheme

The principal objective of the Scheme is to assist farmers purchase new equipment for the upgrading of pig and poultry units on their farms thereby supporting farmers' compliance with animal welfare legislative requirements.

Grant Aid
Grant aid is paid at the rate of 40% up to a maximum investment ceiling of €500,000 per holding. Applicants who receive approval to proceed with investment works at the maximum ceiling of €500,000 under this scheme are not eligible to apply for grants under any other TAMS 3 scheme with the exception of the Low Emission Slurry Spreading (LESS) Equipment Scheme and the Solar Capital Investment Scheme.

Eligible Applicants
The Scheme is open to farmers who:
- Can generate a minimum of 20 production units from farming.
- Have a Department identifier.
- In the case of pig farmers, provide a pig census return for the year of application or the previous year.

Eligible Investments
The scheme covers investment in:
- Energy efficient upgrades for poultry housing, fattener housing, weaner housing and farrowing housing.
- Disease reduction facilities for existing poultry houses.
- Feed systems upgrade for medication reduction and energy efficiency.
- Energy efficient boilers, heat recovery units & heat pumps.
- Solar panels, water meters & medicine dispenser units.

A detailed list of eligible investments can be found on the Department of Agriculture by searching under TAMS 3.

Applications & Further Information
Further information can be had from the www.agriculture.gov.ie. Intending applicants should contact their local ACA or Teagasc advisor.

Animal Welfare and Nutrient Storage Scheme

The Scheme is aimed at improving competitiveness and contributing to the improvement of agricultural incomes and to assist tillage farmers for the storage of animal excreta, soiled water and other farmyard manures and related facilities.

Grant Aid

Grant aid is paid at the rate of 40% up to a maximum investment ceiling of €80,000 per holding. Applicants who receive approval to proceed with investment works at the maximum ceiling of €90,000 under this scheme are not eligible to apply for grants under any other TAMS 3 scheme with the exception of the Low Emission Slurry Spreading (LESS) Equipment Scheme. In the case of an application by two or more eligible partners in a registered partnership, the maximum increases to €160,000.

Eligible Applicants

The Scheme is open to farmers who have a minimum of 5 hectares owned and /or leased that have been declared under the Basic Payment Scheme or equivalent in the year of application or preceding year or in the case of intensive enterprises, generate a minimum of 20 production units from farming.

Eligible Investments

The scheme covers a very comprehensive range of farm investment including animal housing, slurry storage, silage pits, silage pit resurfacing, animal handling equipment, slat replacement along with various items to promote on-farm safety. A detailed list of eligible investments can be found on the Department of Agriculture by searching under TAMS 3.

Applications & Further Information

Further information can be had from the www.agriculture.gov.ie. Intending applicants should contact their local ACA or Teagasc advisor.

Tillage Capital Investment Scheme

The objectives of this Scheme are to facilitate the Tillage Sector to develop a targeted and precise approach focusing on environmental dividends, efficiency and growth, to improve competitiveness and contribute to the improvement of agricultural incomes.

Grant Aid

Grant aid is paid at the rate of 40% up to a maximum investment ceiling of €90,000 per holding. Applicants who receive approval to proceed with investment works at the maximum ceiling of €90,000 under this scheme are not eligible to apply for grants under any other TAMS 3 scheme with the exception of the Low Emission Slurry Spreading (LESS) Equipment Scheme. In the case of an application by two or more eligible partners in a registered partnership, the maximum increases to €160,000.

Eligible Applicants

The Scheme is open to farmers who have a minimum of 15 hectares of eligible crops (Annex D) declared under the Basic Payment Scheme or equivalent in the year of application or previous year. An application may be accepted in the name of a limited company provided that limited company satisfies the eligibility criteria above. A copy of a company's Companies Registration Office Certificate and constitution must be submitted in support of the application.

Eligible Investments
The scheme covers a very comprehensive range of farm investment including grain stores, ventilation systems for grain stores, grain dryers, GPS steering control for tractors, Yield monitors for combines, sprayers, stubble cultivators, fertiliser spreaders mounted with a full GPS control. A detailed list of eligible investments can be found on the Department of Agriculture by searching under TAMS 3.

Applications & Further Information
Further information can be had from the www.agriculture.gov.ie. Intending applicants should contact their local ACA or Teagasc advisor.

Solar Capital Investment Scheme
The Solar Capital Investment Scheme is aimed to encourage the purchase of solar investments thereby reducing dependence on fossil energy. The solar scheme will be ring fenced with its own investment ceiling of €90,000 and will be grant aided at 60%.

Eligibility
The Scheme is open to farmers who prior to submitting the online TAMS 3 application have a minimum of 5 hectares of owned, leased or rented lands which has been declared under the Basic Payment Scheme (BPS) and the Basic Income Support for Sustainability (BISS) or equivalent in the year of application or preceding year, or in the case of intensive enterprises, generate a minimum of 20 production units from farming.

Eligible Investments
A detailed list of eligible investments can be found on the Department of Agriculture by searching under TAMS 3.

Farm Safety Capital Investment Scheme
The Farm Safety Capital Investment Scheme (FSCIS) provides an incentive to farmers to avail of investments to improve their own safety and that of their farm.

Eligibility
The scheme is open to farmers who have a minimum of 5 hectares declared under the Basic Payment Scheme (BPS) or the Basic Income Support for Sustainability (BISS), or equivalent, in the year of application or preceding year; or generate a minimum of 20 production units from farming; for Equine Investments only have and a minimum of 3 equines declared on the Equine Census or equivalent in the year preceding.

Grant Aid
Grant aid is paid at the rate of 60% up to a maximum investment ceiling of €90,000 per holding. Applicants who receive approval to proceed with investment works at the maximum ceiling of €90,000 under this scheme are not eligible to apply for grants under any other TAMS 3 scheme with the exception of the Low Emission Slurry

ARCHAEOLOGICAL & ARCHITECTURAL HERITAGE CONSULTANTS

Archaeological and architectural heritage consultants are involved in solving a number of planning and pre- planning related issues for public bodies and private clients. The professional services offered in relation to archaeological heritage include: pre-development impact assessment, test excavation, full excavation, monitoring of groundworks, conservation and management plans, historic building and monument survey.

The range of services offered in relation to architectural heritage include: impact assessment for protected structures and/or buildings within Architectural Conservation Areas (ACA's). These assessments frequently involve architectural recording and historical research. On foot of an initial assessment, the local authority may request a subsequent condition survey and corresponding conservation method statement. This may be followed by architectural monitoring of any works.

Spreading (LESS) Equipment Scheme. In the case of an application by two or more eligible partners in a registered partnership, the maximum increases to €160,000.

Eligible Investments
A detailed list of eligible investments can be found on the Department of Agriculture by searching under TAMS.

Women Farmer Capital Investment Scheme

The Women Farmers' Capital Investment Scheme (WFCIS) provides an incentive to women farmers to upgrade their agricultural buildings and equipment by providing them with an increased level of support to meet the considerable capital costs associated with the establishment of their enterprises. To promote gender equality, employment, growth, generational renewal, social inclusion and local development in rural areas by supporting the participation of women in farming. To improve competitiveness and contribute to the improvement of agricultural incomes.

Eligility
The scheme is open to farmers who are more than 18 years and under 67 years of age at the date of submitting the application form. They must own or have leasehold title to the site on which it is proposed to carry out the development, have a minimum of 5 hectares declared under the Basic Payment Scheme (BPS) or the Basic Income Support for Sustainability (BISS) or equivalent in the year of application or preceding year, or, for tillage related investments, have a minimum of 15 hectares of eligible crops. In the case of intensive enterprises, they must generate a minimum of 20 production units from farming.

Grant Aid
Grant aid is paid at the rate of 60% up to a maximum investment ceiling of €90,000 per holding. Applicants who receive approval to proceed with investment works at the maximum ceiling of €90,000 under this scheme are not eligible to apply for grants under any other TAMS 3 scheme with the exception of the Low Emission Slurry Spreading (LESS) Equipment Scheme. In the case of an application by two or more eligible partners in a registered partnership, the maximum increases to €160,000.

Eligible Investments
A detailed list of eligible investments can be found on the Department of Agriculture by searching under TAMS.

TAMS Maximum Investment Limits and Grant Rates
Table 1.4 sets out the limits applicable to various collaborative farming arrangements applicable to TAMS 3. A "young farmer" refers to a male or female trained farmer under 40 years. A "woman farmer" is a qualifying person over 18 and under 67. A farmer is a male or a female farmer who does not meet the definition of a "woman farmer" or a "young trained farmer".

Table 1.4: Maximum Investment Limits for Collaborative Arrangements

FARM STRUCTURE	ELIGIBLE GRANT AID
Young and/or woman farmer in partnership with a farmer	Overall investment ceiling of €160k. First €90k @ 60%, remaining at 40%.
Young and/or women farmer in partnership with a young and/or woman farmer	Overall investment ceiling of €160k, all @ 60%
Two farmers	Investment ceiling of €90k, all @ 40%
A company with two farmers	Overall investment ceiling of €90k, all @ 40%
A company with a young and/or woman farmer and a farmer	Overall investment ceiling of €90k, all @ 60%, assuming Young/Women Farmer has a 20% share holding
A company with two young farmers	Overall investment ceiling of €90k, all @ 60%, assuming Young Farmer has a 20% share holding
A company in partnership with a young and/or woman farmer in a registered partnership	Investment ceiling of €160k, of which €90k will be @ 60%,and €70k at 40%
A company in partnership with a young and/or woman farmer in a non-registered partnership where the young and/or woman farmer has a 20% shareholding in the company	Overall investment ceiling of €90k, at 60%
A company in a non-registered partnership with a farmer	Overall investment ceiling of €90k,at 40%

Partnership Dissolution - Clawback of Benefit
Where a partnership dissolves or ceases to trade within a five-year period of claiming an enhanced level of grant aid, the lower ceiling of €90,000 and the 40% grant rate will be re-imposed resulting in a clawback of benefit gained. The rate of clawback will be 100% of the additional benefit gained if the partnership ceases in year 1 reducing by 20% per year over the five years.

Other Pillar II and Government Funded Schemes

National Beef Welfare Scheme
The objective of the National Beef Welfare Scheme (NBWS) is to further increase the economic efficiency of, and enhance animal health and husbandry, on suckler farms. Applicants must be suckler beef farmers, i.e. you have eligible calves born to eligible suckler cows during the period 1 July 2023-30 June 2024. They must do IBR sampling and meal feeding calves pre- and post-weaning.
Payment for IBR testing amounts to €120 up to €300 per herd depending on the number of animals tested. Meal feeding attracts payment of €35 per calf up to a maximum of 40 calves.

Dairy Beef Welfare Scheme
The aim of this scheme is to provide support to farmers who undertake actions to improve the viability of male dairy calves in locally based production systems. The scheme will open for applications in 2024 and the support per calf is set at €20.

Sheep Improvement Scheme (SIS)
The aim of this scheme is to build on the progress made by the Sheep Welfare Scheme (SWS) in the 2014- 2020 RDP by providing support for actions that improve animal health and welfare in the sheep sector. The Sheep Improvement Scheme will contribute to improved welfare through targeted interventions in lameness control, parasite control, genetic improvement, fly-strike and appropriate supplementation. Support amounts to €12 per ewe.

Knowledge Transfer Programme
The aim of this measure is to provide farmers with a platform to share knowledge and to engage in learning. This measure aims to provide support for high quality and targeted advice to farmers, delivered by professional agricultural advisors with the appropriate experience and expertise (KT Facilitator's). Increasing farmers' understanding of topics such as biodiversity, water, climate change, animal welfare and farm management including financial management and succession planning will ensure that the Irish agricultural sector remains resilient. Payment rates of €750 to each farmer and €500 per farmer to the advisor apply.

The National Liming Programme
This programme was introduced in 2023 by the Department of Agriculture Food and the Marine to incentivise the use of Lime as a natural soil conditioner, which

corrects soil acidity by neutralising the acids that are present in the soil. Research has shown that Liming not only increases soil microbial activity but can also unlock soil phosphorous (P) and potassium (K). Liming can improve the response to freshly applied N, P, and K, while providing a valuable source of calcium.

Applicants that have submitted a Basic Income Support for Sustainability (BISS) application in 2023 are eligible to apply. Ground limestone can only be applied in accordance with the lime requirement stated on up-to-date soil analysis reports (maximum of 4 years old from date of purchasing the lime). Farmers that availed of a Nitrates Derogation in 2023 or 2024 and farmers with a grassland stocking rate above 170kg livestock manure nitrogen/ha prior to export in 2023 are ineligible to participate in this programme. Herdowners who are participating or intend to participate in the 2024 Eco-Scheme practice relating to soil sampling and liming are not eligible to participate in this programme.

Approved applicants will receive a financial contribution of €16 per tonne of lime spread, to offset part of the cost of applying Calcium ground limestone (CaCO3) or Magnesium (dolomitic) ground limestone (CaMg (CO3)2). Subject to budget availability payment will be made on a minimum of 10 tonnes of ground limestone and a maximum of 200 tonnes.

Suckler Carbon Efficiency Programme (SCEP)

This scheme aims to provide support to beef farmers to improve the environmental sustainability of the national beef herd. Eligible applicants must calve at least 50% beef breed animals of the yearly reference number between scheme year 01 July 2022 and 30 June 2023 and every scheme year thereafter attend the SCEP training course and an animal handling course by 15th November 2024. Payment will amount to €225 for the first 15 hectares and €180 for the remaining hectares subject to the maximum payable area.

Tillage Incentive Scheme

The Tillage Incentive Scheme (TIS) is a support measure for farmers to incentivise the increase in the eligible tillage crop area and to reduce the dependency on imported feed material. This scheme was available in 2023 but confirmation is awaited on its continuation in 2024. The following details are applicable to the 2023 scheme.

Eligibility

Farmers can prepare for the scheme by declaring the eligible crops- barley, wheat, oats, rye, oilseed rape, maize, beet, triticale - on their current Basic Income Support for Sustainability (BISS) online application. There are two components to the Scheme, each with two key eligibility requirements.

Maintenance Payment

Applicants must have received a payment under the Tillage Incentive Scheme in the previous year and must maintain the overall area under Tillage/Protein as grown in the previous year for the current scheme year.

Newly Converted Payment

There must be an increase in the total tillage crops grown on the holding in the current year versus the previous year and the land on which the additional eligible crops are grown for this scheme must have been in grassland or one of the other specified non-tillage crops in the previous year.

Rates of Payment

A rate of €200 for each eligible hectare under the maintenance option will be paid. A rate of €400 will apply for each eligible hectare under the newly converted land option.

Red Clover Silage Measure

This Measure aims to incentivise farmers to sow red clover silage swards, which will reduce the reliance on nitrogen fertilisers and promote a more sustainable method of farming. Red Clover due to its Nitrogen fixing ability produces fodder higher in protein than conventional silage and combined with its ability to yield over 14t DM/ha will assist farmers in reducing their concentrate feed bills.

Rates of Payment

A payment of up to €300/ha will be provided to participating applicants to offset part of the cost that farmers will incur in the establishment of these swards.

Multi-species Sward Measure

This Measure aims to incentivise farmers to sow multi-species swards, which will reduce the reliance on nitrogen fertilisers and promote a more sustainable method of farming.

Rates of Payment

A payment of up to €300/ha will be provided to participating applicants to offset part of the cost that farmers will incur in the establishment of these swards.

National Farm Safety Measure

This measure is being introduced to incentivise the purchase and use of certain farm safety equipment, which protect farmers and machinery operators from serious and fatal injuries. The measure will provide a financial contribution to participating farmers for a maximum of two quad helmets and four PTO shaft covers. The grant aid will be at a rate of 60% subject to a maximum eligible cost of €100 per PTO shaft cover and €150 per quad bike (ATV) helmet.

Service to Assist Bereaved Farming Families

The Inheritance Enquiry Unit is available to help representatives of a deceased farmer to secure outstanding payments and deal with other farming paperwork. Following the death of a farmer there are generally two issues to be dealt with:

- change to the registration details of the herd number/herd keeper.
- payment of any outstanding monies due to the estate of the deceased and the transfer of any single payment entitlements held by the late farmer.
- The Inheritance Enquiry Unit will help to:
- identify those schemes in which the deceased person participated and establish whether there are any outstanding payments due to the estate of the deceased.
- assist the legal representatives in contacting various sections of the Department.
- advise on what legal documents are required.
- make arrangements for the issue of any outstanding payments due to estate of the deceased and for the transfer of Basic Income Support for Sustainability entitlements.

The principal documents needed to complete the process are copy of will and grant of probate or letters of administration confirming the administrator of the estate where no will exists.

2

Farm Enterprise Planning & Budgets

Effective Farm Planning
The Land, Stock, Capital Expenditure & Financial Plans 70
Budgeting 71

Dairying
Dairy Gross Margin Budgets 2024 72
Dairy Net Profit Budgets 2024 75

Beef Production
Beef Gross Margin Budgets 2024 78
Beef Farm Net Profit Projection... 86

Sheep Production
Sheep Gross Margin Budgets 2024 88
Sheep Farm Net Profit Projection..91

Tillage Crops
Winter & Spring Malting Barley Gross Margin Projections............................... 92
Winter & Spring Wheat Gross Margin Projections...95
Winter & Spring Oats Gross Margin Projections..97
Winter & Spring Oilseed Rape Gross Margin Projections................................. 99
Peas 101
Beans...102
Potato Crops Gross Margin Projections 103
Tillage Farm Net Profit Projections 104

Effective Farm Planning

Whether it's a greenfield start-up, expansion of an existing enterprise or simply a new entrant taking over the family farm, a detailed assessment and analysis of the enterprise will be required. This should take the form of a five-year farm plan as this is vital for charting the medium-term future and setting targets for where you will be in five years' time. The plan should not be viewed as a requirement to secure financing, but rather it should represent a detailed road map for the future, setting down both management and financial objectives and targets. It should represent a whole process which the farmer fully engages with rather than simply a document. A comprehensive farm plan will contain three main components, namely the land and stock management plan, the financial plan and the facilities and infrastructure plan.

The Land & Stock Management Plan
The overall plan should address the following matters over a five-year term:
- Medium to long term sustainable land availability.
- Grazing management plan - rotation & re-seeding.
- Production targets and price assumptions.
- Fertilizer and nutrient management plan.
- Animal waste storage needs assessment.
- The stocking plan.
- Breeding programme.
- Feed budgeting, and;
- Labour needs assessment.

The Capital Expenditure Plan
Expenditure on buildings and equipment associated with expansion or a new start up will require considerable thought and planning. Piecemeal expansion of existing poor infrastructure should be avoided if at all possible, as should over-elaborate structures that are inappropriate to the financial capacity. Good advice should be sought from trusted experts and operators. The key components of the programme should include:
- An inventory and assessment of current infrastructure (paddock fencing and water, buildings, and slurry storage), machinery and equipment setting down age, current condition, expected life span and suitability for use in new/expanded dairy enterprise.
- A five-year forecast of capital investment needs in regard to farm buildings, land improvement works, farm machinery, farm equipment and motor vehicles
- An assessment of planning permission requirement for proposed new structures along with an assessment of planning compliance for existing structures.

The Financial Plan
The financial plan should be based on realistic targets drawn from reliable sources such as the Teagasc Profit Monitor figures or the budgets contained in this handbook. An existing producer will require an assessment of current and past performance as per the annual farm management accounts and herd profile based on three prior

years data such as average yields achieved, crop or forage input costs, concentrate consumption, stocking rate, mortality rates, cow replacement percentage and overhead cost per acre.

The following are essential components of a good farm plan:

- A five-year forecast of personal expenditure to include, home improvements, educational costs, pension funding, dependent relative care etc.
- A current statement of affairs based on realistic physical and financial asset valuations and vouched loan and creditor balances.
- A schedule of exiting bank loans and HP/Lease finance setting out the annual repayments and the end date.
- A five-year schedule of loan/HP financing requirements.
- A five-year annual cash flow budget forecast.
- A five-year annual Profit & Loss and taxation forecast, and;
- A projected balance sheet at the end of the five-year term.

Budgeting

Budgeting in any business is vitally important so that the operator knows what to aim for and expect in predictable circumstances. Budgeting will make for planned and better financial management and will alert the operator to how actual performance matches predicted expectation. The following pages contain sample budgets to establish predicted Gross Margin and Net Profit. Gross Margin is a universal measure of the performance of an individual production unit or a particular enterprise and should only vary from farm to farm insofar as efficiency and land suitability varies. Net Profit on the other hand can vary widely depending on such factors as labour costs, mechanisation cost, overall debt etc.

Dairy Gross Margin Budgets 2024

Gross Margin projection for spring milk production from a Holstein/Friesian herd based on autumn 2023 prices.

Table 2.1: Creamery Milk - Spring Production - Holstein/Friesian/Herd.

Assumptions	€	€	Av. per litre (cent)
Litres per cow	5,150	6,600	
Gallons per cow	1,134	1,454	
Milk Solids per Cow (kg/cow)	400	530	
Standard milk price incl. VAT. (cent)	30	30	
Gross Output			
Milk sales	1,545	1,980	30.00
Calf @ €80 (5% mortality)	60	60	1.02
Cull cow sales	195	195	3.32
Total Output	**1,800**	**2,235**	**34.34**
Variable Costs per Cow			
Concentrates	270	360	5.36
Forage & grazing costs	419	460	7.48
Veterinary & breeding	140	140	2.38
Cow replacement (home rearing basis)	200	200	3.40
Miscellaneous	39	40	0.67
Total Variable Costs - per cow/per litre (av.)	**1068**	**1200**	**19.30**
Gross Margin per cow / litre	**732**	**1,035**	**15.04**
Gross Margin per Ha. (based on 2.5 l.U/Ha.)	1,838	2,597	
Gross Margin per Ha. (based on 2.0 l.U/Ha.)	1,465	1,465	
Impact on Gross Margin of +/- 5 cent per litre	257	330	

Dairy Gross Margin Budgets 2024

Gross Margin projection for spring milk production from a Friesian x Jersey herd based on autumn 2023 prices.

Table 2.2: Creamery Milk - Spring Production - Friesian/Jersey Cross Bred Herd.

Assumptions	€	€	Av. per litre (cent)
Litres per cow	5,150	6,600	
Gallons per cow	1,134	1,454	
Milk Solids per Cow (kg/cow)	440	580	
Standard milk price incl. VAT. (cent)	33	33	
Gross Output			
Milk sales	1,700	2,178	33.00
Calf @ €20 (5% mortality)	19	19	0.32
Cull cow sales	195	195	3.32
Total Output	**1,914**	**2,392**	**36.64**
Variable Costs per Cow			
Concentrates	325	396	6.14
Forage & grazing costs	419	460	7.48
Veterinary & breeding	140	140	2.38
Cow replacement (home rearing basis)	200	200	3.40
Miscellaneous	39	40	0.67
Total Variable Costs - per cow/per litre (av.)	**1123**	**1236**	**20.08**
Gross Margin per cow / litre	**791**	**1,156**	**16.57**
Gross Margin per Ha. (based on 2.5 l.U/Ha.)	1,985	2,900	
Gross Margin per Ha. (based on 2.0 l.U/Ha.)	1,582	1,582	
Impact on Gross Margin of +/- 5 cent per litre	257	330	

Dairy Gross Margin Budgets 2024

Gross Margin projection for winter/spring milk production from a Holstein/Friesian herd based on autumn 2023 prices

Table 2.3: Creamery Milk - Winter/Spring Production - Holstein/Friesian Herd.

Assumptions	€	€	Av. per litre (cent)
Litres per cow	5,150	6,600	
Gallons per cow	1,134	1,454	
Milk Solids per Cow (kg/cow)	400	530	
Standard milk price incl. VAT. (cent)	30	30	
Gross Output			
Milk sales	1,545	1,980	30.00
Winter bonus on 25% production	124	158	3.21
Calf @ €80 (5% mortality)	60	60	1.02
Cull cow sales	195	195	3.32
Total Output	**1,924**	**2,393**	**37.55**
Variable Costs per Cow			
Concentrates	410	430	7.15
Forage & grazing costs	419	460	7.48
Veterinary & breeding	140	140	2.38
Cow replacement (home rearing basis)	200	200	3.40
Miscellaneous	39	40	0.67
Total Variable Costs - per cow/per litre (av.)	1208	1270	21.09
Gross Margin per cow / litre	**716**	**1,123**	**15.65**
Gross Margin per Ha. (based on 2.5 l.U/Ha.)	1,797	2,819	
Gross Margin per Ha. (based on 2.0 l.U/Ha.)	1,432	1,432	
Impact on Gross Margin of +/- 5 cent per litre	257	330	

Dairy Net Profit Budgets 2024

The following budget is based on an established dairy enterprise producing 400kgs of milk solids per cow at 30 cent per litre from an 80-cow spring calving Holstein/Friesian herd in 2024. All calves are sold except for those kept for replacements. The farm carries a total debt of €150,000. All figures are based on 2023 costs and returns.

Table 2.4: Profit Projection for an 80 Cow Dairy Farm.

	€	Cent Per litre
Total Gross Margin (See page 72)	58,592	14.22
Overhead Costs		
Bank interest & charges	6,750	1.64
Light & heat (farm share)	3,360	0.82
General farm repairs	5,600	1.36
Machinery running costs	7,200	1.75
Telephone (farm share)	920	0.22
Motor (farm share)	5,600	1.36
Wages & Social insurance	5,100	1.24
Accountancy/Advisory	2,420	0.59
Insurance	3,400	0.83
Depreciation	8,900	2.16
Sundries	1,730	0.42
Total	**50,980**	**12.37**
Net Profit excluding Gov. & E.U. supports	**7,612**	**1.85**
BiSS & other subsidies (est.)	**11,000**	**2.14**
Net Profit including Gov. & E.U. supports	**18,612**	**3.98**

Dairy Net Profit Budgets 2024

The following budget is based on an established dairy enterprise producing 400kgs of milk solids per cow from a 150-cow spring calving Holstein/Friesian herd in 2024. All calves are sold except for those kept for replacements. The farm carries a total debt of €250,000. All figures are based on 2023 costs and returns.

Table 2.5: Profit Projection for a 150 Cow Holstein/Friesian Dairy Farm.

	€	Cent Per litre
Total Gross Margin (€) (see page 72)	109,860	11.10
Overhead Costs		
Bank interest & charges	15,000	1.52
Light & heat (farm share)	6,300	0.64
General farm repairs	10,500	1.06
Machinery running costs	11,250	1.14
Telephone (farm share)	920	0.09
Motor (farm share)	5,700	0.58
Wages & Social insurance	40,000	4.04
Accountancy/Advisory	2,800	0.28
Insurance	3,334	0.34
Depreciation	11,200	1.13
Sundries	1,800	0.18
Total	108,804	10.99
Net Profit excluding Gov. & E.U. supports.	1,056	0.11
BiSS & other subsidies (est.)	14,000	2.12
Net Profit including Gov. & E.U. supports.	15,056	2.23

Dairy Net Profit Budgets 2024

The following budget is based on an established dairy enterprise producing 530 kgs of solids per cow from a 150-cow spring calving Holstein/Friesian herd in 2024. All calves are sold except for those kept for replacements. The farm carries a total debt of €250,000. All figures are based on 2023 costs and returns.

Table 2.6: Profit Projection for a 150 Cow Holstein/Friesian Dairy by Farm.

	€	Cent Per litre
Total Gross Margin (€) (see page 73)	168,441	17.01
Overhead Costs		
Bank interest & charges	14,000	1.41
Light & heat (farm share)	6,800	0.69
General farm repairs	5,600	0.57
Machinery running costs	10,100	1.02
Telephone (farm share)	920	0.09
Motor (farm share)	5,700	0.58
Wages & Social insurance	38,200	3.86
Accountancy/Advisory	2,320	0.23
Insurance	3,334	0.34
Depreciation	9,300	0.94
Sundries	1,730	0.17
Total	**98,004**	**9.90**
Net Profit excluding Gov. & E.U. supports.	**70,437**	**7.11**
BiSS & other subsidies (est.)	14,000	822.84
Net Profit including Gov. & E.U. supports.	**84,437**	**829.95**

BEEF PRODUCTION

Beef Gross Margin Budgets 2024

Finished Beef from the Dairy Herd

Table 2.7: Gross Margin from Finished Beef from the Dairy Herd.

Assumptions	
Steer weight at sale (kg)	480
Heifer weight at sale (kg)	610
Steer price at sale (€ per kg)	4.90
Heifer price at sale (€ per kg)	4.95
Output per Cow	
Heifers (50% incl. VAT) @54% k.o.	815
Bullocks (50% incl. VAT) @54%	635
Mortality @ 3% of output	44
Less: Calf transfer cost	80
Gross Output	**1,327**
Variable Costs	
Milk Powder	70
Silage cutting, slurry spreading, polythene & acid	255
Fertilizer & Lime	290
Concentrates	320
Veterinary	49
Transport. Levies & Interest	75
Total Variable Costs	**1,059**
Gross Margin Per Livestock Unit	**268**
Stocking rate - L.U./hectare	2
Gross Margin Per Hectare (ex. Gov. & E.U. supports)	**536**

Beef Gross Margin Budgets 2024

Single Suckling - Continental Type Weanlings

Table 2.8: Sucklers, Selling At 18mts in Oct/Nov from March/April Born Calves.

Assumptions	€
Calving rate	90%
Steer weight kg	520
Steer sale price (cent/kg)	275
Heifer wt.	460
Heifer sale price (cent/kg)	280
Output per Suckler Unit	
Sales per cow	1,223
Cull cow sales	150
Less mortality @ 3% of output	37
Less cow replacement cost	205
Gross Output per Suckler Unit	**1,131**
Variable Costs per Suckler Unit	
Concentrates	110
Silage cutting, slurry spreading, polyethene & acid	235
Fertlizer & lime	380
Straw	34
Veterinary & breeding	58
Sundry	28
Total Variable Costs	**845**
Gross Margin Per Suckler Unit (SU)	**286**
Stocking rate - L.U./hectare S.U. = 1.7 Livestock Units)	1.25
Gross Margin Per Hectare (ex. Gov. & E.U. supports)	**358**

Beef Gross Margin Budgets 2024

Single Suckling - Continental Type Yearlings

Table 2.9: Sucklers - Selling Weanlings in Oct/Nov from Mar/Apr Born Calves.

Assumptions	€
Calving rate	90%
Steer weight kg	360
Sale price (cent/kg)	345
Heifer wt.	320
Sale price (cent/kg)	350
Output per Suckler Unit	
Sales per cow	1,063
Cull cow sales	144
Less mortality @ 3% of output	-34
Less cow replacement cost	-215
Gross Output per Suckler Unit	958
Variable Costs per Suckler Unit	
Concentrates	28
Silage cutting, slurry spreading, polyethene & acid	132
Fertlizer & lime	380
Straw	34
Veterinary & breeding	38
Sundry	15
Total Variable Costs	627
Gross Margin Per Suckler Unit (SU)	**331**
Stocking rate - L.U./hectare (iSuckler Unit = 1.7 Livestock Units)	1.66
Gross Margin Per Hectare (ex. Gov. & E.U. supports)	**549**

Beef Gross Margin Budgets 2024

Finishing Weanling Steers

Table 2.10: Weanling Steers (Continental) to Finished Beef.

Assumptions	€
Purchase weight kg.	350
Purchase price (per 100kg cent)	340
Output per animal	
Weight at sale kg.	680
Sales price per kg. (€/kg deadweight)	4.85
Sale price per animal (k.o. 54%)	1,781
Less cost of animal	1,190
Less mortality @ 2%	30
Gross Output per head	**561**
Variable Costs per Suckler Unit	
Concentrates	235
Silage cutting, slurry spreading, polyethene & acid	95
Fertlizer & lime	217
Veterinary	41
Sundry	25
Total Variable Costs	**613**
Gross Margin Per head	**-52**
Stocking rate -animals./hectare (1 store is equivalent to .0.75 L.U and is stocked at 2.1 L.U. per hectare	2.8
Gross Margin Per Hectare (ex. Gov. & E.U. supports)	**-145**

Beef Gross Margin Budgets 2024

Finishing Store Steers

Table 2.11: Continental Stores to Finished Beef - Autumn Purchase & Sale.

Assumptions	€
Purchase weight kg.	420
Purchase price (per 100kg cent)	275
Weight at sale kg.	680
Sales price per kg. (€/kg deadweight)	4.85
Output per animal	
Sale price per animal (k.o. 54%)	1,781
Less cost of animal	1,155
Less mortality @ 2%	29
Gross Output per head	**597**
Variable Costs per Suckler Unit	
Concentrates	165
Silage cutting, slurry spreading, polyethene & acid	85
Fertlizer & lime	268
Veterinary	36
Sundry	52
Total Variable Costs	**606**
Gross Margin Per head	**-9**
Stocking rate -animals./hectare (1 store is equivalent to .0.8 L.U and is stocked at 2.1 L.U. per hectare	2.68
Gross Margin Per Hectare (ex. Gov. & E.U. supports)	**-25**

Beef Gross Margin Budgets 2024
Bull Beef Production

Table 2.12: Calf/Weanling to Finished Beef (Continental Breeds).

Assumptions	€
Purchase weight kg.	340
Purchase price (per 100kg cent)	350
Output per animal	
Weight at sale kg.	680
Sales price per kg. (€/kg deadweight)	4.75
Sale price per animal (k.o. 54%)	1,744
Less cost of animal	1,190
Less mortality @ 2%	29
Gross Output per head	**525**
Variable Costs per Suckler Unit	
Concentrates	290
Silage cutting, slurry spreading, polyethene & acid	85
Fertlizer & lime	235
Veterinary	39
Sundry	25
Total Variable Costs	**674**
Gross Margin Per head	**-149**
Stocking rate -animals./hectare (1 store is equivalent to .0.75 L.U and is stocked at 2.1 L.U. per hectare	2.9
Gross Margin Per Hectare (ex. Gov. & E.U. supports)	**-433**

Beef Gross Margin Budgets 2024

Finishing Summer Grazing

Table 2.13: Store Steers (Apr-May) to Finished Beef in November.

Assumptions	€
Purchase weight kg.	490
Purchase price (per 100kg cent)	275
Output per animal	
Weight at sale kg.	680
Sales price per kg. (€/kg deadweight)	4.85
Sale price per animal (k.o. 54%)	1,781
Less cost of animal	1,348
Less mortality @ 2%	31
Gross Output per head	**402**
Variable Costs per Suckler Unit	
Concentrates	55
Grazing costs	170
Veterinary	24
Sundry	29
Total Variable Costs	**278**
Gross Margin Per head	**124**
Stocking rate -animals./hectare (1 store is equivalent to .0.5 L.U and is stocked at 2.1 L.U. per hectare	4.33
Gross Margin Per Hectare (ex. Gov. & E.U. supports)	**538**

Beef Gross Margin Budgets 2024

Calf to Beef Production

Table 2.14: Calf to Beef (Friesian x Continental Breed).

Assumptions	€
Weight at sale kg.	650
Sale price €/kg deadweight	4.80
Output per animal	
Sale value assuming 54% k.o.	1,685
Less cost of calf	325
Less mortality @ 3%	30
Gross Output per head	**1,330**
Variable Costs per Suckler Unit	
Concentrates	295
Milk powder	70
Silage cutting, slurry spreading, polythene & acid	235
Fertilizer & lime	290
Transport, levies & interest	110
Veterinary	47
Total Variable Costs	**1,047**
Gross Margin Per head	**283**
Stocking rate - L.U. per Ha.	2
Gross Margin Per Hectare (ex. Gov. & E.U. supports)	**565**

Beef Gross Margin Budgets 2024

Net Profit Budget for a 60 Cow Single Suckling Farm Based on Autuimn 2023 Prices

The following projection is based on a 100-acre farm in an Area of Natural Constraint with 60 suckler cows selling the progeny as weanlings in October/November. The farm has €55,000 total debt, is very efficient and is participating in GLÁS/ACRES.

Table 2.15: Profit Projection for a Suckler Farm.

	€
Gross Margin (as per page 80)	19,854
Overhead Costs	
Bank interest & charges	4,500
Light & heat (farm share)	2,650
General farm repairs	4,940
Machinery running costs	8,300
Telephone (farm share)	750
Motor (farm share)	4,937
Wages & Social insurance	1,530
Accountancy/Advisory	1,700
Insurance	2,800
Depreciation	7,800
Sundries	1,300
Total	**41,207**
Net Profit excluding Gov. & E.U. supports.	**-21,353**
Estimated BISS & other scheme payments	17,000
Net Profit including Gov, & E.U. supports	**-4,353**

Beef Gross Margin Budgets 2024

Net Profit for a Calf to Beef Farm Based on Autumn 2023 Prices

The following projection is based on a 100-acre farm in an Area of Natural Constraint carrying 70 livestock units. The farm has €55,000 total debt, is very efficient and is participating in GLÁS/ACRES.

Table 2.16: Profit Projection for a Calf to Beef Farm.

	€
Gross Margin (as per page 85)	**19,786**
Overhead Costs	
Bank interest & charges	4,500
Light & heat (farm share)	2,650
General farm repairs	4,940
Machinery running costs	8,300
Telephone (farm share)	750
Motor (farm share)	4,937
Wages & Social insurance	1,530
Accountancy/Advisory	1,700
Insurance	2,800
Depreciation	7,800
Sundries	1,300
Total	**41,207**
Net Profit excluding Gov. & E.U. supports.	**-21,421**
Estimated BISS & other scheme payments	17,000
Net Profit including Gov, & E.U. supports	**-4,421**

SHEEP PRODUCTION

Sheep Gross Margin Budgets 2024

Early Fat Lamb

Table 2.17: Gross Margin from Early Fat Lamb.

Assumptions	€	€
Lambs sold per ewe put to ram	1.4	1.5
Weight of lams at sale (kg's)	18	18
Price per kg carcass weight (€)	7	7
Output		
Lamb sales	176	189
Less replacement costs	18	18
Gross Output	**158**	**171**
Variable Costs		
Concentrates	38	38
Forage costs	45	45
Veterinary, dipping & dosing	12	13
Transport & other	10	10
Total Variable Costs	**105**	**106**
Gross Margin Per Livestock Unit	**53**	**65**
Stocking rate - Ewes/hectare	8.5	8.5
Gross Margin Per Hectare (ex. Gov. & E.U. supports)	**454**	**553**

Sheep Gross Margin Budgets 2024

Mid-Season Lamb

Table 2.18: Gross Margin from Mid-Season Lamb.

Assumptions	€	€
Lambs sold per ewe put to ram	1.4	1.5
Weight of lams at sale (kg's)	21	21
Price per kg carcass weight (€)	6.40	6.40
Output		
Lamb sales	188	202
Less replacement costs	18	18
Gross Output	**170**	**184**
Variable Costs		
Concentrates	36	36
Forage costs	45	45
Veterinary, dipping & dosing	12	13
Transport & other	10	10
Total Variable Costs	**103**	**104**
Gross Margin Per Livestock Unit	67	80
Stocking rate - Ewes/hectare	8.5	8.5
Gross Margin Per Hectare (ex. Gov. & E.U. supports)	571	677

Sheep Gross Margin Budgets 2024

Hill Sheep

Table 2.19: Gross Margin from Hill Sheep.

Assumptions	€	€
Lambs sold per ewe put to ram	0.9	1.1
Weight of lams at sale (kg's)	18	18
Price per kg carcass weight (€)	5.10	5.10
Output		
Lamb sales	83	101
Less replacement costs	20	20
Gross Output	63	81
Variable Costs		
Concentrates	22	23
Forage costs	27	27
Veterinary, dipping & dosing	8	8
Transport & other	9	9
Total Variable Costs	66	67
Gross Margin Per Livestock Unit	-3	14

Sheep Net Profit Budgets 2024

Net Profit Budget for a Mid-Season Lamb Producing Farm Based on Autumn 2023 Prices

The following projection is based on a 120-acre farm engaged in a 400 ewe mid-season lamb production enterprise finishing 600 lambs. The farm has €50,000 total debt, is very efficient, is participating in Glás/Acres and is in an Area of Natural Constraint.

Table 2.20: Profit Projection for a Mid-Season Sheep Enterprise.

	€
Gross Margin (as per page 89)	31,840
Overhead Costs	
Bank interest & charges	2,400
Light & heat (farm share)	1,580
General farm repairs	4,910
Machinery running costs	7,200
Telephone (farm share)	750
Motor (farm share)	4,345
Wages & Social insurance	1,500
Accountancy/Advisory	1,600
Insurance	3,100
Depreciation	4,940
Sundries	1,580
Total	**33,905**
Net Profit excluding Gov. & E.U. supports.	**-2,065**
Estimated BISS & other scheme payments	28,000
Net Profit including Gov, & E.U. supports	**25,935**

Tillage Crop Production
Crop Gross Margin Budgets 2024

The following projections assume that all machinery is owned except for harvesting equipment. Grain price is based on average harvest 2023 prices.

Spring Feeding Barley

Table 2.21: Spring Barley Gross Margin Projection 2024.

Assumptions	€	€	€
Yield per hectare (tonnes)	5.5	6.5	8.0
Price per tonne @ 20% moisture	200	200	200
Output			
Grain sales	1100	1300	1600
Straw	250	255	260
Gross Output	**1350**	**1555**	**1860**
Variable Costs			
Seed	105	105	105
Fert & Lime	320	320	240
Spray materials	185	195	195
Harvesting & transport	250	260	275
Interest	12	12	12
Total Variable Costs	872	892	827
Gross Margin Per Hectare	**478**	**663**	**1,033**
Overhead costs per hectare (see page 104)	862	862	862
Net Profit per hectare (ex-subsidies)	**-384**	**-199**	**171**
Price per tonne required to achieve a break-even Gross Margin	113	98	71
Price per tonne required to achieve a break-even Net Profit	270	231	179
Yield per hectare required to achieve a break-even Gross Margin	3.1	3.2	2.8
Yield per hectare required to achieve a break-even Net Profit	7.42	7.50	7.15

Overhead costs per hectare drawn from the Net Profit Projection on page 104

Crop Gross Margin Budgets 2024

The following projections assume that all machinery is owned except for harvesting equipment. Grain price is based on average 2023 prices.

Malting Barley

Table 2.22: Malting Barley Gross Margin Projection 2024.

Assumptions	€	€	€
Yield per hectare (tonnes)	5.0	6.0	7.5
Price per tonne @ 20% moisture	268	268	268
Output			
Grain sales	1,340	1,608	2,010
Straw	250	255	260
Gross Output	**1,590**	**1,863**	**2,270**
Variable Costs			
Seed	110	110	110
Fert & Lime	376	376	376
Spray materials	190	190	190
Harvesting & transport	245	256	272
Interest	12	12	12
Total Variable Costs	**933**	**944**	**960**
Gross Margin Per Hectare	**657**	**919**	**1,310**
Overhead costs per hectare (see page 104)	862	862	862
Net Margin per hectare (ex-subsidies)	**-205**	**57**	**448**
Price per tonne required to achieve a break-even Gross Margin	187	157	128
Price per tonne required to achieve a break-even Net Profit	270	227	184
Yield per hectare required to achieve a break-even Gross Margin	3.48	3.52	3.58
Yield per hectare required to achieve a break-even Net Profit	5.04	5.08	5.14

[1]Overhead costs per hectare drawn from the Net Profit Projection on page 104.

Crop Gross Margin Budgets 2024

The following projections assume that all machinery is owned except for harvesting equipment. Grain price is based on average 2023 prices.

Winter Feeding Barley

Table 2.23: Winter Barley Gross Margin Projection 2024.

Assumptions	€	€	€
Yield per hectare (tonnes)	7.5	9.25	11.0
Price per tonne @ 20% moisture	200	200	200
Output			
Grain sales	1,500	1,850	2,200
Straw	200	220	240
Gross Output	1,700	2,070	2,440
Variable Costs			
Seed	105	105	105
Fert & Lime	513	513	513
Spray materials	285	285	285
Harvesting & transport	270	290	310
Interest	12	12	12
Total Variable Costs	1,185	1,204	1,,224
Gross Margin Per Hectare	516	866	1,216
Overhead costs per hectare (see page 104)	862	862	862
Net Margin per hectare (ex-subsidies)[1]	-347	3	353
Price per tonne required to achieve a break-even Gross Margin	158	130	111
Price per tonne required to achieve a break-even Net Profit	158	130	111
Yield per hectare required to achieve a break-even Gross Margin	5.92	6.02	6.12
Yield per hectare required to achieve a break-even Net Profit	5.92	6.02	6.12

[1]Overhead costs per hectare drawn from the Net Profit Projection on page 104

Crop Gross Margin Budgets 2024

The following projections assume that all machinery is owned except for harvesting equipment. Grain price is based on average 2023 prices.

Winter Wheat

Table 2.24: Winter Wheat Gross Margin Projection 2024.

Assumptions	€	€	€
Yield per hectare (tonnes)	7.5	9.25	11.0
Price per tonne @ 20% moisture	210	210	210
Output			
Grain sales	1,575	1,943	2,310
Straw	175	185	195
Gross Output	**1,750**	**2,128**	**2,505**
Variable Costs			
Seed	110	110	110
Fert & Lime	450	450	450
Spray materials	380	380	390
Harvesting & transport	270	290	310
Interest	13	13	13
Total Variable Costs	**1,223**	**1,243**	**1,273**
Gross Margin per hectare	527	885	1,232
Overhead costs per hectare (see page 104)	862	862	862
Net Margin per hectare (ex-subsidies)	**-335**	**22**	**370**
Price per tonne required to achieve a break-even Gross Margin	163	134	116
Price per tonne required to achieve a break-even Net Profit	163	134	116
Yield per hectare required to achieve a break-even Gross Margin	5.82	5.92	6.06
Yield per hectare required to achieve a break-even Net Profit	5.82	5.92	6.06

[1]Overhead costs per hectare drawn from the Net Profit Projection on page 104

Crop Gross Margin Budgets 2024

The following projections assume that all machinery is owned except for harvesting equipment. Grain price is based on average 2023 prices.

Spring Wheat

Table 2.25: Spring Wheat Gross Margin Projection 2024.

Assumptions	€	€	€
Yield per hectare (tonnes)	6.8	8.00	9.0
Price per tonne @ 20% moisture	210	210	210
Output			
Grain sales	1418	1680	1890
Straw	175	185	195
Gross Output	**1593**	**1865**	**2085**
Variable Costs			
Seed	110	110	110
Fert & Lime	360	360	360
Spray materials	240	240	240
Harvesting & transport	260	274	285
Interest	13	13	13
Total Variable Costs	983	997	1008
Gross Margin Per Hectare	**610**	**868**	**1,077**
Overhead costs per hectare (see page 104)	862	862	862
Net Margin per hectare (ex-subsidies)	**-253**	**6**	**215**
Price per tonne required to achieve a break-even Gross Margin	120	102	90
Price per tonne required to achieve a break-even Net Profit	247	209	186
Yield per hectare required to achieve a break-even Gross Margin	3.8	3.9	3.9
Yield per hectare required to achieve a break-even Net Profit	7.95	7.97	7.98

Overhead costs per hectare drawn from the Net Profit Projection on page 104

Crop Gross Margin Budgets 2024

The following projections assume that all machinery is owned except for harvesting equipment. Grain price is based on average 2023 prices.

Winter Oats

Table 2.26: Winter Oats Gross Margin Projection 2024.

Assumptions	€	€	€
Yield per hectare (tonnes)	6.2	7.00	8.0
Price per tonne @ 20% moisture	200	200	200
Output			
Grain sales	1240	1400	1600
Straw	200	210	220
Gross Output	**1440**	**1610**	**1820**
Variable Costs			
Seed	105	105	105
Fert & Lime	345	345	345
Spray materials	200	200	210
Harvesting & transport	260	270	282
Interest	13	13	13
Total Variable Costs	**923**	**933**	**955**
Gross Margin Per Hectare	**517**	**677**	**865**
Overhead costs per hectare (see page 104)	862	862	862
Net Margin per hectare (ex-subsidies)	**-345**	**-185**	**3**
Price per tonne required to achieve a break-even Gross Margin	117	103	92
Price per tonne required to achieve a break-even Net Profit	256	226	200
Yield per hectare required to achieve a break-even Gross Margin	3.6	3.6	3.7
Yield per hectare required to achieve a break-even Net Profit	7.93	7.93	7.99

Overhead costs per hectare drawn from the Net Profit Projection on page 104

Crop Gross Margin Budgets 2024

The following projections assume that all machinery is owned except for harvesting equipment. Grain price is based on average 2023 prices.

Spring Oats

Table 2.27: Spring Oats Gross Margin Projection 2024.

Assumptions	€	€	€
Yield per hectare (tonnes)	5.5	6.50	7.5
Price per tonne @ 20% moisture	200	200	200
Output			
Grain sales	1100	1300	1500
Straw	200	210	220
Gross Output	**1300**	**1510**	**1720**
Variable Costs			
Seed	105	105	105
Fert & Lime	389	389	389
Spray materials	190	190	198
Harvesting & transport	250	261	272
Interest	13	13	13
Total Variable Costs	947	958	977
Gross Margin Per Hectare	**353**	**552**	**743**
Overhead costs per hectare (see page 104)	862	862	862
Net Margin per hectare (ex-subsidies)	**-509**	**-310**	**-119**
Price per tonne required to achieve a break-even Gross Margin	136	115	101
Price per tonne required to achieve a break-even Net Profit	293	248	216
Yield per hectare required to achieve a break-even Gross Margin	8.0	8.1	8.1
Yield per hectare required to achieve a break-even Net Profit	8.05	8.05	8.10

Overhead costs per hectare drawn from the Net Profit Projection on page 104

Crop Gross Margin Budgets 2024

The following projections assume that all machinery is owned except for harvesting equipment. Grain price is based on average 2023 prices.

Winter Oilseed Rape

Table 2.28: Winter Oil Seed Rape Gross Margin Projection 2024.

Assumptions	€	€	€
Yield per hectare (tonnes)	3.7	4.3	5.0
Price per tonne @9% moisture	460	460	460
Output			
Sales	1702	1978	2300
Gross Output	**1702**	**1978**	**2300**
Variable Costs			
Seed	100	100	100
Fert & Lime	420	420	420
Spray materials	275	275	275
Harvesting & transport	230	236	244
Interest	13	13	13
Total Variable Costs	**1038**	**1044**	**1052**
Gross Margin Per Hectare	**664**	**934**	**1,248**
Overhead costs per hectare (see page 104)	862	862	862
Net Margin per hectare (ex-subsidies)	**-198**	**72**	**386**
Price per tonne required to achieve a break-even Gross Margin	281	243	210
Price per tonne required to achieve a break-even Net Profit	514	443	383
Yield per hectare required to achieve a break-even Gross Margin	2.3	2.3	2.3
Yield per hectare required to achieve a break-even Net Profit	4.13	4.14	4.16

Overhead costs per hectare drawn from the Net Profit Projection on page 104

Crop Gross Margin Budgets 2024

The following projections assume that all machinery is owned except for harvesting equipment. Grain price is based on average 2023 prices.

Spring Oilseed Rape

Table 2.29: Spring Oil Seed Rape Gross Margin Projection 2024.

Assumptions	€	€	€
Yield per hectare (tonnes)	3.7	3.0	4.3
Price per tonne @9% moisture	420	420	420
Output			
Grain sales	1554	1260	1806
Gross Output	1554	1260	1806
Variable Costs			
Seed	102	102	102
Fert & Lime	398	398	398
Spray materials	250	250	250
Harvesting & transport	230	234	248
Interest	13	13	13
Total Variable Costs	992.5	996.5	1010.5
Gross Margin Per Hectare	562	264	796
Overhead costs per hectare (see page 104)	862	862	862
Net Margin per hectare (ex-subsidies)	-301	-599	-67
Price per tonne required to achieve a break-even Gross Margin	268	332	235
Price per tonne required to achieve a break-even Net Profit	501	620	436
Yield per hectare required to achieve a break-even Gross Margin	2.4	2.4	2.4
Yield per hectare required to achieve a break-even Net Profit	4.42	4.43	4.46

Overhead costs per hectare drawn from the Net Profit Projection on page 104

Crop Gross Margin Budgets 2024

The following projections assume that all machinery is owned except for harvesting equipment. Grain price is based on average 2023 prices.

Peas

Table 2.30: Peas (Feed) Gross Margin Projection 2024.

Assumptions	€	€	€
Yield per hecttare(tonnes)	4.0	4.5	5.0
Price per tonne	290	290	290
Output			
Crop sales	1160	1305	1450
Gross Output	**1160**	**1305**	**1450**
Variable Costs			
Seed	150	150	150
Fert & Lime	156	156	156
Spray materials	165	165	165
Harvesting & transport	172	178	184
Interest	13	13	13
Total Variable Costs	**656**	**662**	**668**
Gross Margin Per Hectare	**504**	**643**	**782**
Overhead costs per hectare (see page 104)	862	862	862
Net Margin per hectare (ex-subsidies)	**-358**	**-219**	**-80**
Price per tonne required to achieve a break-even Gross Margin	164	147	134
Price per tonne required to achieve a break-even Net Profit	380	339	306
Yield per hectare required to achieve a break-even Gross Margin	2.3	2.3	2.3
Yield per hectare required to achieve a break-even Net Profit	5.24	5.26	5.28

Overhead costs per hectare drawn from the Net Profit Projection on page 104

Crop Gross Margin Budgets 2024

The following projections assume that all machinery is owned except for harvesting equipment. Grain price is based on average 2023 prices.

Beans

Table 2.31: Beans Gross Margin Projection 2024.

Assumptions	€	€	€
Yield per hectare (tonnes)	4.5	5.0	5.5
Price per tonne	290	290	290
Output			
Crop sales	1305	1450	1595
Gross Output	1305	1450	1595
Variable Costs			
Seed	150	150	150
Fert & Lime	156	156	156
Spray materials	175	175	175
Harvesting & transport	172	178	184
Interest	13	13	13
Total Variable Costs	666	672	678
Gross Margin Per Hectare	639	778	917
Overhead costs per hectare (see page 104)	862	862	862
Net Margin per hectare (ex-subsidies)	-223	-84	55
Price per tonne required to achieve a break-even Gross Margin	148	134	123
Price per tonne required to achieve a break-even Net Profit	340	307	280
Yield per hectare required to achieve a break-even Gross Margin	2.3	2.3	2.3
Yield per hectare required to achieve a break-even Net Profit	5.27	5.29	5.31

Overhead costs per hectare drawn from the Net Profit Projection on page 104

Crop Gross Margin Budgets 2024

The following projections assume that all machinery is owned except for harvesting equipment. Grain price is based on average 2023 prices.

Potatoes

Table 2.32: Main Crop Potatoes Gross Margin Projection.

ASSUMPTIONS	€	€	€
Yield per hectare (tonnes)	24.0	25.5	27.0
Price per tonne	300	300	300
Output			
Crop sales	7,200	7,650	8,100
Gross Output	**7,200**	**7,650**	**8,100**
Variable Costs			
Seed	1,700	1,700	1,700
Fertilizer	725	725	725
Spray materials	1,100	1,100	1,100
Harvesting & transport	1,170	1,170	1,170
Destoning	645	645	645
Interest	150	150	150
Total Variable Costs	**5,490**	**5,490**	**5,490**
Gross Margin Per Hectare	**1,710**	**2,160**	**2,610**
Overhead costs per hectare (see page 104)	862	862	862
Net Margin per hectare	**848**	**1,298**	**1,748**
Price per tonne required to achieve a break-even Gross Margin	229	215	203
Price per tonne required to achieve a break-even Net Profit	265	249	235
Yield per hectare required to achieve a break-even Gross Margin	18.3	18.3	18.3
Yield per hectare required to achieve a break-even Net Profit	21.17	21.17	21.17

Overhead costs per hectare drawn from the Net Profit Projection on page 104

Net Profit Projections for a Tillage Farm Based on 2023 Costs & Returns

The following budget is based on a tillage farm of 120 hectares (296 acres), or which 50 hectares are rented in. The cropping programme yielded 407 tonnes of Winter Barley from 44 hectares, 472 tonnes of Winter Wheat from 45 hectares, 70 tonnes of Winter Oilseed Rape from 16 hectares and 68 tonnes of Peas from 15 hectares. Total farm debt including financed equipment is €150,000. Grain, OSR and Pea price is based on average 2023 prices.

Table 2.34: Net Profit Projection for a Tillage Farm in 2024.

Crop Gross Margins (€) (see pages 94, 95, 99, 102)	
Winter Wheat	38,918
Winter Barley	38,948
Winter Oil Seed Rape	14,944
Beans (feed)	11,670
Total Gross Margin	**104,480**
Overhead Costs	
Bank/Finance interest & charges	8,000
Light & heat (farm share)	2,400
General farm repairs	4,750
Machinery running costs	22,650
Land Rent	33,000
Telephone (farm share)	920
Motor (farm share)	5,000
Wages /Farm Relief	3,000
Accountancy/Advisory	2,500
Insurance	3,450
Depreciation	17,000
Sundries	800
Total	**103,470**
Net Profit excluding Gov. & E.U. supports	**1,010**
BiSS & other subsidies (est.)	**29,000**
Net Profit including Gov. & E.U. supports	**30,010**

3
FARM MANAGEMENT DATA

Agricultural Contractor Charges
Indicatives charges for 2024 106
Value of Slurries, Manure & Fertilisers
N,P & K of Slurry, Manure, Chemical & Fertiliser 108
Production Cost
Grass Silage 109
Hay 109
Maze 110
Grazing Grass 110
Fodder Beet 111
Forage & Root Crops 111
Monthly Silage Requirement 111
Relative Values Based on Rolled Barley 112

FARM MANAGEMENT DATA

Guide to Agricultural Contractor Charges

Table 3.1: Guide to Agricultural Contractor Charges for 2024.*

Service	€ (incl. V.A.T.) per acre/item	€ (incl. V.A.T.) per hectare
Hay, Silage & Pasture Operations		
Silage Harvesting (wagon 1st cut)	160-170	395-420
Silage Harvesting (wagon 2nd cut)	150-165	370-408
Silage Harvesting (complete in pit)	175-185	432-457
Maize Silage Harvesting	200-210	494-519
Whole Crop Harvesting	190-200	470-494
Zero Grazer	95-100/load	95-100/load
Grass Mowing	28-32	69-79
Grass, raking, tedding, rowing	16-18	39-44
Silage Bale & Wrap (incl. plastic)	14-16/bale	14-16/bale
Silage, Mow, Bale & Wrap	18-20/bale	18-20/bale
Hay/Straw Baling (4x4)	7-8/bale	7-8/bale
Hay Tedding/Rowing up	15-17/ac.	37-42
Fertiliser Spreading - bulk	50-52/tonne	
Fertiliser Spreading - bags	60-66/tonne	
Lime Spreading	9-12/tonne	9-12/tonne
Complete Grass re-seeding (excl. Seed)	270-285	667-704
Tillage Operations		
Ploughing - lea	58-64	143-158
Ploughing - stubble	52-55	1128-136
Power harrowing per run	60-65	148-161
De-stoning	290-320	716-790
Min till (per run)	42-45	104-111
Plough & One Pass	105-115	259-284
Rolling	16-17	40-42
Cereal Combine Drilling - one pass	56-60	138-148
Maize seeding (ex plastic cost but incl. laying)	100-108	247- 267
Spraying	22-26	54-64
Cereal Combining	74-78	182-193

Agricultural Contractor Charges cont.,	Per acre/item (€)	Per hectare (€)
Sub-soiling/Mole Draining	150-160/hour	
Grain Transport	10-12/tonne	
Disc Harrowing per run	40-45/run	99-111
Fodder Beet - plough, till & sow	120-125	296-308
Plough, till & sow maize	260-285	642-704
Fodder Beet - steering hoeing	25-30	62-74
Fodder Beet - band spraying	30-32	74-79
Fodder Beet Harvesting	180-190	445-470
Oil Seed Rape Harvesting	80-85	198-210
Willow Harvesting	250-260	648-642
Slurry & Muck Handling Operations		
Slurry Spreading 2,500 gls	84-95/hour	
Slurry Spreading 2,500 gls + trailing shoe	105-110/hour	
Slurry Agitation	115-135/hour	
Muck loading & spreading	160-165/hour	
Umbilical spreading (ex-setup charge)	185-200/hour	
General		
Hedge cutting - flail type	75-80/hour	
Hedge cutting - saw head	90-95/hour	
Excavator Mulching	95-105/hour	
Mini Digger	45-48/hour	
Teleporter	65-70/hour	
Mechanical digging - wheeled	65-70/hour	
Mechanical digging - tracked	85-90/hour	
Tractor & Dump Trailer (14 tonne) Hire	70-80/hour	
Tractor Hire (150-200 HP incl. operator)	84-90/hour	
Large Timber Harvester	160-180/hour	
Road Sweeper	55-65/hour	
Sheep shearing	2.80/sheep	

* The price ranges as set out above should be taken as a general indication but not definitive guide.

Value of Slurries, Manure & Fertilisers

Table 3.2: N,P & K Value of Slurries & Manures.

Material	N (units)	P (units)	K (units)
Cattle slurry - 3,000 gallons	21	21	115
Pig slurry - 3,000 gallons	55	21	60
Farmyard manure - 10 tonne	30	24	120
Poultry manure - 10 tonne	110	110	240

Table 3.3: N,P & K Value of Commonly Used Chemical Fertilisers.

Fertiliser type	Nitrogen		Phosphorus	
	%	kg	%	kg
CAN	27%	13.5	0%	0
Urea	46%	23	0%	0
Pasture Sward	27%	13.5	2.5%	1.25
Cut Sward	24%	12	2.5%	1.25
10-10-20	10%	5	10%	5
18-6-12	18%	9	6%	3
0-7-30	0%	0	7%	3.5

Feedstuffs & Forage

The following budgets have been prepared at a time of rapidly rising and volatile fertiliser prices and readers are urged to bear this in mind if using these budgets as a planning aid.

Forage Production Costs

Table 3.4: Grass Silage Production Cost.

Yield/ha - tonnes or bales	Bulk	Bales
	25 tonnes	27 bales
Fertilisers		
250 kgs urea 46%N (227 units N / hectare)	130	130
185 kgs 0.7.30 per hectare	111	111
Slurry spreading cost (7,500 gallons)	90	90
Lime		
5 tonnes / ha / 4 years (€35/ tonne incl. spreading)	44	44
Contractor		
Harvesting	445	
Mow, Bale & wrap (including plastic)		490
Transport		55
Polythene cover	30	
Cost per hectare	**850**	**920**
Cost per tonne	**34**	-
Cost per bale	-	**34**

Table 3.5: Hay Production Cost.

Yield - Bales per hectare	35
Fertilisers	
250 kgs urea 46%N (227 units N / hectare)	130
250 kgs 0.7.30 per hectare	150
Lime	
5 tonnes / hectare every 4 years (€35/ tonne incl. spreading)	44
Contractor	
Cutting, tedding & raking	125
Baling	275
Cost per hectare	**724**
Cost per bale	**21**

Table 3.6: Maize Production Cost.

Target Yield - Dry matter per hectare (utilised)	15
Variable costs per hectare	
Seed	205
Seed bed preparation & sowing	385
Plastic film	310
Fertilizer	570
Spray materials	90
Harvesting & covering	520
Spraying & fertiliser spreading	72
Cost per hectare	**2152**
Cost per tonne dry matter	**143**

Table 3.7: Grazing Grass Production Cost (€).

High Fertilizer regeime	
Variable costs per hectare	
900kg CAN (500 units per hectare)	360
250 kg 0-10-20 per hectare	150
Lime - 5 tonnes / hectare every 4 years	44
Cost per hectare	**554**
ModerateFertilizer regeime	
Variable costs per hectare	
675kg CAN (370 units per hectare)	270
185kg 0-10-20 per hectare	111
Lime -4 tonnes / hectare every 4 years	35
Cost per hectare	**416**
Low Fertilizer regeime	
Variable costs per hectare	
370kg CAN (370 units per hectare)	150
125kg 0-10-20 per hectare	75
Lime - 3 tonnes / hectare every 4 years	26
Cost per hectare	**251**

Table 3.8: Fodder Beet Production Costs Per Acre (Euros €).

Target Yield - Dry matter per hectare (utilised)	14
Variable costs per hectare	
Seed	190
Seed bed preparation & sowing	310
Fertilizer	610
Spray materials	310
Harvesting & covering	470
Spraying & fertiliser preading	150
Cost per hectare	2040
Cost per tonne dry matter	146

Table 3.8 (a): Other Forage & Root Crops - Cost Per Acre Euros (€).

	Rape	Kale	Stubble Turnips
Yield - tonnes per hectare	42	37	25
Yield Dry Matter per hectare	3.4	6	2.5
Variable costs per hectare			
Seed	25	80	30
Seed bed preparation & sowing	240	240	80
Fertilizer	340	410	160
Spray materials	0	65	0
Spraying & fertiliser preading	25	50	25
Cost per hectare	630	845	295
Cost per tonne dry matter	185	141	118

Animal Fodder Requirements

Table 3.9: Monthly Silage Requirement.

	Silage - bulk (tonnes/month)	Bales (670kgs) (number/month)	Bales (1 tonne) (number/month)
Dairy Cows -milking	1.5	2.25	1.5
Dairy Cows - dry	1.1	1.65	1.1
Suckler Cows - Autumn calving	1.4	2.1	1.4
Suckler Cows - Spring calving	1.1	1.6	1.1
Weanlings (240kg)	0.6	0.9	0.6
Cattle 1½-2 yrs (450 kg +)	1.0	1.5	1.0
Calves	0.25	1/3rd	0.25
Ewes	0.15	1/5th	0.15

Relative Value of Feedstuffs

Table 3.10: Relative Values Based on Rolled Barley @ €250 and Soya @ €545/Tonne.

	DM %	UFL/kg	Protein %	€/tonne
Barley	86	1.00	10.5	250
Barley Straw	86	0.40	4.0	119
Beans	87	1.01	27.0	404
Beet Pulp	87	0.96	10.5	243
Brewers Grains DM	100	0.99	24.0	361
Citrus Pulp	87	0.96	6.5	211
Crimped Wheat DM	100	1.14	13.3	296
Distillers Grains	87	1.02	25.5	372
Fodder Beet DM	100	1.10	6.0	226
Grass Silage DM (Good)	100	0.93	16.0	283
Grass Silage DM (Average)	100	0.85	13.0	249
Hay (Good)	87	0.90	12.0	246
Hay (Average)	87	0.80	9.0	204
Kale DM	100	1.03	15.0	294
Maize	88	1.04	8.4	238
Maize Silage DM	100	1.01	8.5	236
Maize Gluten	88	0.96	20.0	318
Molasses (Cane)	74	0.79	4.0	163
Oats	87	0.90	10.5	234
Palm Kernel	88	0.80	16.0	276
Potatoes DM	100	1.10	8.0	246
Rape DM	100	0.85	20.0	319
Rapeseed Meal	88	0.88	35.0	423
Soya Hulls	88	0.91	13.5	265
Soyabean Meal	88	1.01	48.0	545
Sugar Beet DM	100	1.14	5.0	237
Swedes DM	100	1.05	9.0	247
Wheat	87	1.02	11.8	263
Whole Crop Wheat DM	100	0.87	10.0	226

Above information courtesy of Dr. Tom Butler, FBA Laboratories

4

FARM BUILDINGS

Crop & Forage Space Requirements

Crop Storage Requirements..114

Storage Requirement for Settled Silage 114

Animal Housing

Animal Housing - Space Requirements 115

Slurry Accommodation Requirement 115

Guide to Cost of Farm Buildings..116

Planning Permission Requirements 117

Crop & Forage Space Requirements

Table 4.1: Crop Storage Requirements.

Crop	Average Space Required for 1 tonne.	
	Cubic Feet	Cubic Metres
Silage	50 ft.³	1.46 M.³
Hay	330 ft.³	9.63 M.³
Barley	50 ft.³	1.46 M.³
Wheat	45 ft.³	1.31 M.³
Oats	70 ft.³	2.04 M.³
Died molassed pulp	116 ft.³	3.38 M.³
Swedes	65 ft.³	1.90 M.³
Potatoes	54 ft.³	1.58 M.³
Maize silage	49 ft.³	1.43 M.³
Fodder beet	64 ft.³	1.8 M.³

Table 4.2: Storage Requirement For Settled Silage.

Width in metres	Approx. Capacity of Settled Silage in tonnes per metre of length at depths of:			
	1.5 m.	1.8 m.	2.1 m.	2.4 m.
7 metres	7.0	9.0	10.5	12.0
8 metres	8.5	10.2	12.0	13.7
9 metres	9.6	11.5	13.5	15.4

How to measure crop storage requirements

The measurement of feedstuffs in store can be calculated by referring to table 6.11. The first step is to measure the cubic capacity. If the feedstuff is stored in a square or rectangular store or silage pit the cubic capacity is calculated by multiplying the length by the width and by the average height in metres. If the store is cylindrical, as with many meal bins, then the volume is calculated using the formula 3.14 x r2h, where, r = radius and h = average height. Once the volume is known it can be divided by the relevant figure in Table 6.11 to give a measurement in tonnes.

Example 1

A pit full of silage measures 25 m. long by 10 m. wide by 2.1 m. high.

Tonnes of silage in pit = $\dfrac{25 \times 10 \times 2.1}{1.46}$ = 360 tonnes.

Example 2

A circular grain bin is 3 metres in diameter i.e. 1.5 m. in radius and contains wheat to a height of 4 metres.

Tonnes of wheat in bin = $\dfrac{3.14 \times (1.5 \times 1.5) \times 4}{1.31}$ = 21.57 tonnes.

Animal Housing - Space Requirements

Table 4.3: Animal Housing - Space Requirements.

Housing System		Space Requirement
Suckler Cows	Slatted with calf creeps (with passage)	4.5 - 5.2 m²
	Straw bed with calf creeps (with passage)	7.4 - 8.3 m²
Cattle	Slatted incl. passage - weanlings	2.2 - 2.8m² / hd.
	- stores / finishers	2.8 - 3.2 m² / hd
Calves	Individual pens up to 4 weeks	1.12m² / calf
	Individual pens up to 8 weeks	1.8m² / calf
	group pens up to 8 weeks	1.10m² / calf
	group up to 12 weeks	1.50m² / calf
Sheep	Ewe housing - slatted	0.9 - 1.2 m² / ewe
	Ewe housing - straw bedded	1.1 - 1.4m² / ewe

Table 4.4: Animal Housing - Slurry Accommodation Requirement.

Animal type	Accommodation	Space
Dairy Cows	- slatted tank	1.5m³/month
	- uncovered tank	1.8m³/month
Cattle 450 kg.	- slatted tank	1.2m³/month
	- uncovered tank	1.4m³/month
Cattle 250 kg.	- slatted tank	0.6m³/month
	- uncovered tank	0.8m³/month
Suckler Cow	- slatted tank	1.3m³/month
	- uncovered tank	1.6m³/month
Sows	- dry	0.14m³/month
	- suckling	0.56m³/month
Pigs - weaners		0.09m³/month
Pigs - finishers	- dry fed	0.14m³/month
	- liquid	0.17m³/month
Poultry	- layers	0.43m³/100/month
	- broilers	0.26m³/100/month
Sheep - ewes		0.17m³/month

Guide to Cost of Farm Buildings

Table 4.5: Guide to Cost of Farm Buildings 2024.

Housing System	Euros (€)
Cattle Housing	
Calving boxes	3,000 - 3,150/hd.
Weanlings - Slatted house	1.220 - 1,500/hd.
Stores - Slatted house	1,800 - 1,950/hd.
Weanlings - Loose shed	600 - 630/hd.
Stores - Loose Shed	620 - 680/hd.
Calf Housing	800 - 950/calf
Suckler Cows - Straw bed & Slatted passage	1,400 - 1,850/suckler
Suckler Cows - Purpose built slatted	2,900 - 3,500/suckler
Topless cubicles	820 - 1,000/cow.
Topless cubicles + lined slurry lagoon	1,400 - 1,650/cow.
Dairy Facilities	
Dairy Cows - Slatted Easy Feed	2,700 - 3,300/cow
Out-wintering pad - plastic lined, self feed	500 - 520/cow.
Out-wintering pad - plastic lined, easi feed	370 - 400/cow.
Out-wintering pad - clay lined, self feed	260 - 300/cow.
Out-wintering pad - clay lined, easi feed	220 - 250/cow.
Milking Parlour, incl. dairy & plant room	17,600 - 19,000/unit.
Milking Machine (basic to 'state of the art')	5,000 - 10,000/unit.
Milking Machine - Rotary	8,000 - 11,000/unit.
Milking Machine - Robotic	110,000-125,000/unit.
Meal Bin	190 - 250/tonne.
Sheep Housing	
Straw bedded	220 - 240/ewe
Slatted	325 - 340/ewe
Pig Housing	
Sows - rearing to weaner	2,950- 3,200/sow
Fattening	360 - 380/pig
Fowl	
Broiler - Breeding	55/bird
Layers - Free range	46/bird
Layers - Commercial	40/bird
Turkey Fattening	40/bird

Slurry Storage	
Slatted Tank - per cow	€700-€800
Lagoon (lined) - per cow	€380-€420
Circular Tower - per cow	€525-€580
Farm Roadways (compacted hardcore)	8 - 9/m2
Concrete Areas (concrete on hardcore)	37- 42/m2
Silage Slab	37- 42/tonne
Silage Pit Walled	48 - 52/tonne
Sheep Fencing (5 wire)	6.50/m
Paddock Fencing	3.00/m
Timber Post & Rail Fencing (3 rail)	21/m
Water supply system (pipes laid & troughs)	310-330/Ha.
Land drainage (groundwater system)	4,200 - 9,000/Ha.

The assistance Tom Ryan (former Teagasc Farm Buildings Specialist) in preparing this table is gratefully acknowledged.

Planning Permission Requirements

New farm building developments require planning permission by the local authorities in most instances and the payment of farm development grants will be conditional on having acquired planning permission where the floor area exceeds certain limits. However, works consisting of roofed or open structures that do not exceed the prescribed limits are exempt if they fall under the following classes:

Exempt Structures

The following exemptions are set down in the "Planning and Development Regulations and are current as at November 2023.

Type 1: A roofed structure housing cattle, sheep, poultry, donkeys, horses, deer or rabbits, provided that it's floor area does not exceed 200 sq. metres and that the total floor area of all Type 1 structures within the farmyard complex (or 100 metres of it) does not exceed 300 sq. Metres. A roofed structure housing pigs, mink or poultry, provided that its floor area does not exceed 75 square metres and that the total floor area of all such structures within the farmyard complex (or within 100 metres of it) does not exceed 100 square metres.

Type 2: Roofless cubicles, open loose yards, self-feed silo or silage areas, feeding aprons, assembly yards, milking parlours, effluent storage, silage making/storage structures, provided that the floor area of any new structures does not exceed 200 sq. metres and that the total floor area of all Type 2 structures within the farmyard complex (or 100 metres of it) does not exceed 300 sq. metres.

Type 3: A store, barn, shed, glass-house, etc. not exceeding 300 sq. metres in floor area and not used for housing animals or storing effluent, provided that the total floor area of all Type 3 structures within the farmyard complex (or 100 metres of it) does not exceed 900 sq. metres.

Type 4: An unroofed fenced area for the exercising or training of horses not exceeding 2 metres in height nor within 10 metres of a public road;

Type 5: A roofed structure for housing greyhounds, provided that the floor area does not exceed 50 sq. metres and that the total floor area of all Type 5 structures within the same complex (or 100 metres of it) does not exceed 75 sq. metres.

Type 6: A roofless hard-surfaced yard or enclosed area (in connection with the keeping of greyhounds) provided that the total floor area does not exceed 100 sq. metres and that the total floor area of all Type 6 structures within the same complex (or 100 metres of it) does not exceed 150 sq. Metres.

Type 7: Works consisting of a roofed structure for the housing of pigs, mink or poultry, having a gross floor space not exceeding 75 square metres (whether or not by extension of an existing structure), and any ancillary provision for effluent storage. It should be noted that these exemptions are subject to the following conditions:
- The structures concerned must be used for agricultural purposes only and shall not be situated within 10 metres of any public road. No such structure within 100 metres of any public road shall exceed 8 metres in height above ground level.
- No such structure shall be situated, or no effluent from such structures shall be stored, within 100 metres of any dwelling house, school, church or building used for public assembly, save with the consent of the owner and occupier thereof.
- Effluent storage facilities adequate to serve the structure having regard to its size, use, location and the need to avoid water pollution shall be provided. This condition does not apply to buildings where effluents do not arise.
- They must be used for agricultural purposes only (Types 1 to 3) and for the breeding and keeping of greyhounds, as appropriate (Types 4 to 6).
- The exemptions do not apply if the development interferes with sites, features, etc. listed for preservation in the Development Plan or draft plan.

Solar Panels

Rooftop solar installations covering the entire roof of an agricultural structure or roof of any ancillary buildings within the farm are exempt from requiring planning permission, subject to conditions and limitations such as farm buildings located within a Solar Safeguarding Zone (SSZ) which typically will be located near an airport or helipad, in which case there is a rooftop limit of 300 sq. metres. Free standing or wall mounted solar panel installations for agricultural holdings are exempted from the requirement to obtain planning permission subject to a 75 square metre area limit, when taken together with any other such existing installations.

Wind Turbines

There are also exemptions for other renewable technologies including wind turbines. The turbine must not be attached to a building and only turbine is allowed per site. The total height must not exceed 20m and the rotor diameter must not exceed 8m and there must be 3m minimum clearance required between ground and lowest point of blades. There are various other conditions such as noise levels and proximity to other turbines and airports.

Planning Charges

The following scale of charges currently apply:

- Farm buildings are charged at €80 for each building or €1 for each square metre of gross floor area in excess of 200 square metres (50 sq. Metres for greyhounds) subject to a maximum charge of €300.
- The use of uncultivated land or semi-natural areas for intensive agricultural production is charged at €5 per hectare.
- Initial afforestation or replacement of broadleaf high forests by conifer species is charged at €5 per hectare of site area.
- Peat extraction is charged at €80 or €5 for each hectare of site area.
- Erection of a dwelling €65. Alteration of a dwelling €34.

County Council Development Levies

Development levies are charged by County Councils for agricultural developments. These levies are in addition to the planning charge. The amounts charged can vary, ranging from €3 per m^2 upwards but typically are €5.50 per m^2. Farmers contemplating a development should contact their County Council to establish if a development levy will be charged and how much that levy is likely to be.

Forestry and Planning

While most forestry operations are exempt from the requirement to obtain planning permission, some forestry activities require consent by way of licence, from the Department of Agriculture, Food and the Marine. It is an offence to undertake the following forestry activities unless a license is first obtained from the Department:

- Tree felling – a Felling License is required to uproot or to cut down any tree (subject to certain exemptions);
- Aerial fertilisation – an Aerial Fertilisation Licence must be obtained before a person can use an aircraft to apply fertiliser to a forest;
- Afforestation – an Afforestation Licence is required for all afforestation projects where the area involved is greater than 0.10 hectares (approximately 0.25 acres).
- Forest road construction – a licence is required to construct a forest road.

5

FARMING AND THE LAW

The Civil Court System 121

Public Liability 122

Visitors, Recreational Users, Trespassers, Children 122
Contractors 122
Notices or Agreements 122
Animals 123
Public Roads 124
Trees 124
Agricultural Vehicles 127
Towing - Licensing Rules 127

The Land 127
Rights Of Way 127
Squatters Rights 128
Right To A Renewal of a Lease 128
Boundaries 128
Control Of Noxious Weeds 128
Burning of Waste & Agricultural Vegetation 128
Cutting Hedgerows or Destruction of Vegetation 129

Many aspects of the farmers business brings them into contact with the public. This places certain responsibilities to ensure the safety of those with whom he/she comes in contact. Of course, the farmer may also need recourse to the law if they suffered injury or damage.

The Civil Court System

Occasionally a farmer may find himself/herself involved in court action, whether it be because of a road or farm accident, a dispute with a neighbour, negligence on the part of a person supplying a product or service or possibly due to marriage breakdown. For most people, court action will be a totally unfamiliar experience and they will be confronted with a host of unfamiliar terms and documents. The following paragraphs contain simple explanations of some of the likely terms one may be confronted with.

The Adversarial System

The civil action system is based on a for and against system. The Plaintiff is the person who takes the action against a defendant who defends it. Both parties are normally represented by legal advisers-solicitor and barrister. When both sides present their case, it is the function of the Judge to decide the issues between the parties. During the running of the case in the Court these legal advisers may call upon experts to assist the Court in deciding on the extent of the person's injuries or losses.

Court Award Limits

The District Court is the lower court where the maximum award is currently €15,000 The Circuit Court can grant awards up to €75,000 (up to €60,000 in personal injury actions) and the High Court can grant unlimited awards.

Legal Aid Board

Civil legal aid and advice is available for people who cannot afford to pay a private solicitor to represent then. Many farmers will not be eligible but some or indeed their spouses may qualify for assistance. The Legal Aid Board provides advice about certain legal problem. Where a case ends up in court, they may be able to provide a solicitor and/or barrister to handle the case. They may also write letters or conduct negotiations on the person's behalf to settle a dispute amicably. They can provide legal aid in all the civil courts. They will cover matters such as, family disputes – including marriage breakdown, claims for damages because of injuries which have been caused to a person and claims for damages as a result of breach of a contract. They generally will not cover property disputes or disputes that end up before the Workplace Relations Commission or Labour Court. Civil legal aid and advice usually is not free. Clients will have to make a payment, called a contribution, when they first see a solicitor. They will have to make a further payment if it is agreed that they be represented in Court. Sometimes, at the end of the case, a client might have to pay back the cost of the legal aid if they gain or keep money or property arising out of the case.

Public Liability

An occupier of lands owes practically the same duty of care to all persons who entered upon his or her lands. That duty is to take such care and measures for the safety of all persons entering upon the land and not to allow obvious or hidden dangers to remain on the land which would cause injury to a person that has entered upon his/her land. The Occupiers' Liability Act 1995 provides that an occupier of premises now owes a duty of care to the following classes of persons who enter on his/her premises or land.

Visitors

The duty owed to visitors is to take reasonable care that they and their property do not suffer injury or sustain damage by reason of any danger existing on the land/premises of the occupier.

Recreational Users

The duty owed to recreational users is not to injure them intentionally or act with reckless disregard for them. The Occupiers' Liability Act 1995 provides that where a structure on a land or premises has been used mostly by recreational users the occupier must take reasonable care to maintain the structure in a safe condition.

Trespassers

The duty owed to trespassers is similar to that owed to recreational users i.e. not to injure them intentionally or act with reckless disregard for them. However, an occupier may not be liable for injury or damage unintentionally caused to a person who enters upon land or premises for the purpose of committing an offence, unless the Court determines otherwise. The Court's decision will be made on the facts of each case.

Children

An important category of person entering upon the farmer's land are children. The law usually holds that a child under the age of seven is not responsible for his or her actions as their comprehension of danger is far less than that of an adult. The important test, however, is the test of foreseeability. Is it reasonably foreseeable that injury would be caused to a person entering upon the lands? If injury occurs due to a once off or freak accident then the test of foreseeability will not apply.

Contractors

An occupier who has taken all reasonable care when engaging an independent contractor, will not be liable for injury or damage caused to a person entering on the land or premises, or for the contractor's negligence, unless the occupier knows or ought to have known that the work had not been properly done.

Notices or Agreements

Occupiers are now entitled to modify their duty by agreement or notice and in many cases, depending on the particular circumstances, a warning may be sufficient to absolve an occupier from liability. The Occupiers' Liability Act 1995 illustrates the importance of notice in modifying the duty of occupiers to entrants on their lands. Notices will have to be simple, clear, reasonable, placed in prominent positions and carefully drafted to enable occupiers to restrict, or exclude their duties under the 1995 Act. The duty of care that the occupier owes to the entrant is tempered by the test of foreseeability in that the law states that where it is foreseeable that a person would enter the land and would be injured, the farmer or occupier of the land would be liable in negligence for such injury caused to a person entering his/her land. An occupier of land will therefore be responsible for altering his/her land in such a manner as to prevent injury to persons entering on same. An example of this would be traps laid inside a boundary wall for the purpose of catching a wild animal. The position is similar where the farmer might have hidden caves or unsafe ground on his land near a boundary leading on to a public right of way or laneway or roadway. Obviously the further the land is from the public roadway or places where the public congregate, the less foreseeable the danger would be. For example, local beauty spots and places of cultural interest will attract the public and accordingly, the law requires an occupier to ensure that his/her land has no hidden dangers that might cause injury to the public.

Animals
The law imposes certain obligations on farmers in relation to the control of animals.

Domestic Animals
The law provides that dogs, whether working dogs or pets, must be always under the control of a person in public. There are some categories of dog that require to be muzzled in public. Recent legislation has done away with the maxim which stated that the 'dog was entitled to his first bite' and the law now imposes a liability on the owner of the dog for all injury caused to a third party.

Farm Animals
There is a legal obligation on farmers to safeguard their stock by adequate fencing. However, following a successful Supreme Court appeal of the 1995 Act if animals escape onto the roadway and cause damage to cars or persons, the farmer will not be liable for such damage if due care was observed. The law also imposes a duty of care on farmers when moving animals. The more animals that are taken on to the road, the more persons are required to gain control of these animals if a farmer is to comply with his/her duties under the law. It is essential that an adequate warning system be in place to warn oncoming traffic. Warnings and flags should be provided both in front and behind the cattle that are being moved. Farmers have an extra responsibility for dangerous animals, particularly in relation to bulls. It is not advisable for a farmer to place a bull on land near a public roadway or over which land there is a right of way or where the public is known to congregate.

Public Roads

The 1993 Road Act imposes a number of duties on all owners of lands as follows:

- To take reasonable steps to ensure that any structure on the land is not a hazard or a potential hazard to persons using the public road
- To take all reasonable steps to ensure that all trees, hedges and other vegetation are not a hazard to persons using the public road
- To take all reasonable steps to ensure that water is prevented from draining on to the public road
- To take all reasonable steps to ensure that water, soil and other material is prevented from flowing onto the public road. If an owner/occupier does not comply with this duty the local authority may serve him/her with a notice requiring him/her to carry out specified works. Depending on the nature of the breach, the local authority may carry out the work themselves and may seek to recover the cost of same from the owner/occupier of the land.

Trees

Where a landowner has trees growing on his/her boundary fence whether adjoining the public roadway or his/her neighbour he/she is obliged to take care to ensure that such trees are healthy and are not a potential source of danger. Where, for example, a tree displays symptoms of possible decay such as the appearance of fungi on the bark, holes in the trunk or dying off of the foliage on the uppermost branches or any other such abnormalities, it behoves the landowner to further investigate the health of the tree and have it removed if evidence of decay is present or if he/she considers that the tree may present a source of danger to the public. It should be noted that a landowner would be expected to be capable of detecting visible evidence of decay and if he/she is unsure a professional should be employed to investigate and advise the landowner of the best course of action.

Trees - Overhanging

Where a neighbour's tree is overhanging one's property a landowner may cut off any tree branches which overhangs his/her property without giving notice to the owner of the tree, but may not cut down the tree or enter on to the land of the tree owner without permission. In so doing, the landowner must take care not to render the tree dangerous and may only cut on the side of and up to his/her boundary line. It is unlawful to ring bark or otherwise injure trees in such a manner as to cause them to die or decay. All cuttings must be given back to the owner of the tree, or at least offered back. If the owner of the tree doesn't want the cuttings, they must be disposed of in a responsible way and should not be left in the tree owner's property without permission.

Tree Preservation Order

Tree Preservation Orders (TPOs) may be made if it appears to the planning authority to be desirable and appropriate in the interest of amenity or the environment. A TPO can apply to a tree, trees, group of trees or woodland. The principal effect of a TPO is to prohibit the cutting down, topping, lopping or wilful destruction of trees without the planning authority's consent. The order can also require the owner and occupier of the land subject to the order to enter into an agreement with the planning authority to ensure the proper management of the tree, trees or woodland.

Trees - Height
There are no height limits for either hedges or trees and there is no legislation currently available in Ireland to enforce a height restriction.

Trees - Right to Light
Right to light is a specific and complex legal matter and independent advice should be sought on this. A right to light exists only if the owner of a house can satisfy a court that he or she has enjoyed the uninterrupted use of that light for a period of greater than 20 years, before any legal action is brought about the light. This, however, only applies to the windows of a property and not to a garden.

Felling Licence
It is against the law to cut down or uproot any tree unless a Felling Notice has been lodged at the Garda Station nearest to the trees at least 21 days but not more than two years before felling commences. A single license process now operates for tree felling as compared to a general and limited process that obtained previously A Felling Licence is valid for ten years and may be extended for one or more further periods, not exceeding a total of 5 years. Replanting must take place on the same area that has been clearfelled. All replanting must take place within two years of the clearfelling date. Trees replanted must be maintained and protected by the owner of the land for 10 years following the date of replanting. If land under a felling license is sold, the purchaser of the land is also bound by any conditions included in the felling license (e.g.: if someone fells trees and then sells the land, the purchaser must replant if there is a replanting condition on the license). It is the duty of the vendor to inform the purchaser of any licences attached to the land being sold.

Exempted Trees
The law does not apply to any hazel, apple, plum, damson, pear or cherry tree grown for the value of its fruit. Apart from the following exceptions the law applies to every tree of any age or any stage of growth.
- a tree standing within 100 feet of any building other than a wall or temporary structure.
- cutting trees in a hedgerow for the purposes of trimming , provided the tree does not exceed 20 cm in diameter when measured 1.3 metres from the ground. The species hawthorn and blackthorn are also exempt from requiring a licence.
- where a tree is within 30 metres of a building (other than a wall or temporary structure), but excluding any building built after the trees were planted.

- where the trees are within 10 metres of a public road and which, in the opinion of the owner (being an opinion formed on reasonable grounds), are dangerous to persons using the public road on account of their age or condition.
- a tree which is being felled in connection with a Electricity Supply,
- a tree certified by a Local Authority as dangerous to road traffic on account of age or condition,
- a tree uprooted or cut down by direction of the Minister for Transport, Energy and Communications because it is a danger or obstruction to telegraph or telephone wires,
- a tree cut down by a local authority in connection with road construction.

Applications for a Felling Licence

Applications should be made to the Felling Section of the Forest Service, Johnstown Castle, Co. Wexford (053-9160200 or 1890-200223). Application forms can be downloaded from the Teagasc or Department of Agriculture web sites.

Agricultural Vehicles

It should be noted that the Road Traffic Acts, whilst affecting all persons, are of particular relevance to farmers. Every year a significant number of road traffic accidents occur which involve agricultural vehicles. In many cases such accidents could have been avoided if the vehicle was in full compliance with legal requirements. The following list contains some of the more important measures under the Road Traffic Regulations that farmers should be aware of;

- During lighting up hours tractors must be fitted with 2 head lamps, 2 side lamps, 2 rear lamps, 2 rear reflectors, direction indicators and number plate lights.
- The use of white lights such as ploughing lamps at the rear of the tractor are prohibited from being turned on while the tractor is in use on the road.
- All agricultural vehicles must be fitted with a service brake and a parking brake.
- Detached trailers parked in a public place during lighting up hours must show 2 side lamps, 2 rear lamps and 2 reflectors.
- Quads which are being used on the public road must be insured and taxed.They must also fully comply with the Road Traffic Act in relation to brakes, lights etc.

The following regulations currently apply in regard to tractors and trailers:

Braking

Agricultural vehicles that travel at speeds over 40km/h will need a more powerful braking system. Most correctly maintained tractors which have come into use in the past 30 years already meet these requirements.

Lighting & Visibility

Agricultural vehicles will need to be equipped with appropriate lighting systems, flashing amber beacons and reflective markings.

Weights, & Coupling
Trailers carrying weights over 19 tonnes for tandem axles and 22.5 tonnes for triaxles or travelling at speeds over 40km/h, will need a plate showing the trailer's weight and dimensions. They will also need a speed disc. New national weight limits are being introduced. These limits will allow tractors and trailers which don't have plates to remain in use but at limits which are safe for such vehicles. Combinations of tractors and trailers, where either of them is unplated, will not be allowed to tow more than three times the tractor's unladen weight.

Towing - Licensing Rules

Before towing a light trailer, it is important to understand what combinations of towing vehicles and trailers people are allowed to drive depending on the category of driving licence they hold. It is also important to identify the towing capacity of their vehicle, and the load-carrying capacity of the trailer. Light trailers are those with a maximum mass (as specified by the manufacturer) not exceeding 3,500kg. Such trailers typically include anything from small domestic trailers to general duty trailers including flatbed or plant trailers, car transporters, trailer caravans, horse boxes and livestock trailers.
A category B driving licence which authorises a person to drive a car, van or 4 x 4 which has a maximum mass (as specified by the manufacturer) of not more than 3,500kg allows for the towing of a trailer with a maximum mass (as specified by the manufacturer) not greater than 750kg. Where the maximum mass is more than 750kg, the combined maximum mass of the towing vehicle and the trailer can not be greater than 3,500kg. As a general rule, a category B licence does not entitle the holder to tow a horsebox or a livestock trailer because the combined maximum mass would exceed 3,500kg.
A category BE driving licence authorises a person to tow a trailer where the combined maximum mass of the towing vehicle and trailer is greater than 3,500kg. The holder of a Category B Learner permit may not tow any trailer – whatever the size.

The Land

A large percentage of disputes that arise between farmers and their neighbours relate to the question of boundaries and rights of way.

Rights of Way
This is the right to pass over the land of another. The Right of Way exists not for the owner of the lands who uses it but rather as a benefit to the land itself. Consequently, if the property is sold, it carries with it the benefit of the Right of Way. The right may be confined to the right to walk over land, or it may extend to driving animals or the right to bring machinery. The extent of the Right of Way depends on the use to which the Right of Way has been put . The majority of rights of way in Ireland are not granted in writing but are or were acquired by long usage. Under the rules that prevailed until the new Land & Conveyancing Law Reform Act came into effect in 2009, once there was proof of at least 20 years of continuous use of, for example in the case of a laneway, the person using the laneway could establish a Right of Way.

The Land and Conveyancing Law Reform Act 2009 has brought considerable change to the law relating to Rights of Way and Wayleaves (collectively known as Easements). Prior to the 2009 Act coming into force, it was almost impossible for an easement to be extinguished and there was no requirement for the easement to be registered. The new rules provide however that an Easement can only be acquired following 12 years open use after the 1st of December 2009 and must then be confirmed by registering it with the Property Registration Authority. Where a right of way is contested, a Court Order will be required for registration.

Squatters Rights (Adverse Possession)
A claim to squatter's rights can only arise where s person is in continuous possession of land rent free for more than 12 years. That period is extended to 30 years for land owned by the state.

Right to a Renewal of a Lease
Leases of land where rent is being paid do not confer any right of renewal. However, a right to a renewal of a lease can in certain circumstances arise in a case where farm buildings are leased to a tenant at an open market rent after a continuous period of five years. The renewal of the lease in such circumstances will be at open market rent. The important distinction is that where the buildings are ancillary to the land, there is no right of renewal but where the land is ancillary to the buildings, there may be.

Boundaries
What is often thought to be the boundary between two neighbouring farms is sometimes not clearly reflected in the legal documents. All boundaries should be apparent on the Land Registry folio map or on a map attached to unregistered title documents of the property. However, the Registry operates a non-conclusive boundary system in that the Registry Map identifies properties not boundaries. This means that neither the description of land in a register nor its identification by reference to a registry map is conclusive as to the boundaries or their extent. Folio maps may occasionally contain inaccuracies and such matters coming to light should always be brought to the attention of the family solicitor.

Control of Noxious Weeds
Under the Noxious Weeds Act, 1936, it is an offence not to prevent the growth and spread of noxious weeds. Owners and occupiers of land must ensure that they abide by the provisions of the Act. Noxious weeds, which must be controlled, are ragwort, thistle, dock and wild oat.

Burning of Waste & Agricultural Vegetation
It is illegal to burn any household or commercial wastes i.e. backyard burning. It is also illegal to burn garden or park wastes. These should be either home composted, put into the brown organic bin or brought to a civic amenity site. From January 1st 2023 it has been illegal to burn any agricultural, commercial or household waste.

Cutting Hedgerows or Destruction of Vegetation

It is an offence to cut, grub, burn or otherwise destroy during the period beginning on the 1st day of March and ending on the 31st day of August in any year, any vegetation growing on any land not then cultivated. It is also an offence to cut, grub, burn or otherwise destroy any vegetation growing in any hedge or ditch during the same period. However, the following exemptions apply.

- the destroying, in the ordinary course of agriculture or forestry, of any vegetation growing on or in any hedge or ditch.
- the cutting or grubbing of isolated bushes or clumps of gorse, furze or whin or the mowing of isolated growths of fern in the ordinary course of agriculture.
- the cutting, grubbing or destroying of vegetation in the course of any works being duly carried out for reasons of public health or safety by a Minister of the Government or a body established or regulated by or under a statute.
- destroying any noxious weed to which the Noxious Weeds Act, 1936, applies.
- the clearance of vegetation in the course of road or other construction works or in the development or preparation of sites on which any building or other structure is intended.

6

EDUCATION: Third Level Courses & Grants

Third Level Grants

Eligible Persons 131

Eligible Courses 131

Means Test 131

Value Of Grants 132

Special Rate 132

Assessment of Means 133

Student Holiday Earnings 133

Renewing Grants 133

Teagasc Course Charges 134

Third Level Grants

Educational grants are administered by Student Universal Support Ireland (SUSI). Maintenance grants for Teagasc course are available through the Teagasc Maintenance Grant Scheme (see page 131). It should be noted that all grant rates and income limits quoted are those that apply to the 2023/2024 academic year.

Eligible Persons

The grants are available to students who shall be at least 17 years on 1 January following the date of application, and also to mature students i.e., people who are at least 23 years of age on 1 January of the year of entry to an approved course and living away from home.

Eligible Courses

- Full-time third-level courses.
- Recognised PLC courses, student nurse training or student garda training.
- CERT courses of at least one year's duration.
- Full-time Teagasc courses in agricultural colleges.
- Recognised full-time further education courses of at least one year's duration in Northern Ireland.

Means Test

Qualification for grant assistance is means tested in accordance with the income limits set out on table 6.1. Means are assessed when applying for the first years grant and on a random basis thereafter.

Table 6.1: Income Limits for Maintenance and Full Fee Grants 2023/2024.

Number of dependent children	Full Maint.	Part Maint. 75%	Part Maint. 50%	Part Maint. 25%
Less than 4	€40,875	€41,970	€44,380	€46,790
4 - 7	€44,810	€46,022	€48,670	€51,325
8 or more	€48,575	€49,890	€52,760	€55,630

The reckonable income limits for each additional family member attending a full course of at least one year's duration may be increased by €4,950 in the case of full maintenance categories and €4,785 in the case of part maintenance categories The means test is based on your family's income for the previous full tax year. However, if you or your family have had a change of circumstances (which is likely to be permanent) in the meantime, your changed circumstances may be taken into account.

Table 6.2: Income Limits for Student Contribution.

Number of dependent children	50% Tuition Fee & 100% Student Contribution	50% Student Contribution Only
Less than 4	€50,840	€62,000
4 - 7	€55,765	€68,014
8 or more	€60,455	€73,727

Value of Grants

The amount of grant payable will be determined by certain means test limits as set out on table 6.3. Where one qualifies for a maintenance grant, they will also qualify for all elements of the fee grant including all or part of the student contribution, costs of essential field trips and all or part of a student's tuition fees. The rates of grant for the 2023/2024 academic year which includes the Student Contribution element worth €3,000 are as follows:

Table 6.3: Maintenance Grant Rates for 2023/2024.

	Non-Adjacent rate	Adjacent rate
Special Rate	€6,971	€2,936
Full Maintenance	€3,677	€1,613
Part Maintenance (75%)	€2,717	€1,221
Part Maintenance (50%)	€1,887	€886
Part Maintenance (25%)	€1,051	€556

If you normally live 30 kilometres or less from your college, you get the adjacent rate. If you live further away than 30 kilometres, you get the non-adjacent rate. This is based on the distance of where you ordinarily lived in the year before you started college.

Special Rate

Special rates of maintenance grants apply for disadvantaged students who meet a number of conditions. Applicants must have qualified for the standard maintenance grant for the academic year 2023-2024 and total reckonable income in the tax year January to December 2022 must not be more than €25,000, not including Qualified Child Increases and standard exclusions. For students, including mature students, who are assessed on parent(s)/guardian's income, their parent(s)/guardian must, on 31 December 2022, have been claiming long-term social welfare payments, or claiming Working Family Payment or participating in designated programmes e.g., a community employment scheme.

Assessment of Means

In determining a farmer's income for the purpose of establishing means, certain expenses which would be allowable for tax purposes are disallowed and certain income not chargeable to tax is included in determining eligibility. The following expenses are not allowable:

- Leasing charges on equipment or vehicles.
- Interest on loans for capital expenditure or personal use.
- Capital allowances as claimable for tax purposes.
- Stock relief as claimed for tax purposes.
- Income Averaging relief.

The following income items are included in the calculation of your income,

- Part of the proceeds of an endowment assurance policy calculated as follows: policy proceeds less amount of premiums paid into a policy divided by the number of years the policy was in force.
- Income from deposits and investments.
- Income from forest plantations including premiums.
- Part of the proceeds from the disposal of assets.
- Gifts or inheritances.
- Wages paid to dependent children.
- Casual wages.

Payments in respect of retirement annuities are deductible insofar as they are allowable for tax purposes.

Student Holiday Earnings

An allowance of €6,552, in respect of income earned in the reference (tax year 2022 in respect of 2023/24 academic year) period but outside of the approved institution' term time, is deductible from the applicant's earnings.

Renewing Grants

Student grants are reviewed each year. If you had a grant in one academic year and are continuing your studies on the course in the following year, the body that awarded the grant will be in contact with you in order to renew or re-assess your student grant for that next year.

For more information on Educational Grants visit www.susi.ie

Table 6.4: Points Requirements Level 7/8 Courses 2023/2024.

Course	Level	College	Term	Points
Agricultural Science (all preferences)	8	UCD	4 years	400
Agricultural Science	7	MTU Kerry Campus	3 years	239
Agriculture Science	8	SETU Waterford	4 years	382
Agriculture Science	8	MTU Kerry Campus	4 years	308
Agricultural Science	8	UCC	4 years	496
Sustainable Ag./Agri Food Production	8	Dundalk I.T.	4 years	300
Agriculture and Env. Management	7	ATU Galway/Mayo	3 years	270
Agricultural Science and Sustainability	8	TUS Midwest (new)	4 years	308
Equine Science	8	UL	4 years	358
Equine Science	6	UL	2 years	300
Food Science	8	UCD	4 years	498
Food Science	8	UCC	4 years	407
Food Science & Health	8	UL	4 years	430
Forestry	8	UCD	4 years	400
Forestry	7	SETU Waterford	3 years	226
Horticulture	7	SETU Waterford	3 years	181
Horticulture	8	UCD	4 years	400
Rural Enterprise & Agri Business	8	ATU Galway/Mayo	4 years	300
Veterinary Medicine	8	UCD	5 years	589
Veterinary Nursing	8	UCD	4 years	518
Veterinary Nursing	7	Dundalk I.T.	3 years	387
Veterinary Nursing	7	ATU Donegal	3 years	388
Veterinary Nursing	7	TUS Midlands	3 years	400
Bio Veterinary Science	8	TUS Midlands	4 years	293

For further information on Agricultural courses please visit www.careersportal.ie

Teagasc Course Charges

Course charges as set out in Table 8.5 are net of accommodation and food costs. Where an applicant is the holder of a major award at Level 6 or higher, an additional course charge of €1,000 is applied. Teagasc has in place means testing to determine eligibility for the Teagasc Student Maintenance Grant Scheme. This equates with the rate of Maintenance Grant set by the Department of Education and Skills based on the number of course contact weeks.

Table 6.5: Teagasc Course Charges (as of September 2023).

Course	Level	Charge
Certificate in Agriculture	5	€990
Certificate in Horsemanship	5	€990
Certificate in Horticulture	5	€990
Certificate in Forestry	5	€990
Advanced Certificate in Agriculture - Dairy Herd Management	6	€990
Advanced Certificate in Agriculture - Drystock Management	6	€990
Advanced Certificate in Agriculture - Agricultural Mechanisation	6	€990
Advanced Certificate in Agriculture - Crops and Bio Energy	6	€990
Advanced Certificate in Agriculture - Crop and Machinery Management	6	€990
Advanced Certificate in Horsemanship - Stud Management	6	€990
Advanced Certificate in Horsemanship - Equitation	6	€990
Advanced Certificate in Horticulture	6	€990
Advanced Certificate in Forestry	6	€990
Teagasc Distance Education Green Cert for Holders of Non Agricultural Awards (Distance)	6	€2,990
Teagasc Part Time Green Cert - Adult Farmers	6	€1,700
Note: Course charge for a one year programme for a Non-Eu Citizen	n/a	€7,000

Maintenance Grants for Teagasc Courses
Teagasc student maintenance grants are paid through Teagasc and the grant scheme is managed by Teagasc. The maintenance grant scheme is implemented along the lines of the National Student Grant Scheme 2023. Please note that applicants cannot apply to Student Universal Support Ireland (SUSI) to be means tested for a Teagasc Student Maintenance Grant. The application form and closing date can be accessed from the Teagasc website https://www.teagasc.ie/education/going-to-college/student-maintenance-grants/application-process/

Tax Relief on Accommodation
A measure introduced in Budget 2024 allows for payments made by parents in respect of "digs" or rent-a-room arrangements for their children to attend an approved course qualify for the Rent Tax Credit. This is provided the claimant and their child are not related to the landlord. This change will apply retrospectively for the years 2022 and 2023. The credit for 2024 and 2025 is €750 or €1,500 for a jointly assessed couple.

Agricultural College Open Days 2023/2024
Students hoping to pursue higher level courses in Agriculture, Horticulture, Agribusiness, Agricultural Science, Forestry, Pigs, Poultry, Horses & Mechanisation are advised to attend an open day at their chosen college. Visit www.teagasc.ie/education for further information and upcoming open days.

7 FARMING IN HARMONY WITH THE ENVIRONMENT

Organic Farming
Registering and Converting 137
Organic Farming Scheme 140
Advice, Training And Support.. 141

Protection of Water Regulations
Stocking & Fertiliser Restrictions..144
Measures to Prevent Pollution..146

Nitrates Derogation
Training Requirements 150

Installation of Solar Panels
Considering Solar 151
Planning TAMS Grants.. 151

Organic Farming

The aim of organic farming is to produce food of optimum quality in a manner beneficial to the environment and biodiversity. There are currently in the region of 4,000 organic producers in the country. Organic farming has a major role to play in meeting the ever-increasing challenges of depleting oil supplies, climate change, water quality and the provision of a sustainable supply of food. With the higher payments under the Organic Farming Scheme and many farmers after cutting back on fertiliser use in the last few years and increased use of clover swards by conventional farmers, going organic is a viable options for more farmers. All beef and sheep farmers stocked at under 100kgN/ha/year should consider the organic option, if their housing is compliant with the organic rules, as clover swards will maintain their grassland production. For hill sheep farmers, with the reduction of the minimum livestock stocking rate in the Organic Farming Scheme to 0.1 (one ewe) /ha/year, many will have few changes to make to go organic.

Registering and Converting

The first step in considering conversion to organic farming is to contact your local farm consultant (ACA see pages 29-35 or your Teagasc advisor). The Department of Agriculture, acts as the competent authority governing the certification of growers as organic producers. The Department has approved a number of organic certification bodies (OCB). On-farm inspections by the OCB and DAFM constitute part of the certification process.

Organic Certification Bodies

The Organic Certification Bodies provide an inspection and certification service for all Organic Production Units in Ireland. They have been designated and are regulated by the Organic Unit of the Department of Agriculture, Food and Marine, and are responsible for upholding the Organic standards as defined by the EU.

IOA (Irish Organic Association), 16A Inish Carraig, Golden Island, Athlone. Tel: 090 6433680 Email: info@irishoa.ie Web: www.irishorganicassociation.ie

Organic Trust Clg, Unit M4 , Naas Town Centre, Dublin Road, Naas, Co. Kildare, Ireland, W91 F7X3. Tel: 045 882 377. Email: info@organictrust.ie www.organictrust.ie

Global Trust Certificate Ltd. (Aquaculture only), 3rd Floor, Block 3, Quayside Business Park, Mill Street, Dundalk, Co. Louth. Tel: 042 9320912 Email: info@gtcert.com

Converting to Organic

Farmers interested in converting to organic must prepare a plan which involves a detailed description of:

- Management practices on the farm.
- The changes required on the farm.
- Soil analysis, faecal analysis.
- Livestock housing plan.
- Animal health plan (in consultation with your veterinary surgeon).
- And land/crop rotation plan.

The plan can be drawn up by the farmer alone or in consultation with the farm advisor. Attending a QQI accredited "Organic Production Principles" is an excellent way of learning how to complete the conversion plan and the rules of organic farming. See nots.ie or teagasc.ie for these courses. Prospective organic farmers undergo a two-year conversion period before produce can be sold as organic.

Welfare and Housing
- The permanent housing of all stock is prohibited.
- There are specific space requirements for all ages/types of livestock.
- Bedding materials must be provided in all housing and does not have to be organic.
- Provided 50% of the floor area is bedded, up to 50% of the floor area may be slatted.
- Castration and dehorning are permitted before a certain age with anaesthetic, where it is judged to be necessary for considerations of safety and welfare.

Methods of Production
The main features of organic production are:
- Prohibit the usage of synthetic chemicals, fertilisers, pesticides and herbicides.
- Using balanced crop rotations.
- The use of organic manures from organic and specific non-organic systems.
- Use of legumes in rotations and in break crops.
- Using clover in grassland swards to maintain stocking rates and produce quality fodder.
- Specific cultivation techniques: stale seedbeds, mechanical weeding and undersowing.
- Beneficial ecological practices to encourage biodiversity and natural predators for pests.

Well-planned rotations are regarded as an essential part of successful organic production and help to maintain soil fertility, minimise weeds, pests and disease, while achieving sustainable yields and/or providing sufficient organic feed for stock.

Veterinary & Livestock Nutrition
The following rules apply:
- Vaccinations are allowed for known farm problems.
- The system should be designed to maintain the health of the livestock.
- If an animal becomes sick, conventional treatments may be administered to return to animal to full health. However strict recording procedures and at least doubling of the withdrawal periods must be observed.
- Treatment of healthy animals and the routine use of prophylactic drugs is prohibited.
- Antibiotics use is limited to one treatment per animal per 12 months period. If the animal requires further treatment with antibiotics, that individual animal can no longer be sold as organic.
- Supplementary minerals, such as Copper or Calmag may be given where evidence of mineral deficiency exists.
- Each farm must produce a veterinary Health plan outlining the main veterinary issues on the farm and how they are going to be avoided or treated.

Only 100% organic feed can be used for bovines and sheep from the start of the conversion.
The following rules also apply;
• Only where a known dietary deficiency exists in home-grown feeds is mineral supplementation permitted.
• In-feed additives and medications are prohibited unless veterinary need is established.

Purchase of Livestock
Ideally, all purchased livestock should be sourced from organic producers. Breeding males, bulls or rams, can be purchased from non-organic sources. Where breeding females are not available, permission can be sought to bring in a percentage of non-organic females i.e. heifers or hoggets. Stock for meat production must be purchased from other organic farms and must have been born on an organic farm. There are dedicated organic sales in some Marts and both OCB have classified adverts. Sections where stock can be advertised for sale. Organic Hub at organictradinghub.ie is now available to buy and sell organic livestock, fodder and feed. This service is supported by DAFM and is free to use.

Converting to Organic Production Methods
Organic farming involves undergoing a period of conversion in which the land and producer adjust to the organic methods. In general, the producer must comply with the full organic rules from the start of the conversion period. The conversion period for the change from conventional to organic farming depends on the type of enterprise which are outlined in the table 7.1 below:

Table 7.1: Conversion Periods.

Enterprise	Conversion period required
Livestock production (grass based systems)	2 years
Arable and horticultural production	2 years (before sowing the crop)
Perennial crops (eg strawberries):	3 years. Conversion must commence before the first harvesting of the crop

In certain cases the conversion period may be extended or reduced by the inspection body subject to the approval of the Department of Agriculture, Food and the Marine. The earliest date the conversion can begin is when the conversion plan is submitted to the OCB. Prior to commencing conversion, the farmer must submit an application along with a conversion plan, drawn up by either the farmer or a qualified planner to the inspection body for approval. The farm is then inspected by the inspection body who will then adjudicate on the application. For more detailed information on this process, the farmer should contact any of the approved inspection bodies referred to above. After the required conversion period expires, the inspection body may issue organic status to the farmer (unless conversion period is being extended), which allows the farmer to sell his/her produce as organic.

There is often a financial cost associated with conversion. These costs vary widely according to individual circumstances but would be influenced by some of the following factors:
- Output reduction due to changes in production practices.
- Introducing clover to grassland swards.
- Capital investments in land, machinery, livestock housing etc.
- Certification and inspection costs (participation payment under OFS of at least €1400 covers these).
- Inability to command premium prices during the conversion phase.

Advantages of Organic Farming
- It is a healthy, environmentally friendly method of food production.
- There is an increasing consumer demand for organic food, commanding a premium price.
- It is a low input system of farming, based on lower stocking with lesser input costs.
- There is scope for further expansion in the industry.
- Animal health problems are reduced.
- There is an attractive subsidy under the Organic Farming Scheme, Organic Capital Investment Scheme (Organic TAMS) and priority access to Agri Environmental Schemes such as ACRES.
- Farmers continue to claim there their BISS, Eco schemes and ANC payments.

Disadvantages of Organic Farming
- Many consumers are as yet unwilling to pay a premium price for organically grown beef and lamb.
- There are limited markets for some organic produce and farmers may not have a local market available.
- A higher degree of husbandry and farm management skills are necessary to successfully farm organically.

Financial Supports
The main funding sources are the Organic Farming Scheme (page 68) and the Organic Capital Investment Scheme (page 52).

Organic Farming Scheme
The overall objective of the Organic Farming Scheme is to deliver enhanced environmental and animal welfare benefits and to encourage producers to respond to the market demand for organically produced food.

Eligible Persons
As in the previous Organic Farming Scheme, a series of core requirements defines basic eligibility. Key conditions include:
- Requirement of minimum farm area of 3 hectares for livestock and tillage holdings, 1 hectare for horticultural producers (provide that 50% of eligible area for organic payment is cropped each year).

- Registration with one of the Organic Control Bodies, possession of a valid organic license and registration with DAFM.
- Requirement to meet the productivity objective, the minimum stocking levels must equal 0.1 LU per hectare.

Payments

Table 7.2: Organic Farming Scheme Payments.

	Year 1-2 (in conversion) Area <70ha	Year 1-2 (in conversion) Area >70ha	Year 3-5 (fully converted) Area <70 ha	Year 3-5 (fully converted) Area >70ha
Drystock	€300/ha	€60/ha	€250/ha	€30/ha
Tillage	€320/ha	€60/ha	€27/ha	€30/ha
Dairy	€350/ha	€60/ha	€300/ha	€30/ha
Horticulture	€800/ha	€60/ha	€600/ha	€30/ha

Participation payment: Annual payment of €1,400 to cover administrative costs. (€2,000 in year of conversion).

All farmers (in-conversion or fully converted) who are part of the organic farming scheme will be able to avail of the payment rates from 01 January 2024. Learn about the potential payments for your farm using the Departments Organic Payments Calculator.

The OCIS (Organic TAMS) will offer 60% grant aid for a list of funded machinery from the 1st January 2024. This list is only available to registered organic producers including those in conversion and 60% grant aid is also available to Organic farmers on items on the general TAMS list.

Advice, Training and Support

A 25-hour QQI Level 5 'Organic Production Principles' course must be completed within a period after applying for the Organic Farming Scheme (contact nots.ie or teagasc.ie). Organic production, like any other form of production, requires planning, commitment, and dedication to succeed. Preparation can start with any or all of the following bodies and organisations who will be willing to assist;

Agricultural Consultants Association (ACA). See page 28. ACA has two organic specialists to back up all ACA members on information on organic farming.

Teagasc; Teagasc Head office, Oakpark, Carlow 059 9170200

The Organic College (An tlonad Glas): 063 86304 or the website can be visited on www.organiccollege.com.

The Organic Centre: 071 9854338 or www.theorganiccentre.ie

The Leitrum Organic Farmer's Co-op, (071) 9640868 or leitrimorganic.com

National Organic Training Skillnet (NOTS) (071) 9640868 or nots.ie

Protection of Water Regulations

All livestock farmers are obliged to comply with slurry/manure storage requirements; limits on the quantity of organic manure spread on land and the time of spreading it. Furthermore, there are limits on the quantity of chemical fertilisers spread and the time of spreading. Ireland's national Nitrates Action Programme was given statutory effect by the European Communities (Good Agricultural Practice for Protection of Waters) Regulations 2006. This programme forms part of cross-compliance and farmer who do not comply are putting their Basic Payment, Area of Natural Constraints, ACRES and other co-funded scheme payments at risk not to mention the fact that its against the law to fail to comply.

Irelands fifth National Action Programme (NAP) came into effect in March 2022 and will run until 31 December 2025. The following are the existing and new measures set out in this regulation:

- Prevention of direct run-off from farm roadways to waters (i.e. watercourses and dry drains).
- Bovine exclusion from water courses (as identified on 1:5,000 scale OSI mapping or better) on farms with grassland stocking rate above 170 kg N/ha.
- Water troughs to be located at least 20m from watercourses on farms with grassland stocking rates above 170 kg N/ha.
- Prevention of run-off to waters (i.e. watercourses and dry drains) resulting from poaching.
- Increased P build-up allowances for P index 1 and 2 soils. This only applies to farmers with a grassland stocking rate >130 kg N/ha. Farmers availing of these P build-up rates must comply with requirements.
- Soil organic matter testing in designated peaty areas as defined in the Teagasc- EPA Indicative Soils Map.
- Soil sampling area is reduced to 5 hectares and the soil sample is valid for 4 years.
- Provision for the application of 20kg P/ha on winter cereals up to 31st October for P index 1 and 2 soils and P must be incorporated at or before sowing.
- Slurry and Soil Water Storage and Management: Closing dates brought back to 1st Oct in 2023. There must be capacity to store soiled water on the farm for 21 days in 2023 and 28 days in 2024.

Summary of Requirements

Farmers are required to observe the following:

- You must not exceed 170 kg of nitrogen per hectare in a year in the form of animal excretion or organic fertiliser application in the form of Slurry, or Farmyard manure for example.
- There are times of the year when you must not spread any fertiliser at all on your land, either organic or chemical. These are called 'the prohibited spreading periods'.
- You must keep within the overall maximum fertilisation rates for nitrogen and phosphorus (i.e., organic and chemical fertiliser combined), the basic rule being that you only apply as much nitrogen and phosphorus as your crops (including grass) need.

- You must have sufficient storage capacity to meet the minimum requirements of the regulations, and all storage facilities must be kept leak-proof and structurally sound.
- You must follow the rules about ploughing and applying non-selective herbicides.
- You must keep various records, including records of the fertilisers you bring onto your holding or send out of it. You have to keep records for each calendar year, which means 1 January to 31 December, and you must have them ready by 31 January of the following year.

Prohibited Periods for Spreading

Fertilisers and manures cannot be spread during the following periods; Farmers can spread soiled water all the year round if the weather is suitable and if the condition of the land is suitable. However, it is not permitted to spread more than 50,000 litres (25,000 in Extreme Vulnerability Areas or Karst Limestone Aquifers) to the hectare in any six-week period or more than 5 mm an hour by irrigation (3 mm in Extreme Vulnerability Areas or Karst Limestone Aquifers).

Table 7.3: Prohibited Spreading Periods.

Zone	Prohibited Application Period		
	Chemical Fertiliser	Organic Fertiliser	Farmyard Manure
A	15 Sept - 26 Jan	1 Oct - 12 Jan	1 Nov - 12 Jan
B	15 Sept - 29 Jan	1 Oct - 15 Jan	1 Nov - 15 Jan
C (Donegal & Leitrim)	15 Sept - 14 Feb	1 Oct - 31 Jan	1 Nov - 31 Jan
C (Cavan & Monaghan)	15 Sept - 14 Feb	1 Oct - 31 Jan	1 Nov - 31 Jan

Storage Periods for Cattle Manure

The storage periods for cattle shall equal or exceed the limits set down as follows:

Zone A
16 weeks — Holdings in counties Carlow, Cork, Dublin, Kildare, Kilkenny, Laois, Offaly, Tipperary, Waterford, Wexford and Wicklow.

Zone B
18 weeks — Holdings in counties Clare, Galway, Kerry, Limerick, Longford, Louth, Mayo, Meath, Roscommon, Sligo and Westmeath.

Zone C
20 weeks — Holdings in counties Donegal and Leitrim.
22 weeks — Holdings in counties Cavan and Monaghan.

Stocking & Fertiliser Restrictions

Farmers must take all reasonable steps necessary to prevent or minimise the application to land of fertilisers in excess of crop requirement. This will be achieved by a combination of stocking rate and fertiliser application restrictions. The maximum phosphorus fertilisation of grassland shall not exceed that specified for stocking rates less than or equal to 170 kg/ha/year unless a minimum of 5% of the eligible area of the holding is used to grow crops other than grass or a derogation applies in respect of the holding.

Stocking Rate Limit

There is a stocking rate limit to the extent of confining organic nitrogen (animal excreta) to 170 kg per hectare. This equates with 0.8 cows per acre. Stocking rate will be determined by the total amount of organic nitrogen on your farm over the year divided by the number of hectares declared on your single payment form for that year.

Livestock Excretion Rates

Three new excretion rate bands now exist for the dairy cow. Each dairy herd will be assigned to one of the three band's each year, based on the herd's average annual milk yield per cow as set out in Table 7.5. Banding dairy cows' excretion rate based on milk yield reflects the scientific research that shows increasing milk yield also increases the dairy cow's nutrient excretion rate.

Table 7.4: Livestock Excretion Rates.

Band	Herd average Milk Yield	N excretion Rate (kg/cow/yr)
1	<=4,500kgs	80
2	4,501-6,500kgs	92
3	>6,501kgs	106

Table 7.5: Organic Nitrogen and Phosphorus Production Levels.

Livestock type	Total Nitrogen kg/year	Total Phosphorus kg/year
Dairy cow band 1	80	12
Dairy cow band 2	92	13.6
Dairy cow band 3	106	15.8
Suckler cow	65	10
Cattle (0-1 year old)	24	3
Cattle (1-2 year old)	57	8
Cattle > 2 years	65	10
Mountain ewe & lambs	7	1

Lowland ewe & lambs	13	2
Mountain hogget	4	0.6
Lowland hogget	6	1
Goat	9	1
Horse (>3 years old)	50	9
Horse (2-3 years old)	44	8
Horse (1-2 years old)	36	6
Horse foal (< 1 year old)	25	3
Donkey/small pony	30	5
Deer (red) 6 months - 2 years	13	2
Deer (red) > 2 years	25	4
Deer (fallow) 6 months - 2 years	7	1
Deer (fallow) > 2 years	13	2
Deer (sika) 6 months - 2 years	6	1
Deer (sika) > 2 years	10	2
Breeding unit (per sow place)	35	8
Integrated unit (per sow place)	87	17
Finishing unit (per pig place)	9.2	1.7
Laying hen per bird place	0.56	0.12
Broiler per bird place	0.24	0.09
Turkey per bird place	1	0.4

Example of Stocking Rate Calculation:

A farmer has an average over the year of 60 dairy cows in band 1, 15 Cattle (0-1) and 15 cattle (1-2). He is farming 40 hectares of grassland as per his BISS Application form. The calculation of organic nitrogen is as follows:

60 Cows @ 80 kg's/cow	=	4,800 kgs
15 (0-1) Cattle @ 24 kg's/hd.	=	360 kgs
15 (1-2) Cattle @ 57 kg's/hd.	=	855 kgs
Total		5,215 kgs

Total organic nitrogen of 6,015 kgs divided by hectares farmed of 40 = 150 kg's/hectare. This farmer is comfortably below the stocking limit of 170 kg's/hectare and will not need to avail of the 220kg derogation limit.

Temporary Movement of Livestock

The Nitrates Regulations have implications for farmers moving their animals to another holding for grazing on a temporary basis. Where cattle are involved and no sale or purchase has taken place, farmers can obtain credit for the fertiliser produced by these cattle only if they complete a movement form, or by notifying the Department where there are no cattle at the other location.

Table 7.6: Slurry Storage Requirements.

Livestock type	m³/week[1]
Dairy cow	0.33
Suckler cow	0.29
Cattle > 2 years	0.26
Cattle (18-24 months old)	0.26
Cattle (12-18 months old)	0.15
Cattle (6-12 months old)	0.15
Cattle (0-6 months old)	0.08
Lowland ewe	0.03
Mountain ewe	0.02
Lamb-finishing	0.01
Poultry - layers per 1000 birds (30% DM)	0.81

[1] An additional 200 mm freeboard must be provided in all covered tanks and 300 mm freeboard in all uncovered tanks. Allowance must also be made for net rainfall during the specified storage period for uncovered tanks.

Measures to Prevent Pollution

The regulation sets down certain restrictions in relation to the avoidance of pollution as follows:

Spreading of chemical fertiliser, organic fertiliser or soiled water

- At least 50% of slurry produced on the holding shall be applied by June 15th. Low emission slurry equipment shall be used for any slurry applications after the 15th June.
- Chemical fertiliser cannot be applied to land within 2.0 metres of a surface watercourse.
- Organic fertiliser or soiled water shall not be applied to land within 200m (or as little as 30m where the Local Authority allows) of the abstraction point of any surface watercourse, borehole, spring or well used for the abstraction of water for human consumption in a water scheme supplying 100m³ or more of water per day or serving 500 or more persons. The limit is 100 metres (or as little as 30m where the Local Authority allows) if the scheme is serving 50 or more persons or otherwise 25 metres and 20m from a lake shoreline.

- Where farmyard manure is held in a field prior to landspreading it shall be held in a compact heap and shall not be placed within 250m of the abstraction point of any surface watercourse or borehole, spring or well used for the abstraction of water for human consumption in a water scheme supplying 10 (m^3) or more of water per day or serving 50 or more persons. The limit is otherwise 50 metres or 20 metres from a lake shoreline.
- No supplementary feeding points may be located within 20m of surface water or on bare rock.
- Silage bales shall not be stored outside of farmyards within 20m of a surface watercourse or drinking water abstraction point in the absence of adequate facilities for the collection and storage of any effluent arising.
- Fertilisers or soiled water shall not be applied to land if the land is waterlogged, the land is flooded or likely to flood, the land is snow-covered or frozen, heavy rain is forecast within 48 hours, or the ground slopes steeply and, taking into account factors such as proximity to waters, soil condition, ground cover and rainfall, there is significant risk of causing water pollution.
- Organic fertilisers or soiled water shall not be applied to land by use of an umbilical system with an upward-facing splash plate, by use of a tanker with an upward-facing splashplate, by use of a sludge irrigator mounted on a tanker, or from a road or passageway adjacent to the land irrespective of whether or not the road or passageway is within or outside the curtilage of the holding.
- Livestock manures shall not be spread in the Autumn before grass cultivation.

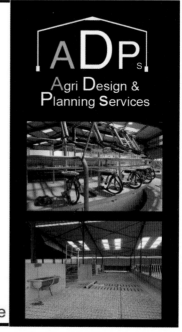

Ploughing and Spraying
- Where arable land is ploughed between 1 July and 30 November, the necessary measures shall be taken to provide for emergence of green cover from a sown crop within 6 weeks of the ploughing.
- Where grassland is ploughed between 1 July and 15 October the necessary measures shall be taken to provide for emergence by 1 November of green cover from a sown crop.
- Grassland shall not be ploughed between 16 October and 30 November.
- When a non-selective herbicide is applied to arable land or to grassland in the period between 1 July and 30 November the necessary measures shall be taken to provide for the emergence of green cover within 6 weeks of the application from a sown crop or from natural regeneration.
- Where green cover is provided to abide by the rules in regard to ploughing or using a non-selective herbicide, it must not be removed it by ploughing or by use of a non-selective herbicide before 1st December, unless a crop is sown within two weeks of removing it.
- No ploughing or tilling may take place within 2m of a watercourse (stream/river) marked on an OSI 6" (1:10560) map except in the case of grassland re-seeding or establishment. The no till zone does not apply to field drains.
- Temporary grassland shall be ploughed in Spring.
- Ploughed grass on all soil types shall be followed immediately by a crop with high nitrogen demand.

Keeping of Records
Records shall be maintained for each holding and shall be prepared for each calendar year by 31 January of the following year and shall be retained for a period of not less than five years.

Nitrates Derogation

A derogation from the normal stocking maximum of 170 kgs/ha is available until 2025 but must be applied for each year. The Nitrates Derogation is a mechanism to allow individual farmers, on application to exceed the standard organic Nitrates upper limit of 170 Kgs of N per annum. The maximum upper N limit for Derogation farmers is 220 Kgs. The main conditions of the derogation are as follows:
- All slurry produced on the holding must be applied using a Low Emissions Slurry Spreader (LESS).
- Adopt a farm scale liming programme.
- Information related to manure transferred off the holding shall be submitted to the Department of Agriculture by 31 October each year.
- Adopt extra measures to prevent contamination of waterways, roadways adjacent to watercourses must be cambered away from the watercourse.
- Water troughs must be more than 20m away from watercourses and animals must be prevented from entering watercourses to drink water.
- All watercourses must be fenced back 1.5m from the top of the bank.

- Livestock manure shall not be spread in the autumn before grass cultivation.
- Temporary grassland shall be ploughed in Spring.
- Ploughed grass on all soil types shall be followed immediately by a crop with high nitrogen demand.
- Grass reseeding on grassland farms shall include a minimum clover content of 1.5kg/ha naked seed and 2.5 kg/ha pelleted seed and not exceed 50% of the sward mixture.
- The entire holding being farmed must be soil sampled. Soil samples must be taken every 4 years. One analysis must be taken for not more than 5 hectares.
- Derogation farmers must record through appropriate software technology the grass produced annually on the farm. If new Derogation farmers haven't the required skills to undertake this measure, they must undertake training in grassland management which must be completed by the end of 2023. Existing applicants must record 20 grass measurements in 2023.
- A maximum of 15% Crude Protein in dairy rations between 1st April and 15th September (if higher levels of crude protein are required, this needs to be certified by the appropriate advisor).
- Leave at least one mature Whitethorn/ Blackthorn tree within each hedgerow or maintain hedgerows on a minimum 3-year cycle or Cut in rotation rather than all at once as this will ensure some areas of hedgerow on your farm will always flower. Cutting annually stops the hedgerow flowering and fruiting.
- A Nutrient Management

Plan (NMP) or Fertilization Plan based on the soil samples and other variables such as stock numbers etc. must be completed using the new Teagasc Nutrient Management Planning system (eNMP) or Farmeye.
- Fertilizer Records must be kept and submitted to the Department of Agriculture by March 31st each year.

The Department of Agriculture and Food will issue Nitrogen and Phosphorus Statements each year to farmers who, in the previous year (a) had cattle recorded on the Department's CMMS and (b) made application under the Basic Income Support for Sustainability Scheme. The Statement will set out the quantities of organic nitrogen and phosphorus produced by your cattle during the previous year. This will give you a clear indication of your organic nitrogen status and whether you were within the 170kg limit in the previous year and will help you to decide whether you need to apply for a Derogation.

Training Requirements
The following training requirements apply to derogation participants.
1. Nitrates Derogation applicants who applied to participate in the Nitrates Derogation in 2022 must have completed all elements of a training programme in nutrient use efficiency and the protection of waters (as per training guidelines issued in 2022).
2. New applicants or applicants who did not apply in 2022 must complete training programmes in nutrient use efficiency and the protection of waters by 31st December 2023.
3. Those farmers who completed a grassland management training course in 2023 will be required to get set up on appropriate software technology (as accepted by DAFM) in 2023. These farmers have two options for grass measuring in 2023 as follows:
   - record 20 grass measurements on appropriate software technology (as accepted by DAFM), or Nitrates Derogation 2023 Terms & Conditions 6.
   - attend two workshops – workshop on using the software technology to record grass measurements AND workshop on grass measuring and take at least 3 grass measurements in 2023,

The assistance of Diarmuid Foley, Farm Consultant, is gratefully acknowledged.

Installation of Solar Panels

Sustainable farming is all about making the most of existing natural resources. The one thing that all farmers have free access to is sunlight. The other thing that most farmers possess is lots of roof space. This puts them in an ideal position to generate power in their own farmyards by installing solar panels. Some farmers have hefty electricity bills, particularly dairy farmers and intensive pig and poultry producers and these bills are only going to increase as the years go by. With the availability of generous grants and tax write-offs, the payback time can be less than two years.

Considering Solar

There are a large number of suppliers in the market and care has to be exercised as to the reliability of the company and the product it is selling. There can be a significant difference in quality and indeed lifespan of the various panels being sold.. In considering solar the first objective must be to meet as much of your own energy use as possible as this will be the most valuable part of the energy you generate. If you sell back power to the grid, it will be at a much lower rate than you are currently paying to receive it. Therefore, solar energy systems work best if you have a daily energy use to balance your generation so that you can consume the energy you generate. This can be assisted by installing a battery storage and water heating system to use any excess energy produced during the optimal daylight hours.

Panels

Solar photovoltaic (PV) cells, which are contained in solar panels, work on the principle that energy in the sun is converted to electricity. The energy available from the sun is measured in kilowatt hours per square metre per year (kWh/m2/year). The quality of the panels is important in terms of their efficiency and longevity. The strong advice is to opt for European manufactured panels. Others may be cheaper, but you get what you pay for. Good quality panels will last for at least 25 years and possibly over 30 years. The angle and orientation of the solar panels is very important. Generally, a large southerly facing roof or field space is the optimal for generation but an east-west orientation, while generating 10-15% less, will spread the generation better during the day and may be a better choice to optimise on-farm consumption of energy generated. An unshaded pitched roof of between 10^0 and 35^0 is the ideal.

Planning

Rooftop solar installations covering the entire roof of an agricultural structure or roof of any ancillary buildings within the farm are exempt from requiring planning permission, unless they are in the vicinity of an airport in which case there is a rooftop limit of 300 sq. metres. Free standing or wall mounted solar panel installations for agricultural holdings are also exempted from the requirement to obtain planning permission subject to a 75 square metre area limit, when taken together with any other such existing installations.

Tams Grants

Grant aid of 60% up to a maximum investment of €90,000 is available. The investment limit is ring-fenced and will not impact on other TAMS grants. The grant will also cover battery storage systems. There is an overall restriction that requires that the system being installed has not the capacity to exceed your previous year's energy bill.

Tax Relief

Solar panel installations which create power for use in the farm business are fully allowable against tax in the year of installation. The relief is available to companies and individuals.

The Costs & Savings

The case study set out hereunder shows that there is a very worthwhile return from installing solar panels. It is a 25 to 30-year investment, so the benefits in many instances will continue to be enjoyed by the next generation, As stated above, the most cost-effective unit will be where the power generated will replace bought in power. The following case study looks at a farm that has an annual usage cost of €5,000 (ex-VAT) and sets out the net cost of installing the system and the likely savings.

CASE STUDY

An annual usage cost of €5,000 equates with g approximately 11,000 units of electricity at an average cost 45 cent per unit. The farm having been surveyed; the advice is to install an 8 Khw system with 5Kwh of battery storage along with a water heating system. This system will take up about 48m² of roof space which is equivalent to a little more than one span of a 30 ft wide shed.

The cost of the system will be in the region of €20,000 incl. VAT@13.5%. After claiming back VAT (which unregistered farmers can do) and claiming the 60% grant on the balance, the net cost of the system is €7,048. As there is 100% tax write-off available on the system in year one, this will save a typical farmer in the lower tax band a further €2,009 between tax, PRSI and USC in the year of installation. This results in an overall net outlay of €5,039. For high-rate taxpayers, the overall net outlay is only €3,629. However, the net outlay for a farming company will be somewhat higher at €6,167 due to lower tax savings.

The system can be expected to generate the equivalent of approximately 6,600 units of electricity annually which at current prices is worth about €2,900 in annual savings to the farmer. This means that the payback period is less than two years or a net return on investment of 57% for a standard rate taxpayer.

The assistance of Pat Smith of Local Power Ltd. in preparing this article is gratefully acknowledged.

2024 SELECTED COURSES

National Organic Training Skillnet

Organic Farming Principles	25-hour QQI Accredited Level 5 course, required for acceptance to the Organic Farming Scheme. Dates: Throughout the year (Multiple locations)
Organic Market Gardening Course	QQI Level 5 accredited course. Taught by Jim Cronin in Clare, this is a 9-month course held every 2nd Wednesday. Begins late February and places fill up fast - contact us ASAP.
Animal Nutrition Course	2-day course taught by Mike Walsh of SETU. Understanding animal gut health and feed support for gut bacteria. Date: Spring 2024 (Contact us for info)
Dairy & Milk Processing Course	Short introductory courses on cheese, yoghurt and ice cream processing. Date: Begins Spring 2024
Intro to Soil Health & Biological Agriculture	6-day in-depth soil health course focusing on biological and regenerative farming methods. Dates: Next course Spring 2024
Soil Health Academy with Gabe Brown's Understanding Ag	3-day course with the Understanding Ag team - focusing on adaptive grazing & regenerative practices. Date: Last week in July 2024
Korean Natural Farming Training with Chris Trump	Learn the fundamental principles of Natural Farming with pioneer of the system Chris Trump. Dates: Late June 2024
Masters (MSc) in Organic and Biological Agriculture	Level 9 Masters Degree. Run in SETU (formerly Waterford IT). 2-year distance learning. Date: Intakes in January and September
BioFarm 2024	Ireland's Biological Farming Conference - learn from the top Irish and international speakers on biological and regenerative farming. Dates: November 2024 (online and in-person)
Bespoke Courses for Our Members	We are always looking to add new courses to our portfolio. If you have any suggestions for future programmes, email us at info@nots.ie

Visit nots.ie or call 071 9640688 for more info

8 FORESTRY

Ireland's Forest Industry

Forestry Programme 2023 – 2027 155
Afforestation (New Planting)...156
Native Tree Area Scheme (Nta) 158
Woodland Environmental Fund (WEF) 158
Environmental Report Grant (ERG) 158

Grant Support for Existing Forests

Forest Roads..159
Reconstitution Of Woodland Scheme 159
Woodland Improvement Scheme..160
Native Woodland Conservation Scheme..160
Climate Resilient Reforestation 160
Forestry Knowledge Transfer Groups (KTGS)..162
Taxation of Forestry...162

Ireland's Forest Industry

Ireland has a mild, maritime climate which is ideally suited to growing trees. There are currently 24,000 forest owners who have planted trees in Ireland. Forests clean the air we breathe, protect our soils and water and increase biodiversity by providing habitats for birds, animals and insects. In addition, forests tackle climate change by sequestering carbon from the atmosphere. Irish forests support over 9,000 jobs and contributes over €2 billion to the Irish economy annually.

Facts on Irish Forestry

- Government has committed €1.3 billion to Irish Forestry for 2023 - 2027.
- National afforestation policy has been a great success, with 690,000 hectares planted in 100 years 1922 -2022, reaching 11.6% of the total land area, the largest land-use change since the foundation of the state.
- At 11.6% forest cover, Ireland is one of the lowest in the EU 27, where the average forest cover is 38%; worldwide forest cover is 31%.
- Over half of the total forest area is in private ownership.
- The forest estate is comprised of 70% conifer and 30% broadleaf.
- The Climate Action plan identifies afforestation as the single largest land based mitigation measure available and sets a roadmap for halving carbon emissions by 2030 and reaching net zero no later than 2050. In order to do this, we need:
  - Area of land under forest to increase to 18% of the total land area.
  - Afforestation rates need to be 18,000 hectares per year to achieve 18% land cover.
  - The further this target is missed the greater the need will be to deliver reductions from other sources, including agriculture.
- There are over 20 million recreational visits to Irish forests every year.
- Over the period 2021 to 2035, roundwood production from Irish forests is forecast to increase from 4.7 million cubic meters to 7.9 million cubic meters, almost all this increase will be from the private sector, mainly farmers.
- Approximately 80% of forest products produced in Ireland are exported, key markets include the UK, Germany and the Benelux countries.
- Every tonne of timber instead of cement is an avoided emission of two tonnes of carbon.

Forestry Programme 2023 – 2027

The Forestry Programme is the main vehicle that the Department uses to encourage the establishment and sustainable management of our forests. There are supports for the creation of new forests, and support for the management and replanting of existing forests.

Afforestation (New Planting)

There are 11 different Forest Types that can be planted by farmers under the new Forestry Programme. The farmer premium duration has been increased to 20 years (15 years for non-farmer). The Afforestation Grant Scheme (AGS) includes an establishment and fencing grant as well as an annual premium payment for 20 years.

Table 8.1: Afforestation Grant Scheme Forest Types & Forest Premium Rates.

Forest Type (FT)		Annual Forestry Premium/Ha	Farmer premium Duration Years
FT1	Native Forests	€1,103	20
FT2	Forests for Water*	€1,142	20
FT3	Forests on Public Lands	N/A	N/A
FT4	NeighbourWoods**	€1,142	20
FT5	Emergent Forest	€350	20
FT6	Broadleaves (Oak/Beech)	€1,037	20
FT7	Other Broadleaves	€973	20
FT8	Agroforestry Silvopastoral (Trees & animals) Silvoarable (Trees & Crops) Forest Gardening	€975 €829 €829	10 10 10
FT9	Seed Orchards	€1,142	20
FT10	Continuous Cover Forestry	€912	20
FT11	Mixed Conifers	€863	20
FT12	Sitka spruce	€746	20

* Additional payment of €1,000 per ha will be paid to landowner on completion of planting

** Grant includes Trails, Seats & Signage Facilities payment

Definition of a Farmer

Applicants that pass the Active Farmer check and who participate in the Basic Income Support for Sustainability (BISS) scheme in the application year and a member of either BISS or Basic Payment Scheme (BPS) in the previous 4 years will be considered a farmer. New and young farmers will only need to be in BISS or BPS from the year they were approved members of either the Young Farmer schemes or the National Reserve schemes. Applicants of inherited or planned inheritance (gifted) land, will benefit from succession/inheritance rules relating to immediate family members and will be able to fulfil the farmer qualifying criteria.

Dawson Rea Ltd

AGRICULTURAL & ENVIRONMENTAL CONSULTANTS

7 Grattan St, Tipperary, E34 R968

Tel: (062) 52166/52040
Mobile: 0868238283
Fax: (062) 52685

www.reagroup.ie
Email: tom@reagroup.ie

Dawson Rea has over 20 years experience in providing Professional Agricultural Consultancy, Advisory Services and Farm Business Advice to farmers and business in the Agricultural Sector.

Clients include Farmers, Solicitors, Insurance Companies, Banks amongst others. We provide Consultancy and Advisory Services in All areas of Agriculture.

Services Include:

BISS & CAP Reform	ACRES Planning & Advice	Nitrates, Cross Compliance & Conditionality
TAMS – Farm Grants	Planning Permissions	Farm Layout & Design
Expert Witness	Agricultural Litigation	Loss Assessment
Family Law Advice relating to Agriculture.	DAFM Scheme Advice	Nutrient Management Planning

Contact:

Tom Dawson B.Agr.Sc., DipFM(ACCA)., DipTax., RAC
7 Grattan Street,
Tipperary Town.
062 52040
086 8238283
tom@reagroup.ie

Richard J Rea B.Agr.Sc., Dip.E.I.A., Mgmt., MACA
7 Grattan Street,
Tipperary Town.
062 52040
086 6070686
richard@reagroup.ie

Native Tree Area Scheme (NTA)

The Native tree Area Scheme (NTA) is for the creation of small native woodlands up to 1ha in size on farms. The NTA scheme does not require an afforestation licence and approval into the scheme is via direct entry as per other agri-environmental schemes. There is an establishment grant and a forestry premium payment for ten years. There are two types of forest that can be established under the scheme and payment is for ten years (a maximum of 1 ha of either NTA 1 or NTA 2, max 2ha in total):

Table 8.2: Native Tree Area Scheme Premium Rates.

	Native Forest Type	Forest Premium/Ha	Duration Years
NTA1	Native Forests on Farms	€2,206	10
NTA2	Native Forests for Water Protection	€2,284	10

Additional Afforestation Grant Supports

Additional grant support towards the planting of land are available through the following schemes.

Woodland Environmental Fund (WEF)

The WEF offers some landowners the possibility of an additional €1,000 per hectare as an incentive to plant Native Forests. This once off payment is paid following satisfactory completion of the planting and is a top up to the €1,103 per hectare annual forest premium payable for native forests under FT1.

Environmental Report Grant (ERG)

An environment report grant is available to help pay for additional environmental reports required with afforestation licence applications. This is paid following satisfactory completion of the planting. The grant rates per application are:
• €450 per ha for first ha.
• €400 for second ha.
• €350 for third ha.
• €50 per ha for subsequent hectares to a maximum of 20 hectares.

Grant Support for Existing Forests

Forest Roads

The COFORD All Ireland Roundwood production forecast projects the roundwood supply will increase from 4.7 million cubic meters in 2021 to 7.9 million cubic meters by 2035. Mobilising this increased volume will require the construction of forest roads. Forest road construction is subject to a license from the Department of Agriculture, Food and the Marine (DAFM). Grant aid for forest road construction of up to 100% of eligible costs is available subject to the following maximum amounts:

Table 8.3: Forest Road Grant.

Category	Max Rate €/Linear metre (Excl vat)	Max Density (Metre/Ha)
Harvesting road	€55	25
Harvesting upgrade or extension	€40	variable
Special construction works	Up to €10,000 per project	
Ecologically Enhanced Forest Roads	€1,000 per project	
Engineering Design Support Measure	€1,000 per project	
Temporary Road Access Solution Measure	€10,000 per project	

DAFM are the single consent authority for forest road applications where the forest road requires a new entrance onto a public road, other than a national road. Forest roads provide additional biodiversity opportunities by increasing the amount of open space and forest edge, providing wildlife corridors and connectivity between habitats.

Reconstitution of Woodland Scheme

This scheme is to assist and support forest owners in restoring forests following significant damage by natural causes such as storms, frost and disease. For example, forest owners impacted by Ash dieback can apply for grant aid under the Reconstitution of woodland scheme. Operations eligible for grant aid include:
- The removal and destruction of diseased trees.
- Ground preparation.
- Replacement trees.
- Planting.
- Vegetation control for up to 4 years.
- Tree shaping.
- Creation of firebreaks and reservoirs.
- Other operations approved in advance.

Woodland Improvement Scheme

This scheme provides support to forest owners to sustainably manage their forests. The primary objective is to offer forest owners a range of schemes to manage their forest sustainably to increase the delivery of ecosystem services, biodiversity, regenerating capacity and vitality. The following table outlines the different funding options available.

Table 8.4: Woodland Improvement Scheme Grant Rates.

Woodland Improvement Measure	Number of payments	Max Grant per Ha	Premium payment per Ha	Number premium years
Thinning, Tending and Agroforestry Maintenance	2	€1,200	N/A	N/A
Continuous Cover Forestry	3	€1,200	€150	7
Coppice and Coppice with Standards	1	€1,200	N/A	N/A
Seed Stand Management	1	€1,200	€500	7

Native Woodland Conservation Scheme

The aim of NW Conservation is to promote and support the appropriate restoration of existing native woodlands and associated biodiversity and the conversion, where appropriate, of existing non-native forests to native woodlands. NW Conservation protects our rate native woodland habitats that are often found on farms. Its emphasis is on minimal site disturbance, species selection based on the most appropriate native woodland type, the use of native planting stock, protection of watercourses and aquatic habitats and long-term 'close-to-nature' management. Support is provided in the form of cost-based grant payment as follows:

- Up to €6,000/ha for approved restoration works.
- Fencing grant.
- A 7-year annual premium payment of €500 per hectare.

Climate Resilient Reforestation

Climate resilient reforestation is support for existing forest owners who wish to replant (reforest) their forest under permanent forest cover. The grant aid per hectare is a "Top up" grant towards additional reforestation costs or in the case of high ecological priority areas a full grant. They also attract a forest premium and ecosystem services payment per hectare for 7 years. The different reforestation types will depend on the suitability of land to support different forest types as well as environmental sensitivities The different forest types and grant support are being piloted as follows:

SWS FORESTRY

- Planting
- Roads
- Management plans
- Investment
- Timber Harvesting
- Land Sales

As they grow so does your income

Earn €22,840 per hectare, tax free

Premium Payments

Forest Type	New Annual premiums	Previous Number of Premiums	New Number of Premiums for Non- Farmers	New Number of Premiums for Farmers
1 Native Forests	€1103	15	15	20
2 Forests for Water*	€1142	New	15	20
6 Broadleaf, mainly oak	€1037	15	15	20
7 Other Broadleaf	€973	15	15	20
8 Agroforestry	€975	5	10	10
10 Continuous Cover Forestry	€912	New	15	20
11 Mixed High Forests: Conifer, 20% broadleaves	€863	15	15	20
12 Mixed High Forests with mainly spruce, 20% broadleaves	€746	15	15	20

ditional payment of €1,000 per ha will be paid to landowner on completion of planting.

Call your local SWS forester today for for information

Freephone: **1800 928 900** www.swsforestry.ie

Table 8.5: Climate Resilient Reafforestation Grant Rates.

Forest Type	Grant per Ha	Forest Premium	Duration Years
Reforestation Continuous Cover Forestry (CCF)	€1,800	€150	7
Reforestation Native woodland - High ecological priority area	€6,000	€500 + €150	7
Reforestation Native Woodland	€2,225	€500 + €150	7
Reforestation for Water	€2,500	€350	7

Forestry Knowledge Transfer Groups (KTGS)

The aim of the KTGs scheme is to increase peer to peer learning and knowledge about all aspects of the forest sector amongst private forest owners. Groups comprise a maximum of 20 participants who meet seven times in both indoor and outdoor events. The groups are typically facilitated by a professional forester. Each participant receives €80 per meeting to attend the KTGs.

Forestry and BISS

If you are in receipt of aid under the Afforestation Grant and Premium Scheme, you are obliged to declare all the land parcels on your holding on your 2024 BISS application. Land which was afforested since 2009 and land which will be afforested in 2024 will be eligible to draw down a BISS payment in 2023 provided that the afforested land meets the following requirements:
- The land to be afforested was declared on a 2008 SPS application form.
- The area must have given a right to payment under the 2008 Single Farm Payment Scheme.
- Farmers who wish to benefit from the Basic Payment on afforested land, must be the person or persons named as forestry scheme beneficiary, or joint beneficiary. This means that you must be the person or persons eligible for payment of the forestry premium in the relevant year.

Taxation of Forestry

All profits or gains from the occupation of woodland in the State which is managed on a commercial basis and with a view to a profit are exempt from Income Tax and Corporation Tax (but not PRSI and Universal Social Charge. For details of how all taxes impact on forestry see page 258.

9

Farm Business Management

Trading & Collaborative Structures for Farmers

Partnerships 164
Limited Companies 167
Share Farming 169
Sharemilking 171
Leasing Out Land for Solar Energy Projects 173

Employing Farm Labour

Guideline Farm Wages 174
Employer's Obligations And Worker's Rights 176
Farm Relief Services 179

Farm Safety

Farm Safety, Health & Wellbeing 180
Farmers Health and Wellbeing 180
Children on Farms 180
Older People on Farms 182
Accident Reporting 183
Information and Training 183

Trading & Collaborative Structures for Farmers

The vast majority of farmers trade as sole traders, a status which has served them well through decades of a relatively benign tax regime and modest profits. However, the dairy sector has seen a substantial increase in average herd size over the past 10 years and the non-dairy sector has seen a similar increase in off-farm employment resulting in those people seeking more tax effective trading structures. The following trading structures represent the current range of options:

- Partnerships.
- Incorporation (forming a Limited Company).
- Share farming.
- Share milking.
- Leasing out the farm.

Farm Partnerships

A farm partnership is essentially a farming operation that is owned and operated by more than one person (i.e. the partners). Typically, the partners could be spouses, children or unconnected persons or a combination of all three. Limited Companies may also be partners. The partners are responsible for the farming operations and will be taxable on any income the farm generates. Under the partnership structure, all farming assets acquired by the partnership are owned by the partnership and the individual partners own an interest in the partnership rather than a direct interest in each underlying farming asset, such as stock and equipment. Assets such as land and buildings will remain in the ownership of the individual partners but will be made available for use by the partnership. Subject to the agreement of the partners, such use may or may not be charged to the partnership.

In the case of family participation, partnerships improve the ability to split taxable income between family members who are partners in the partnership based on their contribution of time and/or capital to the partnership, potentially reducing overall income tax. Furthermore, a farm partnership is also a flexible tool that can be utilised to introduce new family members to the partnership at any time in the future to help facilitate the succession of farming operations to the next generation.

Farm partnerships between unconnected parties offer an opportunity to develop larger farm enterprises and increase scale by managing two or more previously independent enterprises together. Partnerships can also yield a worthwhile social dividend in reducing isolation in farmers' working lives.

Partnership Law in Ireland

Partnerships are not required by law to have a written partnership agreement, but a written agreement is strongly recommended. Unlike a company, a partnership is not a separate legal entity which means that partners have unlimited liability, unlike directors or shareholders in limited companies. As compared to the limited liability that a company would provide, the lack of same means that each partner is liable for the losses of his co-partner in carrying on the partnership business, even where the other partner has carried out acts of fraud.

How Partnerships Operate

Two or more parties decide to enter a partnership arrangement that will have a comprehensive set of operating rules set down in the form of a partnership agreement. The partnership will start out having no assets or liabilities, but the partners may provide land, buildings, machinery, stock and equipment for use by the partnership. The partnership agreement will set out the terms, if any, for the provision of such assets. The partners will agree at the outset how profits are to be shared and how much annual remuneration each partner shall receive, and the terms will be written into the partnership agreement. The partners may agree that individual partners may charge a rent or payment for the use of their assets such as land, buildings or machinery and such matters will be clearly covered in the written agreement. A partnership agreement will generally set down a minimum term such as five years but will also spell out the terms and conditions under which a partnership may be dissolved which could be at any time with the agreement of the partners.

Benefits of a Partnership

- Accommodates farm enterprise expansion.
- Sharing of equipment and facilities.
- Antidote to the solitary nature of farming.
- Economy of scale.
- Brings new skills and abilities to the farming operation.
- Partners may be able to concentrate on their preferred activity.
- Steppingstone to succession in family partnerships.
- Improved access to farm schemes and grant assistance.
- Taxation benefits.
- Better lifestyle/work life balance.

Concerns for Intending Partners

- Loss of independence.
- Intrusion on family privacy.
- Risk of incompatibility and disagreements with partners.
- Issues with introducing intended successors to the partnership.
- Dealing with the eventual dissolution.

Registered Farm Partnerships

A partnership may be registered with the Department of Agriculture, Food and the Marine. Apart from ensuring that the partnership is properly set up, being registered may qualify the partnership for enhanced grant assistance or National Reserve allocations, extended investment limits under the various grant aid schemes, generally to a maximum of double the limit. (See TAMS schemes - Chapter 1). To qualify as a registered partnership, the partnership must be made up of at least two people, with a maximum of 10 allowed. There must be a Category 1 applicant and either another Category 1 or Category 2 applicant. The following are the categories:

Category 1 – a farmer who has farmed greater than three hectares for two years before the date on which the partnership is established, and;

Category 2 – a person with an appropriate agricultural qualification (minimum level 6) whose contribution to the partnership is a minimum of 20% of the profit-sharing arrangement.

Category 3 – other persons, aside from those described in Category 1 and 2 above.

Succession Farm Partnerships

Partners who form a Registered Farm Partnership may apply for admission to the Succession Farm Partnership Scheme whereby, subject to certain conditions as outlined hereunder, they can jointly qualify for an annual income tax credit of €5,000 for up to five years. The credit is split in proportion to the profit-sharing ratio of the partnership between the Farmer and the Successor. Each partner will be entitled to a succession tax credit of the lesser amount of:

- €5,000 per year of assessment divided between the partners in accordance with their profit-sharing ratio, and;
- The assessable profits (after deducting any capital allowances) of that partner's profit share.

Potentially, the scheme is worth up to €25,000 in total between the partners over a five-year period.

Conditions

The key conditions to be met to qualify for the income tax credit are as follows:

1. Make a valid application to be placed on the register of succession farm partnerships maintained by the Department of Agriculture, Food and the Marine.
2. At least one partner in the Succession Farm Partnership must be a natural person (not a company) who has farmed at least 3 hectares in his/her own right for the two previous years. This person is defined as the "Farmer".
3. Aside from the Farmer as referred to above, the other partner(s) must be a young, trained Farmer who is in receipt of at least 20% of the partnership profits. This Partner is defined as the "Successor".
4. The year of transfer must be after 3 years and before 10 years of registering on the succession register to claim the tax credit.
5. The farmer and the successor must sign a succession agreement which contains an undertaking that a minimum of 80% of the farm assets outlined in the succession agreement must be transferred.
6. The income tax credit cannot be claimed in the calendar year where the Successor reaches 40 years of age so in other words the successor can only claim the relief up to age 40.
7. A full clawback of all tax credit claimed will occur where the transfer does not go ahead.

Taxation of Partnerships

The partnership of itself is not a taxable entity but rather, the partners are taxable as individuals at normal personal tax rates on their respective salaries and profit shares and rents if applicable. Apart from the benefits of a Succession Partnership as outlined above, family situations where both spouses and perhaps a son or daughter are in partnership can attract significant tax savings if all three low tax bands can be substantially utilised. Under current tax bands where three family members are in partnership, the combined low tax band would amount to €126,000 meaning that it is possible for that partnership to earn up to that amount and remain in the low tax bracket.

A system of stock relief for registered partnerships, claimable at 50% is available. Similar rules apply to VAT registration as for sole traders which means VAT registration is optional. Partnerships are entitled to the 'Flat Rate Refund' and are also eligible to VAT refunds on items of capital expenditure on buildings, fixed plant and land improvement.

Family members employed by a partnership are liable to PRSI. This does not apply in the case of a sole trader.

Assistance and Information

Farmers considering partnership as an option should firstly consult an ACA or Teagasc advisor who is known to be expert and experienced in the area of partnerships. The Department of Agriculture and Teagasc websites contain a considerable amount of useful information and publications at www.teagasc.ie/collaborativearrangements/.

Limited Companies

Forming a limited company (incorporation) is generally regarded as primarily a legitimate tax saving measure but there may be other worthwhile advantages in terms of farm succession. In practically all cases, only the farming activity and not the farm is transferred to the company. This means that the farmlands and buildings will be rented to the company and the stock and farm implements will be sold into the company. A farmer, subject to certain conditions, is allowed on a concessional basis to apply a rent appropriate to his/her tax profile for his/her land and entitlements which gives him/her a large degree of flexibility in regard to his/her annual personal income.

Farmers Best Positioned To Incorporate

Incorporation will best suit farmers but is not exclusive to farmers who:
- Are currently paying tax at the high rate.
- Have moderate to low levels of debt.
- Have moderate levels of personal drawings.
- Have used up most of their Farm Buildings Allowances.

Tax Implications of Trading as a Company

The big taxation advantage of trading as a company is that retained profits (profits not drawn out of the company for personal use) are taxed at 12.5%. All personal withdrawals from the company are taxed at normal personal tax rates.

In general Capital Acquisition Tax rules do not militate against incorporation. Land, buildings, entitlements etc., continue to qualify for Agricultural Relief (see taxation section) for transfer purposes. Shares in a farming company will not quality for Agricultural Relief but may qualify for Business Property Relief (see taxation section page 269) where the entire farming operation is being transferred as a going concern.

In the case of Capital Gains Tax, farmers will continue to be eligible for Retirement Relief (see taxation section page 276) as they are deemed to be still farming their land. The transfer of shares in a farming company will also qualify providing the farmer is over 55 and has held the shares for 10 years or more.

There are no stamp duty implications in transferring the farming operation to a company provided that no land passes. Young, trained farmers who have already availed of the Stamp Duty exemption and who incorporate the farm business will continue to satisfy the 5-year rule as they are regarded as continuing to farm the land.

Similar rules apply to VAT registration as for sole traders. Accordingly, VAT registration is optional. Companies are entitled to the 'Flat Rate Refund' and are also eligible to VAT refunds on items of capital expenditure on buildings, fixed plant and land improvement.

Basic Income Support Scheme (BISS) Implications

In order for payment under BISS to be deemed income of the Limited Company, it will be necessary to register the herd number in the name of the company and also transfer the entitlements. This can be done by sale or lease or by exercising the 'change of legal entity' provisions as set down by the Department of Agriculture. There is no difficulty in transferring the herd number or entitlements to a company in time for the 2024 scheme provided that the farmer who was in control of the original holding also manages the new holding within the company.

It should be noted that where entitlements are sold to the company by farmers over 55 years, Capital Gains Tax will arise as Retirement Relief is not available unless the relevant area of land also transfers i.e. one hectare per entitlement. It should be further noted that VAT will arise where the entitlements sale proceeds exceed the €40,000 registration threshold.

Advantages of Incorporation

- Potential for substantial tax savings resulting in an opportunity to invest in the farm business.
- No PRSI and no Universal Social Charge on company profits.
- Suitable structure for involvement of family members.
- No audit requirement (turnover less than €8.8m and Balance Sheet value of less that €4.4m).
- Can release a substantial amount of tax-free cash from sale of stock and machinery to company.

- Increased pension opportunities.
- May be a suitable vehicle to accommodate personal debt resolution in a tax efficient manner.
- A company may become involved in a registered partnership.

Disadvantages of Incorporation
- Access to retained profits for personal use may have an income tax cost.
- No tax savings if profits do not exceed personal drawings. Therefore, in years of low or nil profits, a liability to personal tax will still arise that could be greater than if the farmer had remained as a sole trader.
- Farm Buildings Allowance cannot be claimed on buildings which are not owned by the company.
- Exiting or ceasing a limited company may have Capital Gains Tax implications where the company has accumulated some value.
- Future eligibility for Agricultural Relief (see taxation section) may be threatened where the person's company share value has grown.
- Ceasing as a sole trader may have income tax consequences.
- Initial set-up cost and increased annual accountancy charges.

Forming a limited company demands expert professional advice not alone in regard to taxation but also in regard to the implications for BISS Payments, herd numbers, co-op shareholdings etc.

Timing of Entering and Exiting a Limited Company
Given the age profile of the average farmer, creating a company structure for many older farmers may appear to be a case of closing the stable door after the horse has bolted. This is not necessarily so as tax savings can quickly mount up and where a company is in existence for 10 years or more and where the farmer is over 55 years, there are a number of mechanisms to extract tax free money from the company by utilising Capital Gains Tax Retirement Relief in respect of company share buybacks where there is a successor or liquidation if the farmer wishes to cease.

Share Farming

Share farming involves two parties on the same area of land (the landowner and the share farmer) carrying out separate farming enterprises in the one unit, without forming a partnership or company. Both parties share the benefits and the risks. There is no fixed annual payment for the land. The respective parties can independently sell their share of output and equally cover their input costs. Share Farming is approved by the Department of Agriculture and can be fully compliant with the terms of the BISS. Participants are classed as "farmers" so there is no change in their tax status. A legal agreement ensures both parties are protected in the event of difficulties arising.

Benefits for the Landowner

- Retains control of the land to ensure it is farmed to the highest standards while also giving greater security and reward from farming.
- The initiative can be compliant with all support schemes.
- Provides increased buying and selling power as part of a larger unit.
- Higher returns when yields, weight gain and prices increase.
- The share farmer can buy/sell all produce and then invoice/pay the landowner his/her own share if that is the preferred approach.
- The share farmer is responsible to maintain fences, structures etc in good order and condition excluding fair wear and tear.
- The land cannot be used for any other purposes by the share farmer.

Benefits for the Share Farmer

- A tailored agreement allows flexibility to suit individual landowner situations.
- No up front and/or other flat rate payments.
- Input costs shared.
- Increased area/scale allows more competitive purchasing and selling and can also reduce fixed costs.
- An improved and stable land base facilitates better planning in both the short and long-term.

Operating a Share Farm

Trust is an essential part of the agreement. VAT registered farmers/growers and non-VAT registered landowners can successfully operate a Share Farming Agreement.

Setting up a Share Farming Agreement

As trust is a key element of the arrangement the identification of a suitable landowner/share farmer is key. An existing understanding between a landowner and a farmer can be developed into a Share Farming agreement. Discussion on all elements of the agreement is essential before commencement. The agreement document should be in place before farming commences and the practicalities of the arrangement should mirror the agreement. When setting up an agreement the people involved should sit down with their advisors and clarify the exact farming activity they are going to carry out (cropping or livestock or both). Other details to be discussed at this stage include:

- The exact lands involved should be agreed.
- Any machinery necessary and who will provide it.
- If livestock are involved, the livestock should be listed.
- Input and ongoing costs should be worked out.
- A basis of division of produce and costs should be agreed.
- If EU Government Supports are being made part of the agreement, those being contributed by each party should be listed.
- How produce is to be stored and disposed of should be worked out.
- The maintenance of Department of Agriculture and any other statutory records

that are required to be kept, e.g., records for Cross Compliance and records of purchases and sales etc. should be agreed.
• How dispute resolution will be dealt with.

Further Information
The first and essential step is to consult your ACA or Teagasc farm advisor. Teagasc have produced several very useful publications on share farming which include a specimen agreement. These can be found on www.teagasc.ie.

Sharemilking

Sharemilking arrangements provide a steppingstone for young farm workers looking to become farm owners themselves. Two parties exist under a sharemilking agreement, the farm owner, and the sharemilker. Essentially, the parties enter into a sharemilking agreement on the basis that the sharemilker is responsible for operating the farm on behalf of the owner but does not own the land and in return is paid a share of the income from selling milk and anything else produced off the land (e.g., Livestock or fodder). As a result, the legal relationship between a sharemilker and the farm owner is that of principal and independent contractor, not employer and employee or landlord and tenant. The key requirement for a sharemilking arrangement is that the payments are distributed between the parties in accordance with an agreed percentage share of the farm's income.
The farm owner under a typical share-milking agreement provides all the fixed infrastructure. The farm owner also pays for overhead costs such as insurance, rent. repairs to buildings etc. The sharemilker provides the herd, or part of it, and ideally but not necessarily any essential machinery, The sharemilker also provides the labour necessary for the operation and maintenance of the farm. A typical case of a 160-cow operation with the share milker responsible for labour and management and providing half the cow herd, the share milker could expect a 50% profit share.
Sharemilking as a trading structure is popular In New Zealand but is relatively new to Ireland. Given the pace of dairy expansion and the shortage of labour it's potential (or some hybrid variant) as a suitable trading structure is assured for the future.

Further Information
The first and essential step is to consult your ACA or Teagasc farm advisor. Teagasc have produced a comprehensive Specimen Dairy Share Farming Agreement which can be found on www.teagasc.ie.

Leasing out Land
Where there is no obvious successor and the landowner wishes to retire or simply scale back, the option of leasing out land can be quite attractive. Leases should always be based on a written agreement and professional assistance should be employed in drawing up the lease. A properly drafted lease may avoid problems arising at a later stage and will protect you if problems do arise. Leases should always be stamped by

the Revenue Commissioners and registered with the Property Services Regulatory Authority.

Legal Protection with a Formal Lease

A professionally drawn formal lease will contain numerous provisions to protect the landowners' interests such as:

- Payment of rent, when and how.
- Consequences of default in payment of rent.
- Care of the land and access to the land.
- Liability and other insurance requirements.
- Permitted works on the land.
- Terminating the lease.
- Maintenance and repairs.
- Liability for rates and taxes.

The IFA Master Lease is a very good template, but only a template. Professional assistance should be sought in negotiating and agreeing the final terms of the lease as every landowner will have differing requirements and conditions that will need to be addressed and documented.

Renting Out Land - Points to Note

Leasing or renting land can encounter certain hazards where a formal written lease for a definite term is not in place or where the person occupying the land has not paid rent for a period of time, or perhaps never paid rent. Such hazards could be:

- A tenant may acquire rights to a renewed tenancy in circumstances where he or she has been in occupation for a period of more than 20 years.
- A tenant may acquire rights to a renewed tenancy where the tenant has made improvements to the property. If improvements have been made on the property (and the tenant is not entitled to compensation for those improvements under the terms of the lease) and the value of the improvements is one-half of the letting value of the property at that time, then the tenant may acquire an entitlement to a renewed lease.
- Where a person occupies land at no charge for a continuous period of 12 years or more, they may lodge a claim for Adverse Possession (squatters rights). The time limit for lands owned by a state authority is 20 years.

Income Tax Implications of leasing

Depending on one's circumstances, rental income from land (and BISS entitlements where leased with land) may or may not be subject to income tax. Landowners who own the land for a minimum 7-year period and who enter a lease to unconnected persons of a definite term greater than five years will attract varying levels of tax relief depending on the term as set out on table 9.1:

Table 9.1: Tax exempted Amounts on Land Leases.

Term	Tax exempt up to;
Greater than 5 years and less than 7 years	€18,000
Greater than 7 years and less than 10 years	€22,500
Greater than 10 years and less than 15 years	€30,000
15 years or more	€40,000

Connected persons include, grandparents, parents, brothers, sisters, children, grandchildren, the spouse of the lessor or the immediate family of the spouse. Leasing to Limited Companies also attracts the tax relief. Leasing of land to immediate family members does not attract any tax concessions but leases between aunts/uncles and nieces/nephews do qualify.

Capital Gains Tax Implications of Leasing

Land can now be leased up to 25 years before entitlement to Retirement Relief (see Retirement Relief - taxation section page 276) is affected.

Stamp Duty on Leases

Land leases of 6 years or more duration are not liable to stamp duty subject to certain terms and conditions (see Stamp Duty - taxation section page 283).

Leasing Out Land for Solar Energy Projects

Energy companies are currently seeking sites which are suitable for the erection of solar panels. What they are offering in the first instance is a financial incentive to enter into an option agreement, typically for a two-to-three-year period. The Option agreement commits the landowner to entering into a possible 25-year-plus lease agreement with the solar energy company if the option is exercised. Rents being offered are typically in the region of €1,000 to €1,250 per acre per annum.

Income Tax Considerations

Leases of land for the purposes of erecting a solar farm will not qualify under the current land lease tax exemption scheme. Income from the Option Agreement will also be subject to Income Tax.

Capital Acquisition Tax Considerations

Where a site is rented for a solar farm, it retains its agricultural status and qualifies for Agricultural Relief provided no more than 50% of the holding being transferred is occupied by solar panels (see taxation section).

Capital Gains Tax Considerations

A farmer who is over 55 years and, has owned and farmed the land for a 10-year period prior to entering into the lease, will be exempt from Capital Gains Tax if they were to transfer land containing solar panels to a son or daughter provided that less than 50% of the area contained solar panels. Where the value exceeds €3m. the excess over €3m. may be exposed to tax. The capital value of land leased to a solar company and upon which a solar farm is sited will be a multiple of the annual rent being generated and could exceed the current market value of the land. Farmers should seek good tax advice, particularly in the context of succession planning, where they are contemplating leasing to a solar company.

BISS Considerations

Lands occupied by solar panels will generally not qualify for the BISS irrespective of whether it is possible that the lands can be grazed. While cases involving solar panels will be examined on an individual basis, the European Commission advises that the area covered by the solar panels will be deemed ineligible for the purposes of claiming BISS. Furthermore, in line with the Department's current approach on land eligibility, where the area of a parcel covered by solar panels is 70% or greater of the overall parcel, that parcel will be wholly ineligible. If the area in a parcel is reduced by greater than 70% or if there is no agricultural activity in the parcel, or if the applicant does not own, lease, or rent the land, then the parcel will be considered ineligible. If the lands are leased/rented out to a third party, the applicant must have written agreement to access the area throughout the calendar year. If less than 70% is covered by solar panels and the agricultural activity is not hampered by the presence of the solar panels, the area not covered by solar panels may be eligible.

Employing Farm Labour

Deciding to employ a farm worker is not as simple a matter as it might have been in previous generations. There are two principal areas that a farmer should be aware of before a decision is made such as the true cost of employing a farm worker and the obligations placed upon the employer and the workers' rights.

Guideline Farm Wages

The pay and conditions of employees is governed by employment legislation such as the minimum wage which is €12.70 from the 1st January 2024. Agricultural workers are covered under the general employment legislation. Table 9.2 sets out guideline wage rates for farm workers and managers. Rates can vary depending on the level of experience and bonuses or profit shares may also apply.

What Counts as Pay

Pay includes all overtime and bonuses. If a worker receives food (known as board) and, or accommodation (known as lodgings) from the employer, the following amounts are included in the minimum wage calculation:

€61.47 for full board and lodgings per 39 week.
€0.94 per hour worked for board.
€24.81 for lodgings only per week, or €3.55 per day.

Table 9.2: Guideline Current Wage Rates for Farm Managers & Workers.

Position	€
Farm Manager - annual salary	€47-52,000
Dairy operatives - annual salary	€37-44,000
Farm Workers - weekly pay (39 hour week)	€620-€670
Farm Workers - Statutory Minimum hourly rates applicable from 1st January 2024 (based on budget 2024)	
- Statutory Minimum hourly rate < 18 yrs	€ 8.89
- Statutory Minimum hourly rate 18 yrs	€ 10.16
- Statutory Minimum hourly rate 19 yrs	€11.43
- Statutory Minimum hourly rate 20 yrs +	€12.70
- Typical hourly rate	€12-€15

There are some exceptions to those entitled to receive the national minimum wage. The legislation does not apply to a person employed by a close relative (for example, a spouse, civil partner or parent) nor does it apply to those in statutory apprenticeships.

Working Hours

Working hours are generally the hours set out in the contract of employment. "Working hours" include overtime, travel time where this is part of the job, time spent on training authorised by the employer and during normal working hours. "Working hours" does not include time spent on standby other than at the workplace, time on leave, lay-off, strike or after payment in lieu of notice or time spent travelling to or from work. The maximum number of hours that an adult employees can work in an average working week is 48 hours. This does not mean that a working week can never exceed 48 hours, it is the average that is important.

Holidays

The leave year is the year commencing 1 April and ending 31 March. Holiday entitlements are calculated by one of the following methods:

- 4 working weeks in the leave year in which the worker works at least 1,365 hours (unless it is a leave year in which the worker changed employment);
- 1/3 of a working week per month that the worker works at least 117 hours;
- 8% of the hours worked in a year, subject to a maximum of 4 working weeks.

Where a worker falls ill during annual leave and furnishes to his employer a medical certificate in respect of the illness, the days to which the certificate refers shall not be regarded as annual leave. The annual leave of a worker who has 8 or more months of service shall include an unbroken period of two weeks. Holiday entitlements are calculated for part time workers in the same manner as set out above for full time employees. Entitlement to public holidays leave shall only apply where the worker has worked for at least 40 hours in the five weeks before the public holiday.

Bereavement Leave

In the event that a worker suffers bereavement in their immediate family, three days paid leave will be granted in the case of the death of a husband, wife, partner, son, daughter, mother, father, brother, sister or one day in the case of a grandparent, mother-in-law, father-in-law, grandchild.

Paternity Leave

Paternity leave gives new fathers two weeks off work. Leave can start any time in the first six months after the baby's birth. The employer does not have to pay the employee during paternity leave, but they may qualify for Paternity Benefit.

Children

While the employment of children under 16 is generally prohibited by the Protection of Young Persons (Employment) Act 1996, a child over 14 years may be permitted to do light work during school holidays provided it is not harmful to health, development or schooling. A child over 15 may also do such work for up to 8 hours a week during school term. An employer wishing to employ anyone under 18 must first require the production of their birth certificate. Before employing a child under 16 the employer must also get written permission from the parents or guardian. The Act further provides for the setting of limits to the working hours of young people (i.e. 16 and 17-year-olds), provides for rest intervals and prohibits night work. Young people (16 and 17-year-olds) may not work for more than 8 hours in any day or 40 hours in any week. Employers who employ young people under 18 years of age must display a summary of the Act (available in poster form from the Department of Enterprise, Trade & Employment)), and give a summary of the Act to the employee within one month of the commencement of employment.

Employer's Obligations and Worker's Rights

An employer has certain obligations which they owes to their employee as follows:

- To ensure that employees are provided with a written statement of terms and conditions of employment.
- To register employee for tax and give employees a written statement of pay or 'payslip'.
- To pay employees not less than the statutory minimum wage rates.
- To comply with the maximum working week requirements.
- To provide breaks and rest periods during working hours.
- To give annual leave from work.
- To give a minimum amount of notice before termination of employment.
- To maintain records in relation to employees and their entitlements.
- To only engage employees who have permission to work within the State.

Employment Terms & Conditions

A full contract of employment is not obligatory, but every employee must be given written Terms & Conditions of their employment within two months of commencing employment. The Term & Conditions must include the following:

- The full names of the employer and the employee.
- The address of the employer.
- The place of work, or where there is no main place of work, a statement indicating that an employee is required or permitted to work at various places.
- Job title or nature of the work.
- Date of commencement of employment.
- If the contract is temporary, the expected duration of employment.
- If the contract is for a fixed term, the date on which the contract expires.
- The rate of pay or method of calculating pay.
- Whether pay is weekly, monthly or otherwise.
- Terms or conditions relating to hours of work, including overtime.
- Terms or conditions relating to paid leave (other than paid sick leave).
- Terms or conditions relating to incapacity for work due to sickness or injury.
- Any terms or conditions relating to pensions and pension schemes.
- Periods of notice or method for determining periods of notice.

Redundancy

An employee who is employed for two continuous years or more is entitled to statutory redundancy amounting to two week's pay for each year of continuous service between the ages of sixteen and sixty-six (a week's pay is subject to a ceiling of €600) plus one further week's pay. A week's pay is calculated by adding together Gross Weekly Wage, Average Regular Overtime and Benefits in Kind. Employers are not entitled to a rebate of any redundancy paid.

Dismissal Notice

An employee who is in continuous employment for sixteen weeks or more is entitled to certain minimum notice in the event of dismissal as follows:

Table 9.3: Minimum Dismissal Notices.

Length of Service	Minimum Notice
Thirteen weeks to two years	One week
Two years to five years	Two weeks
Five years to ten years	Four weeks
Ten years to fifteen years	Six weeks
More than fifteen years	Eight weeks

Unfair Dismissal

An employee who works for eight hours per week or more and is employed for a year or more is entitled to claim unfair dismissal if he/she should be dismissed or should the conditions of work be made so difficult that he/she feels obliged to leave. Dismissal must be justified on grounds of one or more of the following causes:

- The capability, competence or qualifications of the employee.
- The redundancy of the employee.
- The fact that continuation of the employment would contravene another statutory requirement.
- That there were other substantial grounds for dismissal.

In order to be seen to have complied with the code of practice on grievance and disciplinary procedures, the following actions will have to be followed in as much as is possible before a person can be dismissed other than in the case of gross misconduct leading to instant dismissal:

- An oral warning.
- A written warning.
- A final written warning.
- Suspension without pay.
- Transfer to another task, or section of the enterprise.
- Demotion.
- Some other appropriate disciplinary action short of dismissal.
- Dismissal.

Should unfair dismissal be proven the employer will have to reinstate the person in their old job or reinstate them in an alternative job that the adjudicating bodies consider reasonable, or provide financial compensation to a maximum of two years' pay. An employee found to have been unfairly dismissed but who has suffered no financial loss, i.e. found suitable alternative employment, may be awarded up to four weeks' pay. Further required information regarding the employment terms may be conveyed to the employee by reference to a specific document such as an employment handbook which must be accessible to the employee.

Registering Employees

All employees earning more than €8 a week must be registered under the PAYE system. Failure to do so will cause problems for both the employer and employee.

Farm Relief Services

Farm Relief Services supply a wide range of services to farmers throughout the country. Farmers do not have to concern themselves with PAYE/PRSI registration and fees are fully tax allowable.

Charge Out Rates

Rates will vary between the different FRS areas and the following charges are those as charged in 2023 by the Kilkenny, Carlow and District Farm Relief Services Ltd.

Membership

Annual membership is €350 payable by monthly direct debit. Membership carries benefits such as a 10% reduction in farm services rates, sickness and accident emergency support and accidental death and certain permanent disabilities cover of up to €20,000.

Table 9.4: Farm Relief Charges 2023 (including VAT).

Relief Milking*	Single morning or evening €70 - minimum two hours Daily Milking €140 - minimum 4 hours
Dairy Relief Work	€16.75per hour
Sunday Relief Milking	€85 – minimum of 2 hours
General Farm Relief Work	€14.20 to €18.45 per hour. including work for agricultural contractors
Hoof Care	€95 for 1st. hour, €70 per hour thereafter
Calf dehorning	€40 callout charge plus €4 per head Calves must be under 3 weeks old
Freeze branding	Two digits-€5/hd. Three digits €6.50/hd Four digits €7 per hd

Source: Kilkenny/Carlow District Farm Relief Services Ltd.

Local FRS Offices

- Clare Ph: 065-6844864
- Bandon Ph: 023-8852630
- CLW Ph: (Cavan) 049-8545100
- Kanturk Ph: 029-50750
- Donegal Ph: 074-9145386
- Wicklow FRS, Ph: 0402-38427
- Roscommon Ph: 071-9662781
- Midleton Ph: 021-4613501

- Galway Ph: 091-844551
- South Midlands Ph: 0505-21166
- Kerry Ph: 066-7141099
- South Tipperary Ph 052-7441598
- Kilkenny, Carlow Ph 056-7761671
- Waterford Ph: 051-294277
- Limerick/North Cork Ph: 063-90666

Farm Safety, Health & Wellbeing

Farm safety, health and wellbeing are vitally important. Farming is one of the most dangerous occupations in Ireland with an average of 20 fatal incidents on farms every year. Fatalities on farms account for nearly half of all fatal workplace incidents in Ireland. However, farmers only represent 6% of the workforce. With around 2,800 serious injuries annually on farms, many are life changing and place the farmers' livelihood and farm at risk. Livestock, particularly cows after calving, vehicles and machinery, falls from heights, lifting and handling, slurry and hazardous substances all pose risks, but incidents can be avoided if these risks are properly managed.

There is a common perception that farming is a healthy occupation. However, Irish farmers have a higher incidence of heart disease than other workers. Due to their work environment, farmers also have a higher risk of developing certain illnesses such as skin diseases or infections carried by animals.

Farmers Health and Wellbeing

The principle causes of farmers' ill health is associated with manual handling, lung problems, infections and noise. Half of farmers with occupational ill health suffer from chronic back pain. Irish farmers have a higher incidence of heart disease than other workers, and a higher risk of developing skin diseases because of exposure to damaging ultraviolet sun rays.

To maintain good physical and mental health farmers should:

- reduce lifting or practice lifting safely.
- Eliminate slip or trip hazards.
- Ensure that electrical fittings are in good condition.
- Cover cuts and abrasions with a waterproof plaster or dressing to avoid infection.
- Put a vermin control programme in place on your farm.
- Use earmuffs or ear plugs in noisy areas.
- Sun protection is essential for all outdoor work in agriculture.
- Visit the GP regularly to monitor your general health and physical wellbeing.
- Ensure that you get adequate rest, particularly during busy periods such as calving or lambing.
- Be conscious of your mental health and visit your GP if concerned.

Children on Farms

Farms are a high-risk environment for children, young persons, and other vulnerable persons. Since 2012, 22 children have lost their lives on Irish farms, and around 1 in 10 of all fatalities on Irish farms are children. The overall responsibility for securing the safety and health of children and young people on farms rests with adults. Young children must have a safe play area which is securely separated from the farmyard. The main risks to children on farms are:

- Tractors and machinery: passengers should only be allowed on tractors where there is a passenger seat. Children under 7 years should not be passengers on tractors.

- Self-propelled harvesters, power-driven machines, sprayers, slurry spreaders and chainsaws: children must be kept away from machinery as the operator may not be aware of their presence.
- Drowning: make sure that all slurry tanks and water hazards on the farm are properly covered or fenced off to prevent access by children. Disused slurry tanks and water hazards should either be fenced off, filled in, or adapted so that they can no longer hold water or liquids.
- Tree felling: children should be excluded from areas where chainsaws are in use.
- Falls/building collapse: children tend to climb gates or wheels, particularly large tractor wheels. Gates and pillars should be properly erected, so they do not fall over. Tractor wheel should be stored on the flat or, if upright, should be firmly secured. Stacks of bales, pallets or timber are also temptations for children to climb. Stacks should be built carefully to ensure they do not collapse. Fencing should be erected to prevent children gaining access to dangerous areas.
- Livestock: children should not be allowed near dangerous animals such as bulls, stallions, rams, stags and female animals with new-born young. Children should not be present when animals are being released from buildings after being housed or when animals are being loaded into trailers.
- Chemicals/poisoning: children under 16 should not handle chemicals. Chemicals should be securely locked away in a store in their original containers.

Children between the ages of 7 and 16 may ride on a tractor provided the tractor is fitted with a properly designed and fitted passenger seat (with seat belts) inside a safety cab or frame. Under no circumstances should a child under 7 years of age be carried inside the cab of a tractor. (Irrespective of whether a passenger seat is provided or not). The main causes of child fatal incidents are tractors/machinery and drowning. Adults have a huge responsibility to make sure that the risks posed to children on a farm are assessed and controls put in place to prevent death and injury.

Deaths of Children on Farms 2011-2020 (10% of all Fatalities).

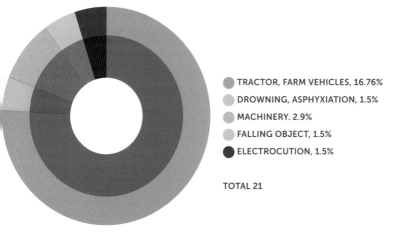

- TRACTOR, FARM VEHICLES, 16.76%
- DROWNING, ASPHYXIATION, 1.5%
- MACHINERY. 2.9%
- FALLING OBJECT, 1.5%
- ELECTROCUTION, 1.5%

TOTAL 21

Older People on Farms

Age is a major factor in farm fatalities and serious injuries. Victims of work-related fatalities in Agriculture were disproportionately older people: 47% of victims were aged 65 years or older. The high rate of work-related fatalities to older workers indicates that older farmers may need to take special precautions to avoid serious injury or fatality when engaged in certain farming activities.

Deaths to Older Farmers (>65 years) 2011-2020 (45% of Total Fatalities).

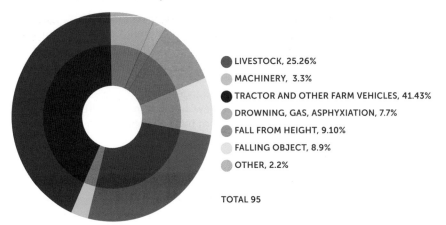

- LIVESTOCK, 25.26%
- MACHINERY, 3.3%
- TRACTOR AND OTHER FARM VEHICLES, 41.43%
- DROWNING, GAS, ASPHYXIATION, 7.7%
- FALL FROM HEIGHT, 9.10%
- FALLING OBJECT, 8.9%
- OTHER, 2.2%

TOTAL 95

Risk Assessment

Like any enterprise on the farm, health & safety requires management. A Safety Statement or Risk Assessment Document identifies the key dangers that may cause death or serious injury. A Risk Assessment Document is the minimum legal requirement on all farms. In this document a commitment is made to:

- Provide a safe place of work and use safe systems of work.
- Provide all machinery with guards, protective equipment, information, training and supervision necessary to protect those at risk.
- Review document at least annually or when there are changes in the business.
- If a dangerous situation arises work should stop immediately until the hazard or danger is controlled.
- Advise all who work on the farm of the hazards.

Precautions

The following precautions must be adopted:

- Prepare and implement a Safety Statement or if three or less people work on the farm, the Code of Practice meets the Safety Statement requirement.
- Plan work to make sure it can be done safely.
- Check machinery and equipment before use.
- Ensure that safeguards are understood by family, workers & contractors

- Train persons to operate tractors and machinery and complete jobs safely.
- Assess and control risks to children and persons with slower reaction time.

Accident Reporting
An accident is reportable to the Health & Safety Authority (HSA) if there is loss of life or if an injured employee or self-employed person is unable to work for more than three consecutive days.

Information and Training
Teagasc has integrated health and safety training into its national training programmes. Teagasc and agricultural consultants who are members of the Agricultural Consultants Association (ACA) provide a training course on the Code of Practice. Coillte provide training for many of the forestry activities, such as chainsaw operation and chemical handling. FRS Training have a course for 14 to 16-year-olds on tractor driving and also provide training in the safe handling of livestock and chainsaws. The Health & Safety Authority can be contacted on LoCall: 1890 289 389 (between 9am and 5pm, Monday to Friday). Email: wcu@hsa.ie. Website www.hsa.ie

10 Succession & Estate Planning

Planning for Succession

Constituents of a Succession Plan 185
Banking Issues...189
Taxation Benefits for Timely Transfers...189
Capital Gains Tax - Retirement Relief (S599) 189
Retirement Relief (S598) 190
Gift Tax - Agricultural Relief...190
Gift Tax -Business Relief 190
Gift Tax Insurance (S73 Policy)... 191
Inheritance Tax Insurance (S72 Policy) 191
Stamp Duty 192
Valuing Farm Property 192
Income Tax Benefits and Consequences of Transferring 192
Transfers Between Spouses..193

Planning for Succession

Over half of Irish farmers are over 55 years. Some may have no identified successor but those who have will at some stage have to face and deal with the matter of handing on their farm. Succession ultimately involves the transfer of the ownership and management of the farm, but this can be a phased process if preferred. The successful outcome of any succession process should meet the needs of all family members and ensure a viable and sustainable outcome for all parties involved.

Constituents of a Succession Plan

- Timing.
- Taxation considerations.
- Spouse's opinion.
- Suitability of prospective successor.
- Successor's opinion.
- Considering and consulting other family members.
- Part or entire transfer of assets and/or management.
- Dealing with the farm dwelling.
- Conditions associated with transfer.
- Post succession income sources for transferor.
- The future care needs question.
- Banking issues.
- Costs associated with transferring.
- Where to begin.

Timing

The timing of handing on the farm should not be solely about your age or your successor's age. Timing will depend on several factors apart from your respective ages such as your preferences, your financial profile, your family circumstances, your successor's circumstances and the risk of adverse changes in taxation legislation.

Taxation Considerations

Taxation in certain instances can present an obstacle to transferring the family farm and accordingly this is best addressed at the outset. The taxes that need to be considered are Income Tax, Capital Gains Tax, Capital Acquisitions Tax and Stamp Duty. These taxes are dealt with in greater detail commencing on page 189.

Spouse's Opinion

Ideally where the landowner is married the decision should be arrived in consultation with his/her spouse. Your spouse may have very definite preferences and ignoring their views may sow the seeds of discord in later years. Both parties should attend all meetings with your accountant, solicitor, and your agricultural advisor.

Suitability of the Prospective Successor
The day is long gone where succession fell to the oldest son or to the least academically inclined member of the family. Modern day farming demands commitment, dedication, and a desire to succeed along with the necessary agricultural educational attainments. Your successor should possess all these traits. If your intended successor does not possess all these traits, maybe you should wait or reconsider. Rushing succession or yielding to pressure should be resisted if you are not sure.

Successor's Opinion
Your intended successor needs to be fully involved in the succession planning process and needs to understand what responsibilities and obligations he/she is undertaking and that they are fully in agreement with same. They may not particularly like some of the conditions associated with the transfer, such as making provision for other family members. Such issues should be discussed maturely and if discussion does not yield a satisfactory outcome the opinion of the family accountant or agricultural advisor should be sought as to whether the suggested provision is reasonable.

Consulting with Other Family Members
The choice of successor is generally a foregone conclusion and seldom generates acrimony from the other siblings. However, it is important that all members of the family are on board with the succession plans. Oftentimes, there may be some level of expectation among the siblings such as the provision of a site or something more and it is important that they are given an opportunity to air these expectations. Their inclusion in the process may avoid disharmony in later years. There will of course be situations where it may be more prudent to proceed without their involvement in the process.

Part or Entire Transfer of Management
Increasingly farmers are choosing to enter partnership or form a limited company with their successor whereby they maintain a meaningful involvement in the running of the farm business even though they have transferred some, or all, of the main farming assets. Such arrangements have a lot to recommend them and can be beneficial from a labour and management point of view and from a taxation and grant aid access perspective. It also enables the parent to retire on a phased basis at whatever pace they so choose.

Part or Entire Asset Transfer
Assuming that if it is your ultimate intention that all your farming assets go to your successor, whether you transfer all or part at the outset may be determined by your personal financial resources. If you are satisfied that you have sufficient resources to grant you a comfortable retirement, you may be happy to transfer the entire. If on the other hand you are unsure of having sufficient resources to meet your retirement needs, it might be wise to retain some portion of the farm and perhaps specify in your will that it goes to your successor. Another valid reason for retaining a portion of the

farm might be as a hedge against your successor running into matrimonial or financial difficulty. On the other hand, you may consider the possibility of future nursing home care as a potential burden that you do not wish to impose on your successor in which case you may choose to transfer all of the farming assets.

Future Care Needs

While one hopes the need will never arise, eligibility for future nursing home care cannot be ignored. Retaining assets such as land or your dwelling, or retaining a right of income, will have a bearing on the means assessment for qualifying for the Fair Deal Scheme and accordingly this needs careful consideration. It may be useful to have your situation assessed by a professional who will compare the potential benefit from Fair Deal in the event of you retaining assets as compared to not retaining assets. See Fair Deal Scheme, page 231.

The Farm Dwelling

Where the farm dwelling is an integral part of the farmyard, it is usual that it would go to successor, whether that be at the time of the transfer of the farm, or it may be left in a will. There may be taxation or future care need issues to be addressed in this decision and the recommended approach in most cases is that the parent(s) transfer the house but retain a right of residence for their lifetimes. This way, the farm dwelling will qualify for Agricultural Relief (see page 265) and will not impact on the Fair Deal means assessment.

Conditions Associated with Transfer

A deed of transfer may contain whatever conditions one chooses to include, and such conditions can be registered as a charge on the title deeds to the farm. Such conditions could be a lifetime right of residence in the farm dwelling or a right of maintenance or income for the transferor. However, care needs to be exercised in terms of the variety and extent of charges on title deeds as such charges may render the title deeds unacceptable to banks for securing loans or may impact on entitlement to means tested state benefits such as the Old Age Pension Increase for a Qualified Adult Allowance or the Fair Deal Scheme.

Post Succession Income for the Transferor

In most cases the transferor will have entitlement to the contributory old age pension, but this may not be sufficient to meet their needs. Assuming they have no personal pension entitlement, income supplementation may have to come from the family farm. This could take the form of a wage, a partnership salary or perhaps rent for lands which were not transferred. It should be noted that persons in receipt of a contributory pension are not subject to means testing and may receive unlimited income from any source. However, the Increase for a Qualified Adult Allowance (spouses' allowance) is subject to a means test and maximum that a person in receipt of that allowance can earn without affecting their allowance is €100 per week or €5,200 per annum.

Banking Issues
It will be necessary to talk to your bank manager if there are existing loans that it is intended that the transferee will take over. Where loans are at a particularly low interest rate you should check with the bank manager if changing the loan to your successor's name will alter the interest rate.

Costs
In all cases you will incur costs which will include the solicitor's fees, Land Registry fees & VAT. There is no set fee for this work, and you should negotiate a figure prior to commencing the process.

Where to Begin: a Step-by-Step Approach
A succession planning process requires consideration, dialogue and consultation. The following is a suggested step by step guide that is designed to involve all the relevant parties at the most appropriate time:

1. Set out your preferences.
2. Discuss with your spouse.
3. Discuss with your successor(s).
3. Consult your succession/tax advisor.
4. Discuss with other family members.
6. Meet with your bank (if necessary).
7. Set a time deadline.
9. Instruct your solicitor and determine the likely cost.

Taxation Benefits for Timely Transfers
The taxation implications of transferring may be a deciding factor in determining whether a transfer is possible. Due to the high age profile of farmers, government have introduced various concessions over the years, many which are still in place, to incentivise farmers to transfer sooner rather than later. These incentives span the full spectrum of taxes.

Capital Gains Tax – Retirement Relief (S599)
Up until recently, Capital Gains Tax was rarely a problem associated with family transfers due to the availability of 'Retirement Relief'. This relief exempts the vast majority of family transfers for persons under 66 years. However, exempted transfers by persons over 66 (70 from the 1st January 2025) are subject to a maximum of €3m in value (€10m from the 1st January 2025). Retirement Relief does not require the transferor to retire in order to avail of the relief but there are certain conditions to be satisfied as follows.
• the person transferring is over 55 years
• the minimum period of ownership must be 10 years.

- the minimum period of use is 10 consecutive years prior to transfer or prior to first letting. All lettings from 31 December 2016 on must be by way of 5-year lease or longer.
- The transferee does not dispose of the farm within six years.

The €3m limit is cumulative and applies for the lifetime of the transferor. Accordingly, splitting the assets or spacing out the transfer will not avoid a liability. If the €3m is exceeded an exposure to Capital Gains Tax may arise if a gain is deemed to have arisen on the basis that a transfer is the same as a sale in the eyes of the Revenue Commissioners.

Retirement Relief (S598)
Occasionally, a succession plan may involve the sale of a part of the farm to generate funds for various purposes. In such cases, the landowner who is over 55 years may quality for an exemption on the first €750,000 or €500,000 if over 66 years (or 70 years from the 1st January 2025). The conditions are similar to those set out above for S599 relief.

Gift Tax – Agricultural Relief
Provided that the combined value of the agricultural assets being transferred from one or both parents is less than €3.35m and the transferee did not receive any prior gifts or inheritances from their parents, most transfers to sons or daughters or favourite nieces or nephews will not attract a liability to Gift Tax subject to certain conditions. This is due to the availability of Agricultural Relief which bestows a 90% reduction in the value of the assets being transferred to active farmers or persons who lease out the land for a 6-year term or longer to a full-time or qualified farmer. However, the recipient must satisfy an asset test that requires 80% of their gross asset value, after receiving the gift, must comprise agricultural property such as land, farm dwellings, livestock, bloodstock or machinery. To qualify for Agricultural Relief, the recipient must;
- qualify as a Young Trained Farmer or
- for a period of not less than 6 years spend not less than 50 per cent of that individual's normal working time farming the holding on a commercial basis and with a view to the realisation of profits, or
- lease out the holding for a period of not less than 6 years to an individual who will either spend not less than 50 per cent of that individual's normal working time farming the holding on a commercial basis and with a view to the realisation of profits or be a qualified farmer.

Gift Tax – Business Relief
Where a successor fails the Agricultural Relief test, they may be entitled to claim Business Relief which also grants a 90% reduction in taxable value. Business Relief only applies to active farms that will continue to be farmed for a minimum 6-year period. So, land that has been or will be leased out will not qualify. Neither do farm dwellings qualify. (See page 269).

CASE STUDY

A farmer's son who is unmarried has a dwelling he received from his late mother, which has a current market value of €250,000 but valued at €200,000 when he received it. He also has savings of €90,000 and a car worth €15,000. He is to receive land (including the farm dwelling), stock, machinery, and entitlements to a combined value of €1m. from his father. The farm dwelling is valued at €200,000. In this case, after receiving the gift from his father, his agricultural assets will only comprise 73.2% of his total asset value in which case he is not entitled to Agricultural Relief' (see taxation section page 265) and the gift is valued at market value giving rise to a liability of €284,460 approx. given that he has already received an inheritance worth €200,000 from his late mother. Clearly, the transfer cannot proceed, and the transferee needs to consider his options to get him over the 80% threshold. These options could be:

- He waits until he gets married, which he intends to do, and transfers his dwelling into joint names with his wife which will result in no liability to gift tax.
- He uses his savings and borrows €100,000 to acquire agricultural property which results in him getting over the 80% threshold and no liability to gift tax.
- He disposes of his dwelling and reinvests the proceeds in agricultural property which results in him getting over the 80% threshold and no liability to gift tax.
- He claims Business Relief which will shelter the agricultural assets to the tune of 90% but will not shelter the farm dwelling so he will have a gift tax of €46,860.

Gift Tax Insurance (S73 Policy)

Currently, the maximum that a son, daughter or favourite niece/nephew can inherit free of tax is now €335,000 which in the case of agricultural assets for qualifying persons means an upper limit of €3.35 million. Where the property value is over this figure there are very few options available to offset this potential liability if considering a lifetime transfer. However, one such option for high-net-worth families facing a definite exposure to gift tax is to consider taking out a type of savings policy know as a Section 73 policy where the proceeds can be used to pay gift tax. The main benefit of such policies is that the funds that were invested in the policy will not in themselves be subject to gift tax. Section 73 policies must be of a minimum of eight years duration before the proceeds can be used for paying gift tax.

Inheritance Tax Insurance (S72 Policy)

Another option could be to will your farm to your chosen successor and deal with the problem by taking out an insurance policy described as a Section 72 policy to cover the eventual liability. The policy will be on your life (and that of your spouse, if you are married), and will be used to pay the Inheritance Tax when it falls due on the death of the longest survivor. A Section 72 policy is a life assurance policy, set up under trust for your beneficiaries. It is designed to pay out sufficient money on your death to meet the Inheritance Tax that will then arise. To the extent that the proceeds of the policy are used to pay the Inheritance Tax bill due, the proceeds will not in themselves be taxable.

Table 10.1 sets out the typical monthly premiums for couples of varying ages. The figures are based on a joint life policy for non-smokers with the sum assured being paid out on the death of the longest survivor. Both the sum assured and premiums are fixed.

Table 10.1: Cost of Section 72 Inheritance Tax Insurance.

Sum Assured	Age next birthday	Monthly premium
€250,000	50	€412.54
€250,000	60	€537.73
€250,000	70	€807.28

Stamp Duty
No stamp duty arises on an inheritance. Transfers between living persons will incur stamp duty unless the transfer is between spouses. Transfers to closely related persons where the transferee is not an eligible young trained farmer, will attract a rate of 1% subject to the condition that the individual to whom the land is conveyed or transferred must, from the date of execution of the transfer, farm the land for a period of not less than 6 years, or lease it for a period of not less than 6 years to a qualified or full time farmer who will farm the land. The 1% rate applies until the 31st December 2028. Transfers to unrelated parties will attract a rate of 7.5% unless the transferee is a young, trained farmer.
Transfers to young, trained farmers may be exempt from stamp duty providing they satisfy certain working hour conditions (see page 284).

Valuing Farm Property
To determine a value for transfer purposes, the farm will be valued by a professional valuer at current market value, in order to determine any liability to tax arising. The value of farm buildings will be considered but it is true to say that farm buildings are generally not separately valued but rather, are reflected in the overall farm valuation. The value of BISS Entitlements, farm machinery, equipment and livestock are not subject to stamp duty.

Income Tax Benefits and Consequences of Transferring
There are several possible benefits that can accrue following transfer, such as,
- The possibility of a more tax efficient trading structure whereby the personal low tax bands and tax credits of transferor and transferee can be more effectively utilised.
- The availability of enhanced Stock Relief for the trading entity.
- Continued involvement of the transferor in the farm business may render certain expenses partially tax allowable that might not otherwise have been tax allowable, such as motor expenses, wear & tear, telephone protective clothing etc.
- Transferring stock or machinery to your successor should not create any additional exposure to income tax as he/she will take over the stock or machinery at the same value as appeared in the transferor's books at the cessation date.

There may also be issues to watch out and plan for in anticipation of a transfer. For example, where the transfer means a cessation of trading there may be an issue where the transferor was availing of income averaging. Where tax has been assessed based on averaging, there may be a clawback of tax saved where averaging resulted in a saving in the year immediately prior to ceasing because in the case of a cessation, profits in that year are taxed on the higher of the actual profit or the averaged profit. Profits in the final year are taxed on the actual profit.

Transfers Between Spouses

There is no exposure to Gift Tax, Capital Gains Tax or Stamp Duty on transfers between spouses. Where such a transfer occurs, the deemed cost for subsequent disposals will refer to the date on which the spouse originally acquired it and not the date on which he/she transferred it to his wife/husband. For spouses over 55 years there is a consequence of transferring in that the transferring spouse will lose part or all of their Retirement Relief threshold in the event of a subsequent sale of all or part of the holding (see Retirement Relief page 276). Where land is transferred into joint names it is important that the recipient spouse is seen to satisfy the 10 year 'use' requirement by being assessed for tax as a farmer whether that be jointly or separately. Transfers to joint names should also be assessed in terms of its impact on the State Pension Increase for a Qualified Adult for the spouse whose name is being added to the title. This allowance is means tested and in the event that the spouse is not otherwise entitled to a contributory pension, he/she may not satisfy the means test as they will now own half of the farm.

11   Wills and Estate Planning

Making Your Will
Altering a Will 195
Being of Sound Mind 195
Revoking a Will...196
Entering a Caveat...196
Lis Pendens..196
Lost Wills..197
Bank Accounts 197
Bank/Building Society Accounts in Joint Names 197
Credit Union & Post Office Accounts..197
Insurance Policies..198
Discretionary Trusts...198
Grant of Probate 199
No Requirement for a Grant..199

Entitlements Under a Will
Spouse/Civil Partner - Where a Will is Present...199
Spouse/Civil Partner - Where no Will is Present 199
Children Where no Will is Present...200
Death of Son or Daughter Where no Will is Present....................................200
Inheritance Rights of a Divorced Person...200
Inheritance Rights of Unmarried Partners..200
Inheritance Rights of Cohabiting Couples 201

Challenging a Will
Challenging the Validity of a Will 201
Challenging the Terms of a Will (S117 applications) 201
Proprietary Estoppel..202

Making Your Will

Anybody who has something to hand on should make a will regardless of their age. A will is a highly important document and should if at all possible be prepared by a solicitor. Making a will ensures that your assets pass to the person of your choice and by having one much unnecessary expense and administration will be avoided after your death.

The other main advantage of making a will is that the question of inheritance tax will presumably have been addressed. If there is a potential problem, you will at least be afforded the opportunity to put measures in place to avoid leaving a substantial inheritance tax bill to your nominated successor. It is important that you speak to your accountant or tax advisor before making your will as he/she will be best positioned to advise you on how best to structure your will from a tax perspective. For married couples it is generally the case that they leave their respective possessions to each other in the first instance and to allow the longest survivor decide on who then gets what. Alternatively, a preferred route for many couples, having discussed and agreed the position, is for the main asset owning spouse to grant the surviving spouse a life interest in the farm and specify who gets what thereafter, thereby taking the decision out of the hands of the surviving spouse.

In the event of you being unable or not wanting to consult a solicitor you should at least ensure that:

- You have made an actual written will that is signed by you and your signature is witnessed by two persons, neither of whom (or their spouses) can benefit under the will.
- You must state your name and address.
- You must revoke all former wills.
- You must appoint at least one and preferably two executors.
- You must be of sound mind.
- You must date the will.
- It should contain a residuary clause, which is a part that sets out how property not specifically covered in the will should be distributed. It usually takes the form of "the remainder of my estate I leave to my daughter, Mary".
- Any references to parts of the farm should be clear and concise to the extent that there is no doubt as to what part of the farm you are referring to.

Altering a Will

Any alterations made to a will, after signing, will be invalid. Where one wishes to alter the content of a will it is essential that the family solicitor is consulted. A will should be reappraised at regular intervals as circumstances can change or tax legislation alter. A will remains in force until it is replaced by a new will.

Being of Sound Mind

In order to make a valid will, you must not only set out your wishes in a written and witnessed document you must also be of sound mind. If you suffer from any mental disorder, it is important that evidence is left with your will (for example, from a doctor) that proves you were mentally competent at the time you made the will. Otherwise, your will can be open to challenge. Your will can also be challenged on the basis that you were acting under pressure or undue influence when you made it, so it is important that you get independent legal advice and not use the services of a solicitor of any potential beneficiary of your will.

Revoking a Will

This refers to cancelling a will, whether for good or with a view to changing its contents. Making a new will and mentioning in it that all former wills are revoked is the most effective method of revocation. Destroying a will may also be an effective means of revocation but not to be recommended unless a new will has been made which revokes all previous wills. A photocopy of a will, in the absence of an original, may be sufficient to take out probate providing the person who made the copy can swear to its authenticity. It should be noted that a will is automatically revoked upon the marriage of the person who made the will, unless it is specified in the will that it was made with the intention of getting married.

Entering a Caveat

A probate caveat is a notice filed (generally by a solicitor) to the Probate Office to state an intention to challenge or oppose an aspect of the will. The caveat is designed to prevent a grant of probate being issued to an executor of a will. A fee of €100 payable to the courts service must accompany the caveat. The next step in the legal process is for the executor to warn (respond to) a Caveat. If the person who lodged the Caveat does not formally acknowledge (described as 'making an appearance') the warning, the Caveat will cease to have effect. If an appearance is lodged, the Caveat may only be set aside by an Order of the Court. In Irish law a caveat can last up to six months before it becomes null and void, but a caveat can be renewed at the end of the six month period. The purpose of a caveat is to notify the probate office that one intends to oppose an aspect of the will. The Probate Office is not concerned with the particulars of the challenge. However, by notifying them of the caveat they are obliged to provide notification of when they intend to grant probate, at which time the person requesting the caveat and his/her solicitor will be notified to act to challenge the will and prevent the grant of probate from being made. The caveat effectively buys the applicant extra time to research their case. A caveat must be lodged with the Probate Office or District Registrar at least one day before a grant of probate is made, so time is of the essence in such cases.

Lis Pendens

Where there is a dispute in relation to title and there is a High Court or Circuit Court case pending, a Lis Pendens can be registered in the Judgments Section of the Central Office of the High Court. Lis Pendens literally means "Litigation Pending" and its purpose is to put on notice that there is a dispute in relation to the property. A Lis Pendans may be lodged in regard to any action in the Circuit Court or the High Court in which a claim is made to an estate or interest in whether by way of claim or counterclaim in the action.

Lost Wills

If the original will has been lost, advertisements should be placed in suitable newspapers to try and find it. A copy will is not normally acceptable, in case the original will was revoked - perhaps by destruction. But, if a copy exists, the High Court may be asked to admit the copy to proof. The solicitor or person who made the copy will must swear that it is authentic. If no photocopy or carbon copy of the original exists, someone with means of knowledge (such as a person who has the original on computer disk) may give evidence so the will can be reconstructed.

Bank Accounts

Where there is money in the bank, family members usually cannot get access until probate is taken out. If the amount of money in the bank is small, the bank may release it provided the personal representatives or the next of kin signs an indemnity form - in effect, this is a guarantee that the bank will not be at a loss if there are other claims on the money.

Bank/Building Society Accounts in Joint Names

If a bank account is in the joint names of the deceased and the deceased's spouse or civil partner, the money can usually be transferred into the survivor's name. You will need the death certificate to do this. If the bank account is in the joint names of the deceased person and someone else, and the bank was given instructions when the account was opened that the other person was to receive the money on the death of the deceased, the money can be transferred into the survivor's name. If there is an account with more than €50,000, you will also need a letter of clearance from Revenue allowing the money to be transferred to the surviving account holder's name pending investigations about any CAT liability. Spouses and civil partners are not liable for Capital Acquisitions Tax (CAT) on inheritances from each other.

Where the bank has no instructions, the intentions of the deceased person will have to be examined (for example, by referring to their will). Where joint accounts are opened with a spouse or child, it is presumed that one party will be fully entitled to the money in the account when the other party dies. Disputes can arise however if someone, perhaps an elderly person or a person with a physical disability, opens a joint bank account with a relative or friend so that the relative or friend can manage his or her finances for him or her. This is because the owner's intention may or may not have been to benefit the relative or friend. A decision in such a case would depend on the intention of the people involved, the amount they each lodged into the account and the terms of their contract with the bank. It is advisable for people with joint accounts to make clear in their contract with their bank or in their will what their intentions are for the money in such accounts.

Credit Union & Post Office Accounts

If the deceased had a credit union account and had completed a valid Nomination Form, when opening the account, nominating someone as next of kin, the proceeds of the account up to a maximum of €23,000 go to the person or persons nominated on the form. They do not form part of the deceased's estate. In the case of Post office accounts. the maximum is €25,000. Any excess over these limits goes into the deceased person's estate.

Insurance Policies

If an insurance policy names a person as the beneficiary, then that person may claim the sum assured directly from the insurance company subject to them furnishing a death certificate. If there is no named beneficiary, then the proceeds form part of the overall estate of the deceased and are distributed with the other assets.

Discretionary Trusts

Discretionary Trusts are commonly used in wills made by a couple with young children or a child with a disability where the couple wish to provide for the children until they reach the age of 21 years or in certain circumstances older than 21 years. Obviously, for a trust to come into being, both parents will be deceased and the two appointed trustees will manage the trust and apply their discretion in caring for the needs of the children. Where the trust extends beyond the youngest child becoming 21 years, Discretionary Trust Tax will apply This will amount to 6% of the trust value at commencement and 1% per annum charge thereafter until such time as the trust is wound up. If a discretionary trust is wound up within 5 years of the initial 6% charge arising, the charge is reduced from 6% to 3%.

Sample Will

This is the last will and testament of John Farmer of Anymore, Co. Westmeath. I hereby revoke all previous wills and testamentary dispositions made by me. I appoint my sister Mary O'Shea and my nephew Pat Farmer as executors of this will and direct them to pay my just debts, funeral and testamentary expenses. I leave £2,000 to the Society of St. Vincent de Paul. To my nephew Pat Farmer of Anyless, Mullingar I leave my farm, farm dwelling and farm outbuildings at Anymore (contaned in Folio WM1234) along with my livestock, farm machinery and farm entitlements. All the residue and remainder of my property of any nature and description and wherever situated, I leave to my sister Mary O'Shea..

Dated this 22nd. day of September 2023

Signed

John Farmer

Signed by the testator as and for his last will and testament in the presence of us, and signed by us in the presence of the testator.

John Power (Witness)   *Mary Power* (Witness)

Caution - Where possible wills should be drawn up by the family solicitor and make sure some reliable person knows of the whereabouts of your will.

Grant of Probate

When a person dies leaving a valid will and appointing an executor, a grant of probate issues to the executor on application. A grant of probate is a document granted by the High Court which gives authority to the executor(s) to deal with a deceased's person's estate. The person's assets are dealt with by the executor, according to the terms of the will. While it is possible for the executor to apply for the Grant, it is generally handled by a solicitor. The solicitor who made the will does not necessarily have to be the solicitor who applies for the Grant of Probate, and it is up to the executor(s) to shop around if they so wish. When a person dies without having made a valid will, they are said to have died intestate. In this case a grant of Letters of Administration issues to the person(s) who were the nearest next of kin at the date of death. The deceased person's assets are then dealt with by that person.

No Requirement for a Grant

A grant is not necessary where:

- A person dies leaving small amounts of money in a bank or other financial institution in his/her own name and that financial institution agrees to release the funds without the necessity for a grant. The financial institution's decision is final.
- A person dies leaving assets which were held jointly with another person. Those assets as a rule become the sole property of the joint owner on the death of the deceased. In cases of doubt, the intention of the deceased at the time the joint account was created is relevant if any evidence of same exists.
- A person dies and leaves no assets, there is generally no need to extract a grant. However, where a grant becomes necessary in such circumstances, contact must be made with the Probate Officer in advance of such application.

Entitlements Under a Will

Spouse/Civil Partner - Where a Will is Present

Where a will is made and the person who made the will is survived by his or her spouse, the surviving spouse may elect to take the following.

- Their entitlement under the will, or,
- One third of the estate where there are children.
- One half of the estate where there are no children.

Spouse/Civil Partner - Where no Will is Present

Where a person dies without a will (intestate) the following are the entitlements of the spouse:

- Where there are no children the spouse/civil partner is entitled to everything.
- Where there are children, regardless of age, the spouse/civil partner is entitled to two thirds and the children to one third in equal shares.

Children Where no Will is Present

Where a person dies without a will the following are the entitlements of the children:

- Where there is a parent with children, regardless of age, the children are entitled to one third in equal shares.
- Where there is no parent alive the estate is divided between the children. If one of the children is no longer living his/her share passes to his/her children.

Rights of Children Where a Will Exists

Unlike a spouse/civil partner, children do not have any absolute right to inherit their parent's estate if the parent has made a will. Children born inside or outside marriage and adopted children all have the same rights and there are no age restrictions. However, a child may make an application to court if he/she feels that he/she has not been adequately provided for. An application must be made within six months of the taking out of a Grant of Probate. The court then has to decide if the parent has failed in his/her duty to the child in accordance with the needs of that child. Each case is considered individually, but it is important to remember that the legal right share of the spouse cannot be infringed in order to give the child a greater share of the estate.

Table 11.1: Minimum Legal Entitlements of Spouses or Children.

Relationship to deceased	Will present	No will present
Spouse/Civil Partner - no children	Half	Entire
Spouse/Civil Partner with children	One third	Two-thirds
Children	Nothing	One third

Death of Son or Daughter Where no Will is Present

Where a son or daughter dies without a will, their estate passes in its entirety to the parent or parents. If the parents are dead the estate passes to the brothers and sisters or the children of deceased brothers or sisters.

Inheritance Rights of a Divorced Person

In the case of divorce, a former spouse who claims that proper provision has not been made for him/her may apply to court for a share of the deceased' estate within 6 months from the date of grant of probate or grant of administration. Personal representatives are required to make reasonable attempts to notify the former spouse. A share will not be given to a former spouse who has remarried. The same rules apply to a separated spouse. These provisions also apply to civil partners.

Inheritance Rights of Unmarried Partners

In the case of non-cohabiting unmarried partners, the "partner" will have no succession rights and will therefore be limited to whatever rights he/she may establish in contract (e.g. where he/she has financially contributed to the purchase of a property) or whatever was left to him/her in a Will.

Inheritance Rights of Cohabiting Couples

If you are in a cohabiting relationship, a pre-existing will still stands. If you enter into cohabitation (i.e., move in with a partner), and you die without a will, your partner has no right to any share of the estate no matter how long you have been together, apart from what was held jointly. There is nothing to prevent you from leaving some or all of your property to your cohabiting partner in your will but if you are still married or in a civil partnership, the law gives your surviving spouse/civil partner a legal right to a share of your estate when you die, no matter what you have said or specified in your will. However, under the redress scheme for cohabiting couples introduced by the Civil Partnership and Certain Rights and Obligations of Cohabitants Act 2010, a qualified cohabitant may apply for provision to be made from the estate of a deceased cohabitant.

Challenging a Will

The circumstances by which the content of a will can be challenged in Ireland are quite limited. The 1965 Succession Act sets down the ground rules as to the legitimacy of the contents of a will.

Challenging the Validity of a Will

It may be possible to challenge the validity of a will on a number of grounds as follows;
- A will that is not witnessed by two people.
- The person making the will was subjected to undue influence at the time of making the will whereby their true intentions are not reflected in the will.
- Mental incapacity.
- The will does not provide for a spouse or children in accordance with the Succession Act 1965.

Challenging the Terms of a Will (S117 applications)

Provided that there is no suggestion of impropriety, and the will has been validly executed, the only person entitled to bring an action to set aside the provisions of a will is a child of the testator, providing that the child's parent i.e. the surviving spouse, is not the sole beneficiary. The Succession Act provides that if on application to a court, that court is of the opinion that the person who made the will failed in his/her moral duty to make proper provision for a child, then the court may order that such provision shall be made for the child as the court thinks just. Such cases are referred to as Section 117 applications so where a son or daughter challenges a will on the grounds that they feel hard done by, the court will take the following matters into account.
- The value of the estate and the amount received by the surviving spouse.
- How the son/daughter bringing the action benefited from the deceased during his/her lifetime.
- The current financial circumstances and prospects of that son/daughter.
- How other siblings benefited from the deceased during their lifetime.
- The current financial circumstances and prospects of the other siblings.

- The financial means of the person who is deceased.
- The conduct of that child towards the deceased during their lifetime.

The onus will be on the child to prove to the court that the parent failed in their moral duty to make adequate provision for them . Similarly, the child must show that there is a need arising in their case which could have been satisfied by a different apportionment of the estate pursuant to the will. An action to challenge a will must be taken within 6 months of probate being granted with no exceptions. Costs are at the discretion of the court but people who fail by bringing what are deemed to be nuisance or unfounded claims will more than likely suffer the costs.

Proprietary Estoppel

Where appropriate grounds for a Section 117 application do not exist, a case for proprietary estoppel may be pursued. Otherwise known as legitimate expectation, the doctrine of proprietary estoppel is regularly applied by the courts where a child, relative or non-relative claims to have a legitimate expectation of benefiting from a deceased person's estate. A typical example of this is where a family member or indeed an unrelated person has worked on a farm for a long period of time, often attending to the owner's welfare as well as running the farm in the belief and on the basis of clear promises or indications made to them that the farm would be theirs on the death of the deceased. The person may have foregone other work or career opportunities by relying on such indications. Such cases can be difficult to establish in court but in many instances the applicant may create a fallback position by also claiming for inadequate or underpaid remuneration in respect of the work he has done, as generally in such cases. remuneration is often token in nature. Such claims for underpaid remuneration may be subject to the statute of limitations which may limit compensation to the previous six years.

12
Pensions, Welfare & Health Benefits

State Benefits & Welfare Entitlements

Contributory State Pension...204
Contributory Pensions For Spouses...208
Changes to Contributory Pensions 209
Widow's Contributory Pension 211
Widowed Parent Grant...212
Carer's Benefit...212
Carer's Allowance 214
Domiciliary Care Allowance 215
Carer's Support Grant 216
Child Benefit..216
Maternity Benefit 216
Invalidity Pension...217
Farm Assist..217
Rural Social Scheme...220
Job-Seeker's Benefit 220

State Health Benefits & Services

Treatment Benefit Scheme 221
Drugs Payment Scheme..223
Medical Cards..223
GP Visit Cards..225
Acquiring Health Care Abroad 226
The Cross-Border Directive...226
The Treatment Abroad Scheme 226
The Northern Ireland Planned Healthcare Scheme 227

Benefits & Services for the Elderly

Medical Cards for Persons Over 70..227
Household Benefits Package..227
Mobility Aids Grant Scheme 228
Housing Aid for Older Persons Scheme 228
Housing Adaptation Grant for People with a Disability............................229
Seniors Alert Scheme...230
The Nursing Homes Support Scheme..231
Nursing Home Loan Scheme 234

State Benefits & Welfare Entitlements

The main welfare entitlements that may concern farmers are:

- Contributory State Pension.
- Contributory Pension for Spouse.
- Widow's/Widower's Contributory Pension.
- Widowed Parent Grant.
- Carer's Benefit.
- Carer's Allowance.
- Carers' Support Grant.
- Invalidity Pension.
- Child Benefit.
- Family Income Supplement.
- Job-seekers Benefit.
- Farm Assist.
- Rural Social Scheme.

Contributory State Pension

The PRSI scheme for the self-employed, which came into effect in 1988, should entitle persons to a pension on reaching their 66th birthday providing they have made the necessary PRSI contributions. It as a non-means tested payment so people are eligible regardless of what wealth they possess. Certain changes which are detailed in this chapter are due to commence in January 2024 but the current system subject to the changes as outlined will continue to operate.

Conditions for a Pension - PRSI Contributions

To qualify you need to have a minimum number of contributions. The yearly average number of contributions will determine if you qualify for a full pension. There are three different options available in order to qualify for a pension as follows:
1. Normal average rule (see below).
2. Alternative average rule (see below).
3. Total contribution approach.

Number of Contributions

You need to have 520 paid contributions (10 years paid contributions). In this case, not more than 260 of the 520 contributions may be voluntary contributions.

Average Number of Contributions

(1) Normal average rule: the normal average rule states that you must have a yearly average of at least 10 appropriate contributions paid or credited from the year you first entered insurance or from 1953, whichever is later to the end of the tax year before you reach pension age (66). An average of 10 entitles you to a minimum pension; you need an average of 48 to get the maximum pension. Farmers who never had PAYE employment will have entered insurance on the 6th April 1988 or when they commenced in farming, whichever is later.

Note: An annual contribution is equivalent to 52 weeks contributions.

2) Alternative average rule: this requires that you have an average of 48 Class A, E, F, G, H, N or S contributions (paid or credited) for each contribution year from the 1979/80 tax year to the end of the tax year before you reach pension age (66). This average would entitle you to the maximum pension. There is no provision for a reduced pension when this alternative average is used.

Table 12.1: Percentage of full pension resulting from yearly average contributions.

Yearly Average	% of full pension	Yearly Average	% of full pension
48 plus	100%	20-29	85%
40-47	98%	15-19	65%
30-39	90%	10-14	40%

3) Total Contribution Approach (TCA): Where the average rules as set out above do not entitle one to a full or possibly any pension, they can opt for the Total Contributions Approach. This is available to new pension applicants and also those who qualified for a pension since 2012. The TCA, also known as the Aggregated Contributions Method, does not use a yearly average to calculate the rate of pension. Instead, the rate is based on the total number of contributions you have paid before you reach the age of 66. The TCA calculation includes the Home Caring Periods Scheme which can allow for up to 20 years of homemaking and caring duties. The **Home Caring Periods Scheme** can only be used with the TCA. Using the TCA, you will qualify for the maximum personal rate of State Pension (Contributory) if you have 2,080 or more PRSI contributions (or 40 years of employment). If you have fewer than 2,080 contributions, you may still qualify for a high rate of pension because up to 1,040 homecoming Periods (20 years) and up to 520 credited contributions (10 years) can be used as part of your pension calculation. However, your combined Home Caring Periods and credited contributions cannot total more than 1,040 (20 years). If your combined total of paid contributions, Home Caring Period and credited contributions is less than 2,080, you will qualify for a reduced rate of pension. For example, a combined total of 1,040 paid contributions, made up of Home Caring Period and credited contributions, would entitle you to 50% of the maximum pension (1,040 / 2,080 = 50%).

CASE STUDY – Total Contributions Approach (TCA).
Jane Farmer will be 66 in February 2024. Jane first paid PRSI when she was 19 but in the intervening years she has only accumulated a total of 270 contributions due to becoming a stay at home mother and home carer of her children up to age 12 and laterally her aged mother for a combined period of 19 years. This leaves her with a yearly average of 9.6 contributions after claiming relief under the Homemakers' Scheme which falls short of the yearly average of 10 contributions to entitle her to even a reduced pension. However, by availing of the TCA option Jane can get 988 credits for the 19 years she spent caring that gives her a total of 1,258 credits which will entitle her to 60.48% of a full pension amounting to a €160.45 weekly payment.

Child Dependent Allowance
An allowance can be claimed for each dependent child up to 18 years of age (or 22 years if in full time education by day) who is living with you. The full rate is payable if you are in receipt of a Qualified Adult Allowance. If your spouse/civil partner is earning less than €400 per week you may qualify for a half rate as payment.

Applying for the pension
You may apply any time from five months of reaching your 66th birthday or from January 2024 onwards, you can defer applying up to age 70 if you need to accumulate more credits. The form is simple to complete and can be had from Old Age Contributory Section, Pension Services Office, College Road, Sligo, (071)69800. Late claims may be backdated for a maximum period of 6 months. Backdating of a late claim beyond 6 months will be considered in circumstances where the failure to claim arose as a result of incorrect information being supplied by the Department or the claimant's incapacity by illness or infirmity.

Rates of Contributory State Pension
The following rates are effective from January 2024:

Personal rate	€277.30
Increase for qualified adult (under 66)	€184.70
Increase for qualified adult (over 66)	€248.60
Child Dependent rate (under age 12)	€46.00
Child Dependent rate (over age 12)	€54.00
Persons over 80 (additional)	€10.00
Living alone allowance	€22.00
Residents of certain offshore islands (over 66)	€20.00

Increase for a Qualified Adult (IQA)

If you are married/divorced, or living with someone as husband and wife, you may get an allowance for him/her as a qualified adult. If you have children living with you and you are single, widowed or separated you may get an increase for the person who is caring for your child(ren), provided the person is living with you and being supported by you. This allowance is means tested with a lower income /earnings limit of €100 per week. However, an allowance will be paid at a reduced rate up to a weekly income/ earnings limit of €310. The means test takes into account any income that the adult dependent is in receipt of. In addition, if he/she has any savings, investments or property the value of these assets will be assessed on the following basis:

First €20,000 - nil.
Next €10,000 - €10 per week.
Next €10,000 - €20 per week.
Remainder -   €4 per €1,000 per week.

By applying these figures, savings/investments of €100,000 would equate with an assessed income of €270 per week. Where property is rented, the rent will be taken into account and not the capital value.

For new applicants the Increase for a Qualified Adult will automatically be paid directly to the adult dependent.

CASE STUDY - Qualified Adult Means Test

Joe Farmer is due to qualify for the contributory pension in March 24. His wife Mary who is 64 years has never worked outside the home. They have combined savings of €60,000 and Mary has shares which she inherited from her mother currently worth €40,000. The following is her assessment of means;

	Per week equivalent
Savings & property	
1st €20,000	nil
Next €10,000	€ 10
Next €10,000	€ 20
Remainder (€30,000)	€120
Total assessed weekly means	€150

As Mary has exceeded the weekly €100 income limit by €50 for a full Qualified Adult Allowance of €184.70, her payment will be reduced to €134.70

Contributory Pensions For Spouses

Generally, spouses working with their partners do not pay social insurance contributions. However, spouses who operate in a farming partnership with their spouses may be brought into the social insurance system and thereby build up entitlement towards a contributory State Pension and other Social Welfare benefits. In reality most farmers' wives are very much involved in the running of the farm business and would fit the criteria that define a business partner. There are two categories of individual for whom this option applies to, namely, those who can become registered now without any backdating and those who are of an age that will require their contributions to be backdated in order to qualify for benefit. Refer to page 205 to determine the number of contributions required to qualify for a contributory pension.

Spouses Not Requiring Backdating

Both spouses must register as a partnership with the Revenue Commissioners and in future, tax returns must be made in joint names. This will mean that the first registered spouse's status as a sole trader will have to cease, which may have income tax implications in terms of benefits recently gained from income averaging. Consult your accountant. It is not necessary to transfer the farm into joint names, nor is it necessary to draw up a partnership agreement for this purpose. However, in order that the partnership is seen as genuine, the bank accounts should be placed in joint names and also, ideally but not necessarily, the herd number.

Spouses Requiring Back Dating

Certain farming spouses could apply to backdate Class S PRSI contributions. Such spouses would have to prove that a working partnership had existed with her/his spouse for the years for which backdating is being requested. The Department of Social and Family Affairs and the Revenue Commissioners will use some but not all of the following factors to decide if a partnership normally exists:

- Each partner writes cheques on the business accounts in their own right.
- There is a joint business bank account.
- It is apparent to those doing business with the partnership that a partnership exists.
- Business accounts and activities are in joint names of the partners.
- Each partner makes a significant contribution to the running of the business.
- The business (but not necessarily the land) is owned jointly by the partnership.
- The profits and losses of the partnership are shared by each partner.
- The business stationery reflects the existence of a partnership.

Where the Department is satisfied that a working partnership exists and where the profit earned would have exceeded the minimum income limit (€5,000 currently) per partner in the relevant years, the newly registered spouse will be required to pay any shortfalls in PRSI if any such shortfalls arise. Shortfalls should only arise where both parties end up being liable for the minimum contribution, or in earlier years where there was a ceiling on income liable to PRSI.

Where a spouse requiring backdating is 66 or over, they will need to have made at least one Class S contribution in order for their request to be considered.

Working in the Home

The Homemakers' Scheme is for people who have been carers who provide full-time care for a child under age 12 or an ill or disabled person aged 12 or over. It does not affect people who were carers before April 1994 and it is not of much use to those who give up work permanently. It is of greatest importance for those who work outside the home for a number of years, then spend a number of years as carers and then return to the workforce. It applies equally to women and men. From 5 April 1994, any contribution year spent as a homemaker may be disregarded in the calculation of the yearly average up to a maximum of 20 years. So, the fact that you do not have any contributions in those years will not affect your entitlement to a pension.

CASE STUDY - Qualifying for the Homemakers Scheme
Joan who has reached her 66th year has a total of 400 PRSI contributions since she started working 45 years ago. This only gives her an average of 8.8 contributions per year which does not entitle her to any pension. However Joan was working in the home for twenty years caring for her children and more recently for her disabled mother. Joan can apply for the Homemakers Scheme whereby the twenty years caring will be disregarded in the calculation resulting in her average being increased to 16 contributions which will entitle her to 65% of a full pension which at current rates will amount to €172.57.

Changes to Contributory Pensions

Changes to the operation of the Contributory State Pension scheme will start to come into effect from the 1st January 2024. These changes comprise the following,

- Improved access for long term carers.
- Flexibility of draw-down age.
- Phased abolition of Yearly Average Method and introduction of Total Contributions Approach (TCA).

Improved Access for Long Term Carers

From January 2024 access to the State Pension (Contributory) will improve for long term carers. If you have spent more than 20 years providing full-time care to an incapacitated person, you may be entitled to enhanced state pension provision. You will get the equivalent of paid contributions (long-term carer's contributions) for periods of over 20 years spent caring to cover gaps in your contribution record needed to calculate your entitlement to the pension. If you have cared for someone full-time, you can apply for these contributions. You can be awarded a Long-Term Carers Contribution on your PRSI record for each week that you provided full-time care to an incapacitated person. These periods can only be used once you have reached a minimum of 1,040 weeks (20 years).

Flexibility of Drawdown Age

From January 2024, the State Pension (Contributory) will become more flexible. You will be able to drawdown your pension at any age between 66 and 70 using flexible options. This will give you the opportunity to continue to work which may improve your contribution record for when you do decide to retire. You will still be able to retire at 66 and drawdown your pension in the same way as you can currently. If you claim your pension beyond the age of 66, you may be entitled to an actuarially increased rate of payment. During the deferral period, you will be able to continue to make PRSI contributions to increase your personal rate of payment or meet the minimum qualifying condition of 520 (10 years) contributions However, you will not be able to increase your contributions past the current maximum of 2080 (40 years). This means that it will be essential to know how many contributions you have before you decide to drawdown or defer drawing down your pension. A contribution statement can be requested by anyone with a MyGovID account.

Introduction of TCA Approach

From January 2025 there will be a 10-year phased removal of the Yearly Average Method, which means that all pensions will be calculated using only the Total Contributions Approach (TCA) by 2034. During the 10-year transition period, pensions will be calculated using two methods:

- The first method will use the full TCA approach. See page 205.
- The second method will, starting in 2025, calculate what your pension would be under the existing Yearly Average Method. The pension rate of payment will then combine 90% of this yearly average rate with 10% of the TCA rate. The proportion accounted for by the Yearly Average Rate will then reduce by 10% over each of the subsequent 9 years until the pension calculation is fully based on the TCA method only.

Widow's Contributory Pension

Widow's/Widower's or Surviving Civil Partner's Contributory Pension is available to such persons provided the necessary employed or self-employed PRSI contributions have been made.

Rates

The rates of widow's contributory pension applicable from January 2024 are:

	Weekly rate
Personal rate age under 66	€237.50
Personal rate aged over 66 and under 80	€277.30
Persons aged 80 or over	€287.30
Additional for each dependent child (under age 12)	€46.00
Additional for each dependent child (over age 12)	€54.00
Living alone allowance (66 or over)	€22.00

Qualifying Persons

The following persons qualify:
- A widow(er) or a surviving civil partner who is not cohabiting with another person as a couple.
- A person divorced from their late spouse before their spouse's death and not remarried and who is not cohabiting with another person as a couple.
- A person who has had their civil partnership dissolved before their partner's death and have not entered into a new civil partnership and not be cohabiting with another person as a couple.

How to Qualify

To qualify for a Widow's, Widower's or Surviving Civil Partner's (Contributory) Pension, either you or your late spouse or civil partner must have a certain number of PRSI contributions. All the PRSI requirements must be met on one person's record - you may not combine the contributions of both spouses or civil partners. All must have been made before the death of the spouse or civil partner. Either you or your spouse or civil partner must have:
- At least 260 paid contributions paid before the date your spouse or civil partner died.

and;
- An average of 39 paid or credited contributions in either the 3 or 5 years before the death of the spouse or civil partner or before he or she reached pension age (66)

or;
- A yearly average of at least 24 paid or credited contributions from the year of first entry into insurance until the year of death or reaching pension age. If this average is used then an average of 24 will entitle you to a minimum pension, you will need an average of 48 per year to get the full pension.

Widowed Parent Grant

A Widowed Parent Grant is a once-off payment designed to assist with the income support needs of a widow or widower immediately following the death of her or his spouse where they have one or more qualifying children. The current rate of payment is €8,000. In any case where a claim to a widow(er)s' pension is being made, there is no requirement to complete a separate application form for the Widowed Parent Grant. The necessary documentation for the pension claim will suffice for the Widowed Parent Grant.

Carer's Benefit

Carer's Benefit may be relevant to those farmer's wife's who are currently in insurable employment but may wish to cease work to care for an incapacitated or elderly relative. You can get Carer's Benefit for a total period of 104 weeks for each person being cared for. This may be claimed as a single continuous period or in any number of separate periods up to a total of 104 weeks.

Eligibility
You may be eligible for Carer's Benefit if:
- You are aged 16 or over and under 66.
- You have been employed for at least 8 weeks, whether consecutive or not, in the previous 26-week period. You must be in employment for a minimum of 16 hours per week or 32 hours per fortnight. You don't have to meet this condition if you were getting Carer's Benefit in the previous 26 weeks.
- You give up work in order to be a full-time carer. Being a full-time carer means you must be living with or in a position to provide full-time care and attention to a person in need of care who is not living in an institution.
- You are not living in a hospital, convalescent home or other similar institution. However, you may continue to be regarded as providing full-time care and attention, if you or the person being cared for is having medical or other treatment in a hospital or other institution for a period not longer than 13 weeks.
- You meet the PRSI contribution conditions.
- The person being cared for is so incapacitated as to require full-time care and attention and is not normally living in an institution. Medical certification is required unless the person being cared for is a child who is getting Domiciliary Care Allowance The carer of a child on a Domiciliary Care Allowance does not need to be the person who receives that allowance on the child's behalf.
- You must not take part in employment, self-employment, training or education courses outside the home for more than 18.5 hours a week. The maximum amount you can earn is €350 per week after taxes.

PRSI Contributions
You must have at least 156 contributions paid at any time between your entry into insurance and the time you make your claim for Carer's Benefit and:
- 39 contributions paid in the Relevant Tax Year, or;
- 39 contributions paid in the 12-month period before the start of Carer's Benefit, or;
- 26 contributions paid in the Relevant Tax Year and 26 contributions paid in the year before that.

Only contributions at Class A, B, C, D, H and E can be counted towards Carer's Benefit. Class S (self-employed contributions) do not count. The Relevant Tax Year is the second last complete tax year before the year in which you make your claim. So, for claims made in 2023, the Relevant Tax Year is 2021. Periods of insurance in another EU member state may be taken into account to meet the PRSI contribution conditions. The last week of insurance must be paid in Ireland.

Rates of Payment
The rate of payment effective from January 2024 for persons under 66 caring for one person is €249 per week. You are not entitled to the Household Benefits package and Free Travel under the Carer's Benefit Scheme but you are entitled to a GP Visit Card.

Carer's Leave
A person's right to carer's leave from employment complements the Carer's Benefit Scheme. Carer's leave allows you to leave your employment temporarily for up to 104 weeks to provide full-time care for people in need of full-time care and attention. The leave is unpaid but people who take carer's leave have their jobs kept open for the duration of the leave. You do not have to be eligible for Carer's Benefit to get carer's leave.

Carer's Allowance

The Carer's Allowance is a payment for carers on low incomes who live with and look after certain people who need full-time care and attention. Carers who are providing care to more than one person may be entitled to up to 50% extra of the maximum rate of Carer`s Allowance each week, depending on the weekly means assessed. It is not unusual in a family farm situation to have an elderly family member in residence who would qualify the person looking after them for this allowance assuming they satisfy the means test.

How to Qualify
The carer must:
- Be aged 18 or over.
- Satisfy a means test.
- Live with the person(s) you are looking after.
- Be caring for the person(s) on a full-time basis.
- Not be engaged in employment, self-employment, training, or education courses outside the home for more than 18.5 hours a week.
- Be living in the State.
- Not be living in a hospital, convalescent home or other similar institution.
- during your absence, adequate care for the person requiring full-time care and attention must be arranged.

The person receiving care must:
- Be so disabled as to need full-time care and attention (medical certification is required).
- Not normally living in a hospital, home, or other similar institution.
- Ne over the age of 16 and so incapacitated as to require full-time care and attention, or;
- Be aged under 16 and getting a Domiciliary Care Allowance.

Meaning of 'full-time care and attention'
The person(s) being cared for must be so disabled or invalided as to require:
- continuous supervision and frequent assistance throughout the day in connection with his/her normal personal needs, for example, help to walk and get about, eat or drink, wash, bathe, dress etc., or;
- continuous supervision in order to avoid danger to themselves, and
- so incapacitated as to be likely to require full-time care and attention for at least 12 months.

The requirement to provide full-time care and attention will be assessed on an individual basis. It is not intended, nor is it desirable, that a carer would be expected to provide care on a twenty four hour basis. In this regard, the above arrangements will be applied in a flexible manner, having due regard to both the needs of the carer and the person requiring care.

Note: The person being cared for may attend a non-residential course of rehabilitation training or a non-residential day care centre approved by the Minister for Health and Children.

Earnings limit

With effect from June 2022 the first €350 of weekly income is disregarded in the case of a single person. In the case of married co-habituating persons the first €750 of combined weekly income will not be taken into account when assessing your means.

Investments and Savings

Your means are any income you or your spouse/partner have or property (except your home) or an asset which could bring in money or provide you with an income. The means test is similar to that operating under Farm Assist in regard to savings and investments. Savings or investments up to €50,000 in the case of an individual are not counted or €100,000 in the case of a couple.

Rate of Payment

In addition to the Carer's Allowance a Carers' Support Grant is also automatically paid to persons in receipt of the allowance. The following rates of payment are currently effective and will apply for 2024;

Full rate caring for one person (under 66)	€248.00
Full rate caring for one person (over 66)	€296.00
Carers' Support Grant	€1,850
Additional for each child dependent under age 12 - full rate	€46.00
Additional for each child dependent over age 12 - full rate	€54.00

Carer's Allowance will continue to be paid for a period of 12 weeks when the person being cared for moves permanently into residential care. The allowance also continues for not longer than 13 weeks where the carer or the person being cared for (an adult) is having medical or other treatment in a hospital or institution.

Domiciliary Care Allowance

Domiciliary Care Allowance is a monthly payment for a child aged under 16 living in the home with a severe disability who requires ongoing care and attention, substantially over and above the care and attention usually required by a child of the same age. The allowance is not means tested.

Rate of Payment

The rate for 2024 is €340 per month. Where the child is in part time residential care, a half rate may be payable.

Carer's Support Grant

The Carer's Support Grant, previously described as the, Respite Care Grant is an annual payment made to carers by the Department of Social Protection. Carers can use the grant in whatever way they wish. They can use the grant to pay for respite care if they wish, but do not have to do so. The grant is paid automatically to carers getting Carer's Allowance, Carer's Benefit, Domiciliary Care Allowance or Prescribed Relative's Allowance but is also paid to certain other carers providing full-time care and who are;

- Aged 16 or over and ordinarily resident in the State,
- Caring for the person on a full-time basis,
- Caring for the person for at least six months – this period must include the first Thursday in June,
- Living with the person being cared for or, if not, be contactable quickly by a system of communication (for example, telephone or alarm),
- not working more than 15 hours per week outside the home or taking part in an education or training course for more than 15 hours a week.

Rate of Grant
A grant of €1,850 is paid once each year, usually on the first Thursday in June, for each person that is cared for. It is not taxable.

Applications
Application forms can be had from your social welfare local office or Citizens Information Centre.

Child Benefit

Child benefit is payable to qualifying children under age 16 or under 18 years if they are physically or mentally handicapped or in full-time education. The current rate is €140 per child monthly, with twins attracting one and a half times that rate.

Maternity Benefit

Self-employed persons including farmers can qualify for maternity benefit if they have 52 PRSI contributions (or one annual contribution) paid in any of the three years preceding the year in which they make a claim. The person making the claim must have paid PRSI themselves.

Rate of Payment
A standard rate of €274 per week applies from January 2024.

Duration of Payment
Maternity Benefit is payable for a continuous period of 26 weeks.

Taxation
Maternity Benefit is subject to income tax but not subject to USC or PRSI.

Invalidity Pension

Invalidity Pension is available to self-employed persons including farmers. It is a weekly payment to people who cannot work because of a long-term illness or disability. To qualify you require 5 years PRSI contributions but voluntary contributions do not qualify (see page 288). The start date of permanent incapacity (as decided by the Department) is usually after you have been incapable of work due to illness for one year At 66, recipients transfer automatically to the State Contributory Pension (Contributory) at the full rate. Recipients are entitled to a Free Travel Pass and may also get extra social welfare benefits such as the Household Benefits Package (see page 227). The pension is taxable.

Rates
The current rates of payment are set out at table 12.2. It should be noted that increased payments for an adult dependant and any child dependants will only apply if your spouse, civil partner or cohabitant has an income of less than €400 a week. You get a half-rate child allowance if your spouse, civil partner or cohabitant earns between €310 and €400 a week.

Table 12.2: Rates of Invalidity Pension (from 1ˢᵗ January 2024).

Personal rate	Increase for adult dependant	Child dependent rate
€237.50	€169.70	Child under 12 - €46
		Child over 12 - €54

Farm Assist

Farm Assist is a weekly means-tested payment for low income farmers. Farmers who have income from another source (such as other self-employment, insurable employment, capital etc.) may still qualify for a payment under Farm Assist.

Eligible Farmers
Farmers between 18 and 66 years who farm land within the state may be eligible. It is not necessary for you to own the land you farm to be eligible however if you rent or lease your land to another person you are not eligible.

Means Test
To qualify for this scheme your means as determined by Social Welfare must be below a certain level. Your means include any income or property (excluding your home) you may have and any other assets that may provide you with an income. On completion

of form Farm 1, a Social Welfare Inspector will visit your home and examine all of your farm income and expenditure documentation. It is important that you have as much documentation as possible available in order to provide the Inspector with adequate information to determine your eligibility. Failure to provide sufficient information, or withholding information, may give the inspector no choice but to turn down your application or at least postpone a decision until such information as he or she deems necessary is available. Applicants are entitled to receive a copy of the farm income calculation.

Calculation of Means

Means can arise from a number of sources and are treated as follows :

Means from Self Employment Including Farming: Your income from farming and any other form of self-employment are added together and the costs involved are deducted. 70% of these means are then added to your means from other sources. A disregard of €254 for each of the first two dependent children and €381 for each subsequent child applies are deducted in arriving at the 70%.

Means from GlAS, ACRES, SAC'S and most other Agri-Environment and Agri-support schemes: Income from these schemes but excluding direct payment schemes (BPS/BISS) is assessed separately from other farm income in that €5,000 is deducted from your annual payment and half of the balance remaining after deduction of expenses incurred in complying with these schemes is taken as means.

Means from Insurable Employment: €20 per day worked is deducted from your (or your spouse's) net weekly earnings, subject to a maximum of €60, and 60% of the remaining earnings is assessed as weekly means.

Seasonal Work: If you have seasonal work you are assessed with your earnings only during the period while you were actually working

Means from Investments and Savings: The actual income from such savings or investments is not taken but rather a notional income is arrived at as follows:
- First €20,000 not counted
- €20,000 to €30,000 is assessed at €1 per €1,000
- €30,000 to €40,000 is assessed at €2 per €1,000
- Over €40,000 is assessed at €4 per €1,000.

Means from Spouse's/Partner's Earnings: Income from insurable or self-employment is the same as that set out above for the principal earner.

Rate of Farm Assist

The maximum personal rate is €232 from January 2024. The additional payment for a dependent spouse/partner is €154 and €46 for a dependent child under age 12 and €54 for a child over age 12. The amount actually paid is the difference between your assessed means and the maximum rate of payment that you could be entitled to.

CASE STUDY

Joe Farmer has assessed means are €70 per week and he is married with a dependent spouse and three dependent children over 12.

Calculation of entitlement

Personal rate	€232.00
Dependent spouse	€154.00
Dependent children x 3	€162.00 (all over age 12)
Sub -total	€548.00
Less:	
Assessed means	€70.00
Farm Assist payable	€786.00

It should be noted that if you qualify for a full allowance for your spouse or partner you will get the full rate child dependent allowance, otherwise you will get half the child dependent allowance.

Taxation & PRSI

Farm Assist being an assistance based payment is not subject to income tax or the Universal Social Charge. However, by being in receipt of Farm Assist, you are not exempt from paying PRSI on your farm profits.

When and How to Apply

You can get a form Farm 1 from your local Social Welfare Office and complete and return same to that office.

Rural Social Scheme

The aim of the scheme is to provide income support for farmers and fishermen in Ireland who are receipt of long-term social welfare payments. In return, those participating in the scheme will provide certain services that benefit rural communities. The Department of Social Protection has overall responsibility for policy in relation to the Rural Social Scheme, including eligibility criteria. The Department monitors the implementation of the scheme and supports the various bodies that manage the scheme locally. At a local level, the Scheme is managed by implementing bodies such as local development companies and in the Gaeltacht areas, by Údarás na Gaeltachta.

Rules

In order to participate in the scheme you must be currently in receipt of Farm Assist or have a herd or flock number, be submitting a Basic Payment application and be a recipient of certain social welfare payments, The scheme provides participants with part-time work for a specified period. That is 19.5 hours per week for an initial 12-month period. These hours are based on a farmer/fisherman-friendly schedule. This is to ensure participation in the scheme does not affect your farming/fishing. At the end of each 12-month period on the scheme you may re-apply to participate again. While it is not intended that anyone would remain on the scheme permanently, there is no definite time limit for participation.

Family Members

Farmers who are eligible but do not wish to participate in the RSS, can have their dependent spouse take the available place. A child/sibling of a herd number owner that can certify that they are resident and/or working on the farm and are getting one of the qualifying social welfare payments may also be eligible to participate in the RSS on the basis of the parent's/sibling's herd number.

Rates of Payment

Payment will be equal to your current (January 2024) rate of benefit payment, presumably Farm Assist, plus a €27.50 top-up giving a minimum weekly payment of €259.50.

Job-Seeker's Benefit

Where a person has been employed, but is now out of work, they may be eligible for Jobseeker's Benefit if they have paid enough PRSI contributions.

Requirements

To qualify you need at least 104 weeks of Class A, H or P PRSI paid contributions or at least 156 Class S PRSI contributions since you first started work, and, 39 weeks of A, H or P PRSI paid or credited in the relevant tax year (a minimum of 13 weeks must be paid contributions).

Job-Seekers - vs – Farm Assist

Where a person is entitled to both Jobseeker's Benefit and Farm Assist, they can choose the more favourable payment. However, it is worth noting that Jobseeker's Benefit is taxable, and Farm Assist is not. If one is receiving Jobseeker's Benefit, they must also be available for and actively seeking work.

Rates of Payment

The rate of payment is determined by the average weekly earnings prior to ceasing work. The maximum rate from 1 January 2024, based on earning of €300 or over, is €232 plus €154 for a qualified adult, €46 for each child under 12 and €54 for each dependent child over 12.

Duration of Payment

Jobseeker's Benefit is paid for 9 months (234 days) for people with 260 or more Class A, H or P PRSI paid contributions. It is paid for 6 months (156 days) for people with fewer than 260 Class A, H or P PRSI paid contributions.

State Health Benefits & Services

Treatment Benefit Scheme

The Treatment Benefit Scheme covers self-employed people who pay Class S PRSI which includes most if not all farmers. The Treatment Benefit Scheme is a scheme run by the Department of Social Protection that provides dental, optical and aural (hearing aids) services to qualified people. The scheme is available to people who have the required number of PRSI contributions. The scheme is available to people who have the required number of PRSI contributions.

Contribution Conditions

Individuals must have paid Class A, E, P, H or S social insurance contributions. The amount of social insurance you need depends the persons age. Any farmer who has been paying PRSI for five years or more will be eligible. Farmer's sons or daughters who have been in employment paying Class A PRSI may also be eligible as will those sons or daughters who are in farm partnerships and who have made the n necessary contributions. The following is a table of the required number of contributions for people in different age categories;

Table 12.3: PRSI Contribution Requirement - Treatment Benefit Scheme.

Age	Minimum required contributions
Under 21 years	39 at any time
21-24	39 in the 2nd last year and 13 in a recent contribution year, or 26 in each of the second and third last contribution years.
25-28	260 (reducing to 39 from June 2022) and 39 in the 2nd last year and 13 in a recent contribution year, or 26 in each of the second and third last contribution years.
29-66	260 and 39 in the 2nd last year and 13 in a recent contribution year, or 26 in each of the second and third last contribution years.
Aged 66+	260 and 39 in any of the two contribution years before reaching age 66 and 13 paid in a recent contribution year

Spouse, Civil Partner or Cohabitant

A spouse, civil partner or cohabitant may, qualify in their own right if they have enough social insurance contributions. However, if they do not have enough social insurance contributions, he/she may still qualify for Treatment Benefit on the spouse's/partner's social insurance record. To qualify, the spouse, civil partner or cohabitant must be dependent on their spouse/partner and be earning less than €100 per week.

Dental Benefit

Under this scheme, the Department pays the full cost of an oral examination once in a calendar year. A payment of €42 towards either a scale and polish or - if clinically necessary - periodontal treatment, is also available once a calendar year. If the cost of either cleaning or periodontal treatment is more than €42, you must pay the balance - capped at €15 for a scale and polish. There is no cap on the balance charged for periodontal treatment. The examination is provided by private dentists who are on the Department of Social Protection's panel which includes most dentists. If the case of a dependent spouse or civil partner, they should apply under the PPS number of the insured person.

Optical Benefit

The Treatment Benefit Scheme entitles eligible applicants to a free eyesight test every second year and a contribution of up to €42 for glasses. However, sight tests for VDUs, driver's licenses etc., are not covered under the scheme. The examination is provided by opticians who have a contract with the Department of Social Protection. Where contact lenses are required on medical grounds on a doctor's recommendation, the Department will pay half the cost up to a maximum of €500. This applies to a small number of eye conditions that make wearing glasses impossible. Disposable lenses are not covered under the scheme. Contact lenses are not available on purely optical or cosmetic grounds.

Hearing Aids

Hearing aids may be provided by suppliers who have a contract with the Department of Social Protection. The Department pays the full cost of a hearing aid up to a maximum of €500 (€1,000 for a pair) once every fourth calendar year. It also pays the full cost of repairs to aids, up to a maximum of €100, once every fourth calendar year..

Applications

Applications for dental services are made by completing a form D1 (form D2 for a dependent spouse, civil partner or cohabitant). Forms are available from the dentist. Applications for optical services are made by completing a form O1 (form O2 for a dependent spouse, civil partner or cohabitant). Forms are available from the optician. Applications for aural services are made by completing a form MA (form MA2 for a dependent spouse, civil partner or cohabitant). Forms are available from the suppliers. Applications are made to the Treatment Benefit Section, Department of Employment Affairs and Social Protection, St. Oliver Plunkett Road, Letterkenny, Co. Donegal.

Drugs Payment Scheme

Under the Drugs Payment Scheme you have to pay a maximum of €80 per month for approved prescribed drugs, medicines and certain appliances for use by yourself and your family. Family expenditure covers the nominated adult, his or her spouse/partner and children under 18 years or under 23 if in full-time education. A dependent with a physical or mental disability/illness living in the household who does not have a medical card and who is unable to fully maintain himself/herself, may be included in the family expenditure regardless of age. This scheme covers the cost of drugs over €80 per month for the entire family.

Medical Cards

Medical cards are available to individuals or families where the health board is satisfied that the income level is below a certain limit. Persons in receipt of a medical card are entitled to the following services free of charge:

- General practitioner services.
- Prescribed drugs and medicines.
- All in-patient services in a public hospital.
- All outpatient public hospital services.
- Dental, ophthalmic and aural services and appliances.
- Maternity and infant care service.

Eligibility

Eligibility is determined by a means test. Your income as determined for tax purposes will be a major determining criterion but the criterion of income alone may not ensure eligibility and the final decision lies with the HSE. It should be noted that savings and investments are considered only insofar as the income they generate with certificates of interest/dividends being required. In other words the notional calculation of income from savings or investments used in assessing eligibility for Farm Assist or other non-contributory benefits does not apply in this case. The following expenses can also serve to reduce your assessable means:

- Childcare costs.
- Reasonable mortgage payments on family home and other land or property.
- Mortgage protection insurance and associated life assurance.
- Home insurance.
- Maintenance payments you make.
- Nursing home, private nursing or home care costs for the applicant or spouse.

In certain cases of serious conditions requiring ongoing expensive treatment, the HSE may grant a card to that individual and not to the entire family, where the income limit is exceeded. Reasonable expenses incurred in respect of childcare costs and rent/mortgage payments will also be allowed. The weekly income limits (gross less tax and PRSI deductions) as set out on table 12.4 are effective as at November 2023.

Table 12.4: Income Limits for Medical Card Eligibility.

Category	Aged Under 66 €/week	Aged 66-69 €/week	Aged 70 or over €/week
Married couple	266.50	298.00	1,050
Single person (living alone)	184.00	201.50	550.00
Single person (living with family)	164.00	173.50	
Allowance for each of 1st. two children under 16	38.00	38.00	
Allowance for 3rd. and subsequent children under 16	41.00	27.00	
Allowance for each of 1st. two children over 16		39.00 39.00	
Allowance for 3rd. and subsequent children over 16	42.50	42.50	
Allowance for other dependants over 16 in full time non grant aided education	78.00	65.00	

Applications

Contact the Community Care section of your local HSE area or down load form from www.oasis.gov.ie/health

GP Visit Cards

Certain people in Ireland who do not qualify for a medical card may apply for a GP (family doctor) Visit Card. GP Visit Cards allow individuals and families who qualify, to visit their family doctor for free. The GP Visit Cards are aimed at those who do not qualify for a medical card on income grounds but for whom the cost of visiting a GP was often prohibitively high. In situations where for example, someone has an ongoing medical condition that requires exceptional and regular medical treatment or visits to the doctor, then the HSE (Health Services Executive) may grant a Card to that individual or family even where their income is greater than the guidelines. Largely the HSE will only consider these applications where an ongoing medical condition is causing or likely to cause undue financial hardship.

Eligible Persons Where no Means Test Applies
The following people are eligible for a GP visit card without a means terse:
- All children under age 8 are eligible.
- People in receipt of Carer's Benefit or Carer's Allowance, at full or half-rate,
- Everyone aged over 70.

Table 12.5: G.P. Visit Card Income Limits.

Category	Aged under 66	Aged 66-69
Single person living alone	€304.00	€333.00
Single person living with family	€271.00	€286.00
Married couple	€441.00	€492.00
Additional allowance for:		
First 2 children aged under 16	€57.00	€57.00
3rd and subsequent children under 16	€61.50	€61.50
First 2 children aged over 16 (with no income)	€58.50	€58.50
3rd and subsequent children over 16 (no income)	€64.00	€64.00
Dependants over 16 years in full-time non-grant aided third-level education	€117.00	€117.00

Means Test
Eligibility for all GP Visit Cards is means tested. That is, your income is assessed by the HSE as part of the application process. Broadly speaking, you will qualify for a GP Visit Card if the combined income of you and your partner (if any) is less than the income guidelines set out below that relate to you or the HSE decide that financial hardship would occur because of your medical costs or other exceptional circumstances even where your combined income is greater than the income guidelines below. The weekly income limits (gross less tax and PRSI deductions) as set out on table 12.5 and are effective as at November 2023.

Acquiring Health Care Abroad

It is possible to acquire healthcare outside of the state where such care is not available here and for which the cost will be refunded by the HSE. There are currently three possible options available as follows:
- The Cross Border Directive.
- The Treatment Abroad Scheme.
- The Northern Ireland Planned Healthcare Scheme.

The Cross-Border Directive

The Cross Border Directive (CBD) allows for EU residents to access health services in EU member states other than their own. The Cross Border Directive allows for Irish residents to avail of healthcare in other EU member states that they would be entitled to within the public health system in Ireland, which is not contrary to Irish legislation. The costs must be borne by the individual and he/she then seeks reimbursement upon return to Ireland. The HSE operates the European Union Cross-Border Healthcare Directive (CBD) for persons entitled to public patient services in Ireland who may seek to avail of those services in another EU member state. If you decide you wish to access the healthcare in question in another EU State then ask your referring clinician to provide you with the appropriate referral letter. The letter should stipulate the healthcare required, the health professional abroad you are being referred to and the clinic/hospital/location where that health professional operates from. The cost of the services you avail of under the CBD in another EU member state will be reimbursed at the cost of the service in the country where you availed of it or the identified cost here in Ireland – whichever is the lesser. Further information can be had by emailing crossborderdirective@hse.ie.

The Treatment Abroad Scheme

If you are a public healthcare patient and require treatment that is not available to you in Ireland, you may be able to apply for the Treatment Abroad Scheme (TAS). This allows you to get the medical treatment in another country in the European Union (EU), the European Economic Area (the EEA also includes Iceland, Liechtenstein and Norway) or in Switzerland. Only a public hospital consultant based in Ireland can refer you for treatment abroad. A GP cannot refer you for this scheme. If you are a private patient, you cannot be referred for the scheme by a private hospital consultant. You should apply to your private health insurance provider to fund the treatment abroad. If your private health insurance provider declines your application and you have been refused on appeal, you can then apply to the Treatment Abroad Scheme. Applications can be made to Treatment Abroad Scheme Office, Health Service Executive, Seville Lodge Callan Road, Kilkenny. Tel: 056 778 4900

The Northern Ireland Planned Healthcare Scheme

You can no longer use the Cross-Border Healthcare Directive to access healthcare in the UK but the Northern Ireland Planned Healthcare Scheme is a temporary scheme that allows you to receive healthcare in Northern Ireland in a similar way to the Cross-Border Healthcare Directive. The healthcare must be publicly available in Ireland. You must pay for the healthcare and then claim the cost from the HSE. The Scheme is available until a permanent statutory scheme is approved.

Benefits & Services for the Elderly

Medical Cards for Persons OVER 70

Eligibility is subject to a gross income limit of €550 per week for a single person and €1.050 per week for a married couple. Where one spouse is aged over 70 years and the other spouse is aged under 70 years, they will both qualify for a medical card if their income is below €1.050 per week. If your spouse or cohabiting partner dies and you are aged over 70, you can keep your medical card for three years, provided that your income is less than €1.050 per week. After the three years, the relevant income limit for a single person applies. All medical cards have an expiry date and are subject to review. In general, medical cards currently issued to people aged 70 and over were issued for a period of 2 years. All persons over 70 are entitled to a GP Visit Card regardless of your income.

Household Benefits Package

This package comprises:

• Electricity Allowance, or;
• Natural Gas Allowance, or;
• Cash Electricity Allowance, or;
• Cash Gas Allowance, and;
• Television license.

The Gas/Electricity allowance amounts to €35 per month.
The package is available to:

- All persons over 70 years of age and is not means tested,
- Persons who are in receipt of carers allowance except in the case of new applicants who are not living with the person for whom they are providing care,
- Persons over 66 years who live alone or with an 'Excepted Person' and are in receipt of the State Contributory or Non-Contributory Pension including a Widow's Pension. Excepted people are a qualified adult (your spouse, civil partner or cohabitant is considered a qualified adult if you are receiving an allowance for him or her with your payment or if he or she earns less than €310, including income from a social welfare payment),
- Persons under 66 in receipt of Disability Allowance or Invalidity Pension.

Mobility Aids Grant Scheme

The Mobility Aids Grant Scheme provides grant aid to cover a basic suite of works to address mobility problems, primarily, but not exclusively, associated with ageing. The effective maximum grant is €6,000, which may cover 100% of the cost.

Means Test

The maximum grant of €6,000 is available to applicants with gross household income (based on all household members) of up to €30,000 per annum.

Type of Work Allowable

The types of works allowable under the scheme can be varied and may include the provision of grab-rails, access ramps, level access showers and stair-lifts.

Applications

Contact the Housing Adaptation Grants Section of your local authority.

Housing Aid for Older Persons Scheme

The Housing Aid for Older Persons Scheme is used to improve the condition of an older person's home. In general, this scheme is aimed at people 66 years of age and above. However, if there is a case of genuine hardship the local authority may give assistance to people under 66 years of age.

Means Test

The Housing Aid for Older Persons Scheme is a means-tested grant. This means that your total household income is assessed to find out if you qualify for the grant and at what level of assistance.

Type of Work Allowable
The type of worked that can be grant aided includes, structural repairs or improvements, re-wiring, repair or replacement of windows and doors, the provision of water, sanitary services and heating, cleaning and painting, radon remediation and any other repair or improvement work considered necessary.

Grants
Where the household income is less than €30,000 the maximum grant can be 95% of expenditure subject to an upper limit of €8,000. Where the household income is greater than €30,000 the grant rate is reduced on a tapering basis. No grant is payable where household income exceeds €60,000.

Applications
Contact the Housing Adaptation Grants Section of your local authority.

Housing Adaptation Grant for People with a Disability
The Housing Adaptation Grant for People with a Disability Scheme is administered by local authorities and provides grant aid to applicants to assist in the carrying out of works that are reasonably necessary for the purposes of rendering a house more suitable for the accommodation needs of a person with a disability. The effective maximum grant in respect of a privately owned house is €30,000, which may cover 95% of the approved cost of works.

Eligible Applicants
A person with a disability who requires adaptation works to render a house more suitable for their accommodation needs or a home-owner on behalf of a person with a disability who is a member of the household. An occupational therapist must confirm that the works are fit for purpose and that they meet the applicant's needs in the most economical way.

Rate of Grant and Means Test
The maximum grant for houses over 12 months old is €30,000 and is available to applicants with gross household incomes of up to €30,000 per annum, tapering to 30% for applicants with gross household incomes of between €30,001 to €60,000. The maximum for houses under 12 months old is €14,500. The applicant must be Local Property Tax compliant.

Type of Work Allowable
The types of works allowable under the scheme can include the provision of access ramps; stair-lifts; downstairs toilet facilities; accessible showers; adaptations to facilitate wheelchair access; extensions; and any other works which are reasonably necessary for the purposes of rendering a house more suitable for the accommodation of a person with a disability.

Applications
Contact the Housing Adaptation Grants Section of your local authority.

Seniors Alert Scheme
The Seniors Alert Scheme provides grant support for the supply of equipment to enable older people without sufficient means to continue to live securely in their homes. The grant assistance is made available through community and voluntary groups registered with the Department of the Environment.

Eligible Applicants
The scheme provides assistance to older people. To be eligible you must be aged 65 or over and have limited means or resources. You must be living alone or with someone who also meets the eligibility criteria. You must be living in the area covered by the community group administering the grant support and be able to benefit from the equipment being supplied. You must also be willing to maintain contact with the community group.

Type of Equipment Supported
Grant support is provided towards the cost of purchasing and installing safety and security equipment. Grants are available for, monitored personal alarms, monitored smoke detectors, monitored carbon monoxide detectors, external security lights and internal emergency lights. Equipment supplied under the scheme remains the property of the community group.

Applications
An application for a grant is made by the registered community group for your area. When a community group identifies an older person in its area as needing assistance, it assesses the person's eligibility for the scheme, completes the application form, identifies the equipment required, obtains quotations from suppliers and also submits the application with supporting documentation to the Department.

The Nursing Homes Support Scheme

Otherwise known as the Fair Deal Scheme, this scheme is a scheme of financial support for people who need long-term nursing home care. Under the Nursing Homes Support Scheme, you will make a contribution towards the cost of your care and the State will pay the balance. This applies whether the nursing home is public, private or voluntary.

Applications

There are three steps to the application process. Step 1 is an application for a Care Needs Assessment. The Care Needs Assessment identifies whether or not you need long-term nursing home care. Step 2 is an application for State Support. This will be used to complete the Financial Assessment which determines your contribution to your care and your corresponding level of financial assistance ("State Support"). Step 3 is an optional step which should be completed if you wish to apply for the Nursing Home Loan (see below).

Care Needs Assessment

The Care Needs Assessment identifies whether or not you need long term nursing home care. Its purpose is to ensure that long-term nursing home care is necessary and is the right choice for you. The assessment will consider whether you can be supported to continue living at home or whether long-term nursing home care is more appropriate.

Financial Assessment

The Financial Assessment looks at your income and assets in order to work out what your contribution to care will be. The HSE will then pay the balance of your cost of care. For example, if the cost of your care was €1,000 and your weekly calculated contribution to care was €300, the HSE will pay the weekly balance of €700. This payment by the HSE is called State Support. The Financial Assessment looks at all of your income and assets (see case study below). In the case of couples, an individual's income will be based on half of the couple's combined income and assets. A couple is defined as (a) a married couple who are living together or (b) a heterosexual or same sex couple who are cohabiting as life partners for at least three years. The assessment will not take into account the income of other relatives such as your children.

Contribution Towards Care

Having looked at your income and assets, the Financial Assessment will work out your contribution towards care. You will contribute 80% of your assessable income and 7.5% of the value of any assets per annum. However, the first €36,000 of your assets, or €72,000 for a couple, will not be counted at all in the financial assessment. Your principal residence will only be included in the financial assessment for the first 3 years of your time in care. This is known as the 22.5% or 'three year' cap. It means that you will pay a 7.5% contribution based on your principal residence for a maximum of three years regardless of the time you spend in nursing home care. In calculating your contribution towards care, you are allowed deduct any tax you pay including property tax along with any medical expenses incurred in the previous year.

CASE STUDY – Financial Assessment

Joe Farmer is 74 years of age and has 70 acres valued at €800,000. His dwelling is valued at €140,000. He has co-op shares to a value of €50,000 and both he and his wife both have State pensions worth €28,120 in total. Joe's wife, Mary, has been suffering from dementia for some time and now needs nursing home care. Their son Pat is farming the land and qualifies as a family successor.

Assessments of Assets

Land	€800,000
Dwelling	€140,000
Shares	€ 50,000
TOTAL ASSETS	€990,000
Les exempted amount	€72,000
Assessable Assets	€918,000
Assessable assets deemed return @7.5%	€68,850

Assessment of pensions and other income

State pensions	€28,120
Dividends on shares	€1,300
Total assessable income @80%	€23,536

Combined assessment of income & assets €92,396

Assessed income for Mary €46,198 (or €888 per week)

Result: Mary is deemed to have means of €888 per week which is what she will be required to pay. If we assume that the nursing home is costing €1,300 per week, the Fair Deal Scheme will contribute the shortfall of €412 per week. After three years have elapsed, the farm and dwelling are no longer assessed, and Mary's care cost will drop from €888 per week to €226 per week.

Three Year Cap for Farm and Businesses

The cap is broadly similar to the dwelling house cap but is far more restrictive and subject to several conditions as follows.
- The applicant must apply to the HSE for the appointment of their family successor. The HSE will review each appointed family successor to make sure that they comply with the conditions of the Scheme. The application can be reviewed at any time during the 6-year period post application and the appointed family successor will need to provide official documents as proof that they are continuing to run the farm or business.

- The successor must be 18 years or older and a relative of the person who needs care or the partner of the person who needs care or a son-in-law or daughter-in-law of the person who needs care or their partner. A relative can include cousins, grandchildren or grandnieces or nephews.
- The family successor must commit to run the farm for at least 6 years beginning from the day they are appointed. The commitment is by way of a signed statutory declaration declaring that a substantial part of the successors normal working time will regularly and consistently be applied to running the family asset for a period of 6 years beginning on the date of the appointment. While it is not entirely clear, it is presumed that persons with off-farm employment are not ruled out.
- A substantial part of the working time of the applicant, their partner or their family successor must have been devoted to running the family farm for at least 3 of the last 5 years immediately prior to the applicant entering care.
- Where the asset is a transferred asset, each owner of the transferred asset must consent to the making of the application for the appointment of the family successor.
- As part of the application, both the applicant and their family successor must complete a further Statutory Declaration confirming that the above conditions will be met.

Farms and businesses that have not been actively worked by the applicant, his/her partner or the proposed family successor cannot be considered for the 3-year cap. If a family successor does not comply with the conditions of the Scheme, this may lead to money being refunded to the HSE. For example, if the successor decided to lease the farm, this would constitute a breach of the conditions and would result in a repayment of benefit already received. Where the family successor can no longer comply with the conditions of the scheme, they must contact their local nursing homes support scheme office as soon as possible. An application for the appointment of a new family successor will be required in order to continue to avail of the 3-year cap on the farm or business assets.

Legal Charge on Land
The applicant must agree to HSE placing a charge in favour of the HSE on the farm. This must be agreed by the applicant, his/her partner and any other owners of the farm or business. A charge is a type of mortgage that will be placed on the property until the successor's commitment period of 6 years has ended. The charge will be removed once all other conditions of the 3-year cap have been met.

People with Reduced Capacity
If a person in/entering care is incapable of making an application, certain people may apply on their behalf. These people include:
- person appointed as a care representative (a person appointed by Circuit Court).
- a committee for Ward of Court (a person appointed by Office of Ward of Courts).
- a holder of a registered enduring power of attorney (chosen to act on behalf of another person). A registered enduring power of attorney needs to be in place before the applicant becomes unable to make decisions.

Clearly the number of people that can sign on the applicant's behalf is very limited which underlines the importance of establishing power of attorney if not in all cases, at least in cases where there is a concern that the person's capacity may be diminished in the future.

Nursing Home Loan Scheme

The Nursing Home Loan is an optional element of the Fair Deal Scheme. Where your assets include land and property in the State, the 7.5% contribution based on such assets may be deferred. This means that you do not have to sell your land or dwelling to find the money to pay the Nursing Home. during your lifetime. Instead, if approved, the HSE will pay the money to the nursing home on your behalf, and it will be collected after your death. This does not mean that the property will necessarily have to be sold after your death as it will be up to the beneficiaries of your will as to how the loan is repaid. Interest is not charged if the loan is repaid within 12 months after the death of the person in care, but the consumer price index is applied to the amount due. Where the loan is not repaid within 12 months, interest will be applied, and the interest will start from the date of death. Loan repayment deferrals may be granted in certain situations. If the property is sold or transferred when a person is still in care, the loan must be repaid within 6 months of the date of sale or transfer. Interest will be charged with effect from 6 months after sale.

Amount of Loan Provided
The level of care cost covered by the loan is determined by the value of security provided. A maximum of 7.5% of the value of the security on an annual basis can be provided to fund the cost of care. The following example sets out how the loan scheme works.

Example
Mary Farmer requires nursing home care. Her assessed means are €1,000 per week and the cost of care is €1,200 per week. She has income comprising land rent and a pension amounting to the equivalent of €500 per week of which she is prepared to contribute €400 towards her care cost. Mary will qualify for €200 support under the Fair Deal Scheme (being the difference between her assessed means and the cost of care) but that along with the €400 she is prepared to contribute herself will leave her short by €600 per week. Mary's only option is the Nursing Home Loan Scheme, and she is happy to provide her house and 20 acres as security which is valued at €500,000. This will entitle her to loan funding of up to €721 per week which well exceeds her current shortfall. If the cost of care increases Mary may have to have her property value updated or if that is not sufficient, she may have to contribute more or provide further security.

Further Information: You can call the HSE info line on 1850 24 1850 for more information or visit www.hse.ie

13
Taxation

Income Tax 237
Taxation of Married Couples & Civil Partners 238
Taxation of Persons Over 65 Years 239
Taxation of Separated and Divorced Persons 239
Personal Tax Credits 2024 240
Personal Tax Reliefs 2024 242

Other Farm Tax Credits & Reliefs
Succession Farm Partnership Credit 245
Averaging Of Farm Profits 245
Stock Relief.. 246
Stock Relief - Points to Note.. 247
Compulsory Disposal of Livestock 247
Carbon Tax Relief on Farm Diesel... 248
Claiming Tax Relief on Motor Expenses 248
Capital Allowances 250

Tax-Free Or Tax Efficient Activities
Leasing Of Farmland 252
Investing in Personal Pensions 253
Employing Family Members 255
Taxation of Horses.. 257
Taxation of Private Forestry... 258
Vacant Homes Tax 259
Residential Zoned Land Tax... 259
Forming a Limited Company.. 259
Taxation of Biss Payment Entitlements.. 262
Taxation of Rental Properties.. 263
Tax Relief Check List   264

Capital Acquisitions Tax
Agricultural Relief... 265
Business Property Relief 269
Family Home Relief... 269
Favourite Nephew Relief..271
Other CAT Reliefs 271

General Points to Note 272

Capital Gains Tax
Entrepreneur Relief 275
Retirement Relief.. 276
Farm Restructuring Relief... 279
Section 604A Relief 280
Some General Points on Capital Gains Tax 282

Stamp Duty
Special Relief for 'Young Trained Farmers'....................................... 284
Stamp Duty Rates 286
Self Employed PRSI.. 286
Benefits from Paying PRSI 287
Income Liable to PRSI 287
Voluntary Contributions 288
Value Added Tax.. 290
Universal Social Charge (USC) 291

Income Tax

Self-employed people pay income tax under the self-assessment system once a year. Self-assessment means that people are responsible for making their own assessment of tax due whether that be by themselves or on their behalf by an accountant or tax consultant. Preliminary Tax (an estimate of tax due for your current trading year) is required to be paid on or before 31 October in that tax year and a tax return for the previous year not later than 31 October. Filing on line will generally extend the deadline by two weeks. Where a person fails to file a tax return on time or at all, they may be subject to a surcharge, interest, fines and penalties.

Interest on Late Payment of Tax

Interest is chargeable at 0.0219% per day or 8% per annum. Interest on refunds of tax amounts to 0.011% per day or 4.0% per annum, Such refunds must be claimed within four years of the year in which the refund arises.

Surcharge on Late Submissions

Where a tax return is submitted less than two months after the return filing date, currently the 31st October (or mid-November in the case of returns filed on line), there is a surcharge of 5% of the tax liability, subject to a maximum surcharge of €12,695. Where a tax return is made two months or more after the return filing date, a higher surcharge of 10% of the tax liability will apply. However, even though the income tax return may be filed on time, this surcharge may also apply where a person has not filed all outstanding Local Property Tax (LPT) returns or has not paid whatever LPT is due.

Farming Losses

Relief for losses incurred may be claimed against other income in three consecutive years or four consecutive year in certain cases. Where there is no other income or where relief is denied because of the three-year rule, such losses can be set off against future profits. Where a profit is earned in any year, losses incurred in subsequent years can be claimed against other income subject to the three-year rule. In certain exceptional cases where ongoing losses are incurred due to farm debt and where the debt can now be serviced only by the farmer or his spouse obtaining an alternative source of income or diverting income from an existing source and where the farming is being carried on a commercial basis, relief may be allowed on the losses in the fourth and subsequent years. Where a sole trader ceases his sole trade to enter a partnership, prior sole trade losses cannot be offset against partnership profits.

Taxation of Married Couples & Civil Partners

Where both parties are earning, it is important that best use is made of tax credits and tax bands but there may be certain situations where couples may wish to be treated partially separate or entirely separate for tax purposes. The following options are available:

- Joint Assessment/Aggregation.
- Separate Assessment.
- Assessment as a Single Person (Separate Treatment).

Joint Assessment

Joint Assessment (also known as aggregation) is usually the most favourable basis of assessment for a married couple. It is automatically given by your Regional Revenue Office once you have advised them of your marriage, but this doesn't prevent you from electing for either of the other options. Under Joint Assessment, the tax credits and standard rate cut-off point (in respect of PAYE earnings) can be allocated between partners to suit their circumstances. For example, if only one partner has taxable income, all tax credits and the standard rate cut-off point will be given to him or her, however if both partners have taxable income, they can decide which partner is to be the assessable partner and request their Revenue Office to allocate the tax credits and standard rate cut-off point between them in whatever way they wish.

Separate Assessment

Under Separate Assessment your tax affairs are independent of those of your partner. The main tax credits are divided between each partner and the balance of the tax credits are given to each partner in proportion to the cost borne by them. The Employee tax credit and employment expenses, if any, are allocated to the appropriate partner. Any other tax credits which are unused by one partner may be claimed by the other partner. The tax credits may not generally be adjusted until after the end of the tax year. Any unused tax credits (other than the PAYE tax credit and employment expenses) and standard rate tax band can be transferred to the other partner, but only at the end of the tax year. The increased standard rate tax band for working partners is not transferable between partners.

Single Assessment

Assessment as a Single Person, (also referred to as Separate Treatment) should not be confused with Separate Assessment. Under assessment as a Single Person each spouse is treated as a single person for tax purposes and both partners are taxed on their own income as unrelated persons. This method of assessment is uncommon but may be suited in certain instances where there is an informal separation arrangement in place.

Taxation of Persons Over 65 Years

Taxpayers of 65 years or over are entitled so an additional tax credit of €245 for a single or widowed person and €490 for a married/civil partners couple, if either is over 65. This means that from January 1st, 2024, single persons over 65 who are entitled to claim the Employee/Earned Income Credit can earn up to €19,975 free of tax. Married couples can earn up to €39,950 free of tax.

Tip: In a family farm situation it may be possible for the son/daughter to pay the parent(s) a wage to use up their tax-free threshold where the parent has some active involvement on the farm. Such payments could satisfy a maintenance contribution or some other obligation that was agreed under the transfer terms. For example, if both parents were in receipt of State pensions amounting to €29,394 they could receive a further €10,556 without paying tax.

Deposit Interest Retention Tax

Deposit Interest Retention Tax (DIRT) is deducted at a rate of 33% from the interest payable on savings in banks, building societies, etc. DIRT is deducted whether or not you would normally be liable for tax. If you are aged 65 or over or your spouse or civil partner is aged 65 or over or if you are permanently incapacitated, you may not be liable for DIRT if you are exempt from income tax. You can notify your financial institution so that they can pay your interest without deducting DIRT. Where DIRT exceeds €300 in any year, the financial institution is required to return details of that account to Revenue. DIRT is not liable to Universal Social Charge but is liable to PRSI for persons under 66 years.

Persons in Receipt of Qualified Adult Allowance

Persons in receipt of the Contributory State Pension are entitled to the employee tax credit, currently amounting to €1,875 from January 1st 2024. However, where the person's spouse is in receipt of the Qualified Adult Allowance, even though that allowance may be payable directly to the dependent spouse, she/he is not entitled to claim the employee tax credit, nor is she/he entitled to avail of the extended lower tax band in respect of this income.

Taxation of Separated and Divorced Persons

The manner in which such persons are taxed will depend on the nature of their separation.

Living Apart: Where the separation is genuine and likely to be permanent and there are no legally enforceable maintenance payments, then the couple are assessed on a Single Assessment basis. i.e., as if they were two totally unrelated individuals. Any maintenance payments made are disregarded. Maintenance payments in respect of the children are neither taxable or tax allowable.

Legal & Judicial Separations: If there is no legally enforceable maintenance agreement in place the individuals are assessed to tax on a Single Assessment basis. Any maintenance payments passing between the spouses are not taxable or tax allowable. If there are legally enforceable maintenance payments passing between the couple who are both resident in the state and they opt for Single Assessment, the payments are allowable against tax for the paying spouse and taxable for the spouse receiving the payments. However, maintenance payments in respect of the children are neither taxable or tax allowable. It should be noted that in cases of single assessment where there are dependent children and where custody is shared even to a very limited degree both spouses in such circumstances will be granted the single parent tax allowance.
If the couple are resident in the country they may opt for Separate Assessment whereby the payments are ignored for tax purposes.

Divorced Couples: The same provisions apply as for separated couples but if either party remarries the option of Separate Assessment no longer applies.

Personal Tax Credits 2024

Personal tax credits reduce the amount of tax that would otherwise be payable. Table 10.1 sets out the value of tax credits available in 2024 and the amount of tax free income that these credits represent at the 20% tax rate.

Home Carers' Credit
A credit of €1,800 is available to married persons who are jointly assessed and where one spouse works at home to care for children, the aged or incapacitated persons. The Carers income cannot exceed €7,200 to avail of the full credit but a reduced rate applies if the income is less than €10,600. The tax credit is not available to Married Couples or Civil Partners who are taxed as single persons.

One Parent Family Credit
The main tax credit which a separated or divorced person may be entitled to is the Single Person Child Carer Credit of €1,750 but only one parent is entitled to the credit. The child must be under 16 or in full time education.

Table 13.1: Tax Credits 2024.

Personal Tax Credits	2024	
	Credit €	Tax Free €
Single person	1,875	9,375
Married couple/Reg. Civil Partnership/	3,750	18,750
Widowed person	2,415	12,075
Single person child carer	1,750	8,750
Widowed person with dependent child (additional)		
Bereaved in 2023	3,600	18,000
Bereaved in 2022	3,150	15,650
Bereaved in 2021	2,700	13,500
Bereaved in 2020	2,250	11,250
Bereaved in 2019	1,800	9,000
Child credit- Incapacitated	3,500	17,500
Dependent relative credit	245	1,225
Blind person	1,650	8,250
Both spouses blind	3,300	16,500
Age Credit- Single / widowed	245	1,225
- Married couple	490	2,450
Home carer	1,800	9,000
Employee Credit	1,875	9,375
Earned Income Credit	1,875	9,375
Farm Partnership Credit	5,000	25,000

Earned Income Credit

This credit of €1,875 is available to taxpayers earning self-employed trading or professional income, such as farmers. It will not be available to persons in receipt of the Employee Tax Credit.

Employee Tax Credit - Family Members

Family members who are full time employed on the farm are entitled to the Employee Tax Credit provided they earn a sufficient farm wage to incur a tax liability. This tax credit is currently €1,875 which means that when added to the single person's tax credit, an unmarried employee with no other earnings can earn up to €16,500 before incurring any tax.

Personal Tax Reliefs 2024

Tax reliefs differ from tax credits in that tax credits are a deduction from you tax bill whereas tax reliefs are a deduction from your income and can save tax at the lower rate or marginal rate depending on the particular relief.

Third Level Education Fees

Tax relief at the standard rate, subject to certain restrictions, is granted in respect of fees paid to a college or Institute of Higher Education within the state or to publicly funded or duly accredited universities or similar third level colleges in the EU or outside the EU. Undergraduate courses must be of at least 2 academic years duration, and in the case of courses carried out in colleges and institutions that require approval by the Department of Education and Science, the course must be approved by that Department.

Postgraduate courses must be carried out in an approved college and be of at least 1 academic year but no more than 4 academic years in duration, and lead to a postgraduate award based on either a thesis or an examination. The person taking the course must already have a primary degree or equivalent qualification.

The maximum limit on qualifying fees is €7,000 per person per course. Relief is not available in respect of:

- any part of the tuition fees that is or will be met directly or indirectly by grants, scholarships, by an employer or otherwise.
- administration, registration, or examination fees.
- Student's Centre levy or Sports Centre charges.

Tax relief at 20% is allowable in respect of tuition fees including the Student Contribution (for the second and subsequent students), but not examination fees, registration fees or administration fees, however the tax relief only applies where expenditure exceeds €3,000 for full time students which is equivalent to the Student Contribution.

Fees Paid for Training Courses

Relief for fees is available to individuals who partake in approved courses of less than two years duration in the areas of information technology and foreign languages subject to the conditions that the course will result in the awarding of a certificate of competence. Relief at the standard rate is available for fees in excess of €315 to a maximum of €1,270.

Rent a Room Relief

Rent a room relief entitles homeowners to up to €14,000 rent free of tax USC and PRSI when they rent a room as residential accommodation in their principal primary residence. No deductions are allowed and if the gross rent exceeds €14,000 no relief is available. This relief is not available in respect of a son or daughter and is not available in respect of short-term letting of less than 29 days. Relief will apply to shorter term residential accommodation which is not leisure or business such as lettings for respite care for incapacitated individuals, accommodation for full or part time students, including language students and four-day-a-week 'digs'. The room must be located in your main residence which is your home for most of the year and where friends would expect to find you. You do not have to own the property to claim relief. The rented room or rooms can be a self-contained unit within the house, such as a basement flat or a converted garage. If the unit is not attached to the property it cannot qualify for the relief.

Medical Expenses
Tax relief is available on non–recoverable medical expenses incurred by the tax payer, his spouse and children. Certain items are not allowed such as ophthalmic or routine dental treatment. This relief is confined to the 20% rate.

Health Expenses: Dependent Relative
Medical expenses incurred by an individual in respect of a dependent relative can be claimed against tax at the 20% rate provided such expenses cannot be recouped. Where a dependent relative is being maintained at a nursing home or hospital, tax relief at your marginal rate can be claimed but the allowable amount is reduced by 50% of the dependant's old age pension.

Nursing Home Charges
Nursing home charges are allowable against tax at the marginal rate whether they relate to yourself or another person.

Child Minding Income Relief
Earnings from child minding up to €15,000 per annum are tax free. However, if the earnings exceed €15,000 the entire amount earned is subject to tax. The childminding must be done in the carer's home and a maximum of three children can be minded. In order to qualify for the relief, you must notify the HSE that are providing childcare services and also claim the relief on your annual self-employed tax return which means you have to make a tax return even if this is your only source of income.

Permanent Health Insurance Premiums
Payments made to a health insurance scheme which provides regular income in the event of sickness or disability are fully allowable against tax. The premiums being paid must not exceed 10% of current income.

Deeds of Covenant
A possible means of a family member supporting a parent in a tax efficient manner is to covenant money, particularly if you are a higher rate taxpayer. The person to whom you covenant must be 65 or over or be permanently incapacitated. If the conditions are met, you can claim tax relief on an amount up to 5% of your taxable income; however, there is no limit if the person is permanently incapacitated.

Covenants are most effective if the recipient does not have a taxable income. The amount you covenant may be taxable in the hands of the recipient. It is important to note that money covenanted to people receiving a non-contributory pension or means-tested allowance may affect their entitlement to the allowance in question. As a general rule, tax relief on covenants to children is not allowable. The types of covenant payments that are allowed are as follows:

- Payments to permanently incapacitated adults.
- Payments to permanently incapacitated nieces, nephews or other unrelated children.
- Payments to elderly individuals who are not incapacitated. The amount allowable is restricted to 5% of the income of the person making the payments.
- Payments which are part of a maintenance agreement between separated spouses.

Employing a Carer

If you employ a carer for yourself or on behalf of a family member, you can claim the tax relief on the cost of that care. A family member is a spouse, civil partner, child or a relative, including a relation by marriage or civil partnership. The cared for person must be totally incapacitated for the complete tax year (January to December) in which you are claiming the tax relief, but the carer does not have to be employed for the full tax year. The term totally incapacitated means the person is disabled and requires a carer. Relief is also available on the cost of care service providers or agencies, such as, charitable or voluntary organisations or commercial organisations that provide home care services. The maximum allowance is €75,000 for employing a carer and is allowable at your marginal rate of tax.

Tax Allowable Life Assurance

Tax relief on life assurance premiums is available on certain policies. Such policies that can be stand-alone policies or be included in a personal pension contract. Payments to these policies are allowable against income tax up to 5% of relevant income. However, where tax relief is also being claimed for personal pension payments the overall limit which applies to pension premiums also covers the combined payments. Certain restrictions apply to these policies:

- The policy is straightforward life cover and cannot include any savings.
- Cover must be taken on a single life basis only.
- The term must end between age 60 and 70.
- This type of policy is non assignable i.e. it cannot be assigned to a bank as security against borrowings.

Where a high-rate tax paying farmer is contributing say €1,000 per annum towards straight life cover on a 25 year policy he would save €10,000 in tax over the lifetime of the policy.

Mortgage Interest Tax Relief

Mortgage Interest Tax Relief is available for 2024 for homeowners who had an outstanding mortgage balance of between €80,000 and €500,000 on their primary home on 31 December 2022. The Mortgage Interest Tax Relief will be available on the increased interest you paid on your mortgage in 2023 when compared with the amount you paid in 2022. The tax relief on the increase will be 20%, which is the standard income tax rate. The relief will be capped at €1,250.

Other Farm Tax Credits & Reliefs

Succession Farm Partnership Credit

There is an incentive in registering a Succession Farm Partnership by way of an annual income tax credit of €5,000 for up to five years. The credit is split annually based on the profit-sharing ratio of the partnership between the Farmer and the Successor. For example, if a father and son had a 50:50 partnership they would each save themselves €2,500 in tax, providing the partnership earned sufficient profits to utilise the credit. The maximum credit available is limited to the lower of,

(i) €5,000 per year of assessment divided between the partners in accordance with their profit-sharing ratio under their partnership agreement, or

(ii) the tax arising on the assessable partnership profit shares (after deducting capital allowances).

What this means in effect is that if the partnership makes no profit there will be no credit available to set off against other income that the partners might be in receipt of. It is important that the partnership is structured in a way that will make best use of the tax credit. Potentially, the scheme is worth up to €25,000 over a five-year period. The credit will not be available to either partner from the tax year that the successor reaches his/her 40th birthday.

Averaging of Farm Profits

A concession is available whereby a farmer can opt to be taxed on an average of five years' profits, the current year and two/four previous years. This means that an unusually high profit in a particular year could be reduced by adding it to the profit of the four previous years and taking an average of the five years. The problem with the system is that once you opt onto it, it is not easy to opt out again. A farmer is obliged to remain in the system for a minimum of five years and thereafter opting out may result in the benefit that was gained in the four years prior to the last year of averaging being clawed back.

Temporary Step-Out Concession

Farmers may avail of an option to step-out of the income averaging regime for a single year. This allows farmers to pay tax based on the actual profits of the particular year as opposed to the average amount that would normally be due. The resulting deferred tax will be payable in instalments over the following 4 years. An individual shall only be entitled to make an election to opt out of averaging once every 5 years. Any outstanding deferred tax becomes due and payable immediately if a farmer elects or is deemed to have elected to opt out of averaging permanently.

Ceasing Averaging

Where it is decided to cease averaging, the final year of averaging is unaffected but the four previous years are reviewed and if the averaged profit in any or all of those years is lower than the averaged profit of the final year, the assessable profit in each of those years is increased by the difference.

Ceasing Averaging to Incorporate

Where a farmer on income averaging forms a limited company he is deemed to have ceased farming as a sole trader. When this happens, the cessation of averaging rules do not apply, but rather the cessation of business rules apply. This means that the final year or part year is assessed on the actual profit earned and the second last year is assessed the higher of the actual profit earned or the averaged profit. All previous years remain unaffected.

Income Averaging - Points To Note

- Averaging to rise should only be considered when profits are rising and likely to continue to rise in the years subsequent to opting in to the system.
- Where profits are falling, averaging will result in a profit that is higher than the income for the current year. In a year of small profits this may have serious cashflow implications as the resources may not be present to pay a tax bill which is in effect the result of a postponement of an earlier tax liability.
- Farmers can only opt into averaging in a situation where taxable profits (before capital allowances) were recorded in each of the previous four years.
- If a taxable loss was recorded in one or more of the four years prior to the year you intend to commence averaging, it is not possible to enter averaging. However, when on averaging it is possible to include years in which losses were incurred.
- As stock relief is treated as if it were a trading expense so profits for averaging purposes are the profits after deduction of stock relief.
- A farmer may opt out of averaging only if he has been on averaging for the five years prior to the year he wants to opt out. No revision will be made to the last year of averaging but the four years prior to the last year are reviewed and if the existing assessment for either year is less than the amount of the assessment for the last averaged year, an additional assessment is made for the difference.
- Where a farmer ceased as a sole trader or partnership to form a Limited Company, he must cease income averaging but normal cessation of business rules apply (not cessation of averaging rules).

Stock Relief

There are currently three systems of stock relief in place.

General Relief

A deduction of 25% of the increase in value in trading stock is allowed against profits in the accounting year. There is no clawback provision and when he comes to dispose of his stock he will be taxed only on the amount by which the sale proceeds exceed the actual value that had been placed on those stock for tax purposes. This scheme runs until the 31st December 2024.

Relief for Young Qualifying Farmers

A system of stock relief claimable at 100% (with no claw-back) for young qualifying farmers under 35 years of age is available for four years from commencement. The scheme runs until 31 December 2024. The cash equivalent amount of stock relief at the 100% rate which a young-trained farmer can receive is limited to €40,000 in a single year and €100,000 in aggregate over the four years of the scheme. This overall limit also includes the cash equivalent of tax relief granted from the Succession Partnership Scheme and Stamp Duty Relief for Young Trained Farmers. The cash equivalent is the amount of tax that was saved by availing of the reliefs.

Qualifying young farmers must meet the following conditions:
- From the year in which the qualifying young farmer first becomes chargeable to tax in respect of income from farming is under 35 at the start of that tax year and at any time in that tax year satisfies the required academic and training standards.
- Submits a business plan to Teagasc unless a business plan has otherwise been submitted to Teagasc or the Department of Agriculture for any other purpose.

Relief for Registered Farm Partnerships

A system of stock relief for registered partnerships, claimable at 50% is available until the 31st. December 2024. There is a rolling three-year limit of €20,000 in aggregate on the cash equivalent of the amount claimed.

Stock Relief - Points to Note

- Stock relief cannot be claimed to create or increase a loss.
- Where stock relief is claimed, it is not permitted to carry forward prior year losses or excess capital allowances against future profits.
- Stock Relief is not available in the year in which a farmer ceases to farm.

Compulsory Disposal of Livestock

A relief for farmers is available in respect of profits resulting from total herd depopulation due to statutory disease eradication measures. There are two separate reliefs as follows:
- The farmer may elect to have the excess, i.e., the difference between the amount of compensation received and the opening stock value in that accounting year, excluded from the computation in the year in which it arises and to have it taxed in four equal instalments in each of the four succeeding accounting periods. Or he may elect, if it suits him, to have the excess taxed in four equal instalments in the year in which it arises and the three immediately succeeding accounting periods.

- Where the receipts from the compulsory disposal of livestock are reinvested in livestock, the farmer may elect to claim stock relief at 100% during the four-year deferral period. However, where he does not invest the full amount received the stock relief will be reduced proportionately.

Carbon Tax Relief on Farm Diesel

Carbon tax on farm diesel refers to the carbon component of Mineral Oil Tax for farm diesel. Tax relief is granted on the difference between the rate that obtained when the relief was first introduced which was €41.50 per 1,000 litres and the current rate which is €131.47 per 1,000 litres.

Example

In 2023 a farmer purchased 3,000 litres of agricultural diesel. The diesel cost €3,900 and this included carbon tax of €394.41 (based on the rate applicable from the 1st of May 2023 of €131.47per 1,000 litres). In accordance with the terms of the relief, the farmer is entitled to an additional allowance of €270.51, which is the difference between the carbon tax included in the cost of the 3,000 litres of farm diesel (i.e., €394.41) and the carbon tax that would have been included in the cost if the rate had remained at €41.30 per 1,000 litres (i.e., €123.90). So, in addition to the relief on the purchase price the farmer will get relief on the carbon tax giving him total relief on €4,170. The value of the additional relief to this farmer is approximately €141 by way of savings in income tax, PRSI and USC assuming he is paying tax at the high rate, or €77 for a farmer on the 20% rate band.

Claiming Tax Relief on Motor Expenses

The manner in which you can claim tax relief on motor expenses will depend on a number of factors such as:
- Whether you are a sole trader or partner.
- Whether you are a company director or an employee.
- The extent to which you use the vehicle for the business.
- Whether the business or the individual purchases the vehicle which can apply in the case of limited companies.
- Whether the vehicle is classed as a commercial vehicle.

Sole Traders and Partners

Sole traders and equity partners (non-employee) can only claim motor expenses based on actual expenses incurred rather than on a rate per mile or kilometre travelled. This means retaining invoices for all expenses incurred such as fuel, repairs, tax and insurance. Revenue will accept that it may not always be feasible to retain all dockets for fuel purchased but any claim made will have to be consistent with expected norms.

deally fuel should be purchased by way of credit or debit card whereby evidence of payment is readily available.

Company Directors and Employees

A farmer trading his farming enterprise as a limited company will be allowed claim motor expenses on the basis of a rate per kilometre travelled on behalf of the business assuming that the vehicle is owned by him personally and not by the company. The rate is usually linked to the Civil Service mileage rate as set out on table 13.2. It should be noted that where mileage is claimed the farmer must bear the full cost of running and maintaining the vehicle himself. The company cannot pay mileage and also bear the associated costs. Employee's motor expenses are also dealt with in a similar manner.

Table 13.2: Revenue Approved Mileage Rates.

Distance Band	Engine up to 1,200cc	Engine 1,201 - 1,500 cc	Engine 1,501cc upwards
Up to 1.500km (Band 1)	41.80	43.40	51.82
1,501km to 5,500km (Band 2)	72.64	79.18	90.63
5,501km to 25,000km (Band 3)	31.78	31.79	39.22
25,001 upwards (Band 4)	20.56	23.85	25.87

Use for Business Purposes

The extent to which you use the vehicle for business purposes will determine the proportion of total expense incurred that is allowable. Typically, a one-car farming family might be allowed up to three quarters of the total expense incurred but this may also depend on whether either spouse is using it for accessing or servicing off farm employment in which case the proportion allowed may be reduced. Where there is a commercial vehicle such as a jeep or crew cab available, the allowable expenses incurred on the family car may be further restricted. In summary, the proportion of allowable motor expenses will be determined by the number of vehicles present and to what extent the vehicles are used for the farm business. Once the claim being made is reasonable and makes sense Revenue will not object.

Company Owned Vehicles

Farmers trading as companies will frequently consider the option of having the company purchase a vehicle whether that be a commercial or a non-commercial vehicle. This option is best suited to commercial vehicles that are used exclusively for the farm business as all cost is incurred by the company with no impact on the individual's personal tax position. However, purchasing a typical family car, a passenger jeep or a crew cab through the company may not be very tax efficient as the individual can be hit with a tax adjustment known as Benefit in Kind (BIK). For a farmer doing less than 26,000 business kilometres per annum this will typically amount to 30% of the new list price of the vehicle even if the vehicle was purchased second hand. So, a company car with a new list price of €30,000 will result in €9,000 being added to

your annual taxable income. Partial relief will apply in respect of cars made available between 1 January 2023 and 31 December 2025. This relief applies by reducing the Open Market Value (OMV) of the vehicle as follows.
- €45,000 for cars acquired in 2023.
- €20,000 for cars acquired in 2024.
- €10,000 for cars acquired in 2025.

Where the relief reduces the OMV to nil, a BIK charge will not arise. Any OMV in excess of the reduction is liable to BIK in the usual manner.

Commercial Vehicles

Commercial vehicles for use exclusively in the business such as jeeps, vans and crew cabs benefit from similar treatment in terms of lower VRT and being VAT refundable. For a vehicle to be regarded as being used exclusively for the business it presumes that there is also a vehicle available for private use. All running costs for such vehicles are fully tax deductible unless there is an element of private use, in which case a proportionate adjustment must be made. Benefit in Kind (BIK) may also apply in the case of company owned vehicles where there is some element of private use unless such vehicles qualify for an exemption because they are pooled vehicles that are available to more than one employee and are not generally used by only one employee. In addition, any private use must be incidental to the business use and the vehicle must not normally be kept overnight at the home of any of the employees or directors. Where the vehicle does not qualify as a pooled vehicle, a BIK rate of 5% applies to vans and commercial jeeps but crew cabs are subject to the higher motor vehicle rate which in the vast majority of cases is 30% of the new list price.

Capital Allowances

Purchasing machinery and erecting farm buildings is not allowed as deductible expenses in the normal way but is allowable over a number of years and the amount that is allowed is called, 'Farm Buildings Allowance' or in the case of plant and machinery or motor vehicles a 'Wear and Tear Allowance'.

Plant & Machinery Allowance

All Plant & Machinery is written off over 8 years at 12.5% per year. Where a machine is sold or traded in for a sale figure that exceeds the tax written down value, a balancing charge amounting to the excess arises providing the proceeds exceed €2,000. The amount of the balancing charge can be rolled over against the cost of a replacement machine purchased in that year but where no replacement is purchased the balancing charge is subject to income tax. Where the disposal resulted in a lesser figure than the tax written down value, a balancing allowance arises. The amount of the balancing allowance can be offset against farm profits.

Farm Buildings

Farm Buildings and land improvement can be written off over 7 years at a rate of 15% for the first 6 years and 10% in the 7th year.

Slurry Storage Facilities

From 1 January 2023 until the 31st December 2025 the capital cost incurred in constructing slurry storage facilities can be written off over two years.

Motor Vehicles

Capital allowances on motor vehicles first registered prior to 1 July 2008 amount to 12.5% of the cost each year for eight years but subject to a maximum purchase price of €24,000. Capital allowances on motor vehicles first registered on or after 1 July 2008 depend on the emissions category. Categories A, B & C are allowed at 12.5% of the cost but subject to a maximum cost of €24,000 regardless of whether the vehicle cost more. Categories D & E are restricted to 12.5% of 50% of the cost of the car subject to a maximum expenditure of €24,000. Categories F & G will not be entitled to any capital allowances.

Capital allowances at 100% are available on cars coming under the category "Electric and Alternative Fuel Vehicles". The accelerated allowance is based on the lower of the actual cost of the vehicle or €24,000.

Accelerated Capital Allowances Scheme

The Accelerated Capital Allowance is a tax incentive which aims to encourage companies and sole traders to invest in energy saving technology and runs until 31 December 2025. The scheme allows participants to write off 100% of the purchase value of qualifying energy efficient equipment against their profit in the year of purchase. Claiming the relief is similar to that which applies for the standard Capital Allowances. The following categories of equipment which may be relevant to farm businesses will qualify where they meet the specified energy criteria and are designed to achieve high levels of energy efficiency:

Heating and electricity provision equipment and systems. This includes wind turbines and solar panels.
Electric motors and drives
Lighting equipment and systems.
Building energy management systems.
Information and Communications Technology (ICT) equipment and systems.
Process and heating, ventilation and air-conditioning (HVAC) equipment and systems.
Electric and alternative fuel vehicles and equipment.
Refrigerating and cooling equipment and systems.
Electro-mechanical equipment and systems.

Tax-Free or Tax Efficient Activities

Leasing of Farmland

Where a person, of any age, leases his/her land for a period of 5 years or more, some or all of that income including rent from Basic Payment entitlements may be exempt from income tax but not PRSI or USC. For qualifying leases which were made on or after 1 January 2015 the exempted amounts are set out at table 13.5.

Table 13.3: Land Lease Income Exempted Amounts.

Lease Duration	Exempted Income
5 years or more but less than seven years	€18,000
7 years or more but less than 10 years	€22,500
10 years or more but less than 15 years	€30,000
Fifteen years or more	€40,000

A qualifying lease must be in writing or evidenced in writing which:
- Contains the names and addresses of the lessor(s) and lessee(s), specifies the acreage, address, location etc. of the land which is the subject of the lease and sets out the terms of the lease and is signed by all parties.
- Is for a definite term of five years or more and is expressly set out. This means that opt-out or revocation clauses are not permissible.

A qualifying lessee cannot be:
- The lessor's immediate family (e.g. grandparents, parents, brothers, sisters, children, grandchildren, etc.).
- The spouse of the lessor or the immediate family of the spouse.
- A person with whom the lessor is in partnership or the spouse of that person or the immediate family of that person or of the spouse of that person.
- A company which the lessor, or the lessor and persons connected with him, controls, and;
- A person who is the settlor of a settlement of which the lessee is a trustee and the land is let in the course of the lessor's capacity as a trustee.

Points of Note:
- Nieces or nephews qualify as eligible lessees.
- Where lands are jointly held, e.g., husband and wife, both parties can claim the exempted amount.
- Where a person inherits a farm that is currently leased, the rent continues to attract it's tax exempt status.
- A lease must be for a definite term of at least 5 years. Accordingly, it cannot include

a break clause or early termination provision.

- There is no clawback of relief provisions related to early termination of a lease but general anti-tax avoidance provisions may apply.
- From the 1st January 2024, purchased land must be owned for 7 years before it qualifies for this relief.

Tip: Where the leased lands are in joint names, both spouses are eligible for up to €40,000 in exempt income each, including rent from payment entitlements.

Investing in Personal Pensions

Contributions towards Personal Pension Schemes are fully tax allowable subject to certain limits (see Table 13.4 below). More importantly, single premium contributions can be made right up to the filing date for your annual tax return which means that you have at least 10 months in which to determine how much you could or should pay to minimise your tax liability.

Personal Pension Contributions Relief
Payments to approved personal pension schemes for persons with non-pensionable incomes, subject to certain limits (see table 13.4) are allowable against tax at the marginal rate. The income ceiling for tax relief on pension contributions is €115,000. In other words, you are only allowed claim relief on income up to €115,000.

Table 13.4: Personal Pension Allowable Limits.

Age	% of Income
Under 30 years	15%
30 - 40 years	20%
40 - 50 years	25%
50 - 55 years	30%
55 - 60 years	35%
60 years and over	40%

For those fortunate enough to have a pension fund of €800,000 or more, the maximum tax-free lump sum is €200,000. Above that amount any excess up to €300,000 is subject to income tax at 20%. Above that amount, tax is charged at the taxpayer's marginal rate.

Pension Options
When your pension matures, it depends on which option you take with your fund as to how and when you will be taxed. It is assumed that the option to take a 25% tax free lump sum will be exercised in all cases in which case the options for the remaining fund are as follows:

- Invest the balance of the fund in an Approved Retirement Fund (ARF). You can draw money at any time from this fund subject to normal income tax treatment, The remaining fund does not die with you and be passed on to whomsoever you wish.
- Take an annuity (pension) for life. This will typically amount to an annual pension of between 2% and 4% of the value of your fund, depending on your age and will be subject to normal taxation treatment. If this option is exercised, unfortunately the remaining fund dies with you.

imputed Distribution
An imputed distribution is where tax is levied each year on a certain percentage of your ARF fund as if it had been drawn down. Where the ARF owner reaches 61 years of age or over during the tax year an imputed distribution is calculated as a percentage (currently 4%) of the market value of assets in the ARF on 31 December each year. The imputed distribution rises to 5% where the ARF owner reaches 71 years of age. Actual distributions made during the year normally may be deducted from the "imputed distribution" to arrive at a "net" imputed distribution (if any) . If you opt for an ARF, table 10.4 sets out a summary of the position in relation to income tax and capital taxes:

Table 13.5: Taxation Treatment of ARF's and AMRF's.

ARF owned by/ inherited by	Income tax & USC due	Capital Acquisitions Tax ('CAT') due
Self	All withdrawals liable to Income Tax & USC	None
Surviving spouse	None where transferred into an ARF of the surviving spouse.	None
Child aged 21+ at date of your death	Income tax at 30%.	None
Child aged less than 21 at date of your death	None	Normal inheritance tax rules will apply.
Non-blood relative (anyone else not being your surviving spouse or children)	This will be treated as a distribution by the deceased in his/ her year of death.	Normal inheritance tax rules will apply.

Transferring Funds
It is possible to transfer funds accumulated with one provider to another during the lifetime of the pension fund, however there may be costs involved in doing this. At maturity one may shop around to ascertain what company will pay the best annuity or provide the best terms for an ARF or AMRF.

Employing Family Members

Registering family members who help out, or indeed work full time on the farm, can be very beneficial from a tax point of view and generally will not incur a liability to PRSI for either the employer or employee. Most employees are liable to pay PRSI but exceptions to this general rule apply in the case of certain family employment. A family employment describes a situation in which a farmer either employs, or is assisted in the running of the business, by a spouse or by other family member(s). However, if the business does not operate on a sole trader basis, for example if it is a Limited Company or a Partnership - it is not family employment. The following categories of family employment are not liable to PRSI:

- If you are employed as an employee by a prescribed relative i.e. a parent, grandparent, stepparent, son, daughter, grandson, granddaughter, stepson, stepdaughter, brother, sister, half-brother, or half-sister and the family employment relates to a private dwelling house or a farm in or on which both you and the employer reside.
- If you assist or participate in the running of the family business but not as an employee. For example, a son/daughter who is attending full-time education who participates in the business (e.g. farm) after school hours or a spouse who carries out book-keeping work for the business, but is not an employee.

It should be noted that where annual earnings exceed €13,000, the Universal Social Charge will apply to all income earned by the employee. Under labour law, a young person between 14 and 15 years may be employed for light work provided it does not interfere with their schooling. Children aged 15 may do 8 hours a week light work in school term time. The maximum working week for children outside school term time is 35 hours. The maximum working week for young people aged 16 and 17 is 40 hours with a maximum of 8 hours a day.

Tip: Wages to children which are claimed against tax must be seen to be paid. However, it is perfectly in order for that wage to put into a bank account in the child's name or in joint names of the child and parent for future use by that child.

Forming a Partnership with Your Spouse

Where tax returns are being made in the sole name of the farmer and where tax is being paid or is likely in the future to be paid at the high rate, a partnership between the two spouses may be beneficial. In 2024 a married person with a non-earning spouse can earn a maximum of €51,000 at the 20% rate whereas a couple in partnership can earn up to €84,000. For younger couples there may be the added benefit of having the spouse pay PRSI contributions (which will be at no added cost as the contribution is a percentage of profit share) whereby she secures future entitlement to a contributory pension and possibly maternity benefit. On a note of caution, the overall benefit in forming a partnership with one's spouse in certain situations may require a degree of forward planning. Such situations might be:

- Where the farmer is currently on income averaging, he/she may be required to continue in averaging as it may not be feasible to cease averaging. In such situations there may be a significant added tax cost in the first three to four years of the partnership due to the fact that the averaging calculation in the early years of the partnership will include the full profit for the relevant years in which the farmer was a sole trader. In such situations it may be worth assessing the benefit of exiting averaging if that is possible.
- Where the farmer is nearing pension age and where the intention is that his spouse will qualify for a Qualified Adult Allowance, there may be little point in forming a partnership as the Qualified Adult Allowance is means tested and her profit share may disqualify her from entitlement.

CASE STUDY – Benefit of partnership with Spouse
Farmer Joe earns a taxable profit on the family farm of €70,000. His wife Mary is working full time in the home and on the farm. They have two school going children. Joe has been advised by his accountant to create a partnership with his wife as there is a distinct tax advantage in so doing. The following case study details the extent of the tax savings.

CASE STUDY – Benefit of partnership with spouse
Farmer Joe earns a taxable profit on the family farm of €70,000. His wife Mary is working full time in the home and on the farm. They have two school going children. Joe has been advised by his accountant to create a partnership with his wife as there is a distinct tax advantage in so doing. The following case study details the extent of the tax savings.

	Joe - Sole Trader	Partnership with Mary
Taxable farm profit	€70,000	€70,000
Tax @ 20%	€10,200	€14,000
Tax @ 40% on	€7,600	nil
PRSI	€2,800	€2,800
USC	€2,105	€1,410
Less:		
Personal Tax Credit	€3,750	€3,750
Earned Income Credit	€1,875	€3,750
Home Carer Credit	€1,800	nil
Tax due	€15,280	€10.710

Creating the partnership represents a saving of €4,570. There is no need for a formal partnership agreement, but it is advisable that a joint bank account be set up and the herd number placed in joint names.

Paying a Wage to your Spouse

As an alternative to creating a partnership with your spouse, it may be equally beneficial to pay your spouse a wage in order to extend the 20% tax band. In the vast majority of cases, farming spouses are involved in the farming operation and can well justify a wage. It should be noted that a wife who receives a wage from her sole trader husband on the farm is not covered under Class S PRSI. However, if the husband and wife were in a partnership both would be covered under Class S PRSI or if the husband was in partnership with a person other than his wife or was trading as a company and the wife was paid a wage in excess of €5,000, she would also be covered under class S PRSI.

Registering as an Employer

In order to claim tax relief on any wages paid, be it to family members or others, it is necessary to register as an employer with the local Inspector of Taxes. This cannot be done retrospectively as only wage payments made and recorded on the Revenue online system are allowed for tax purposes.

Taxation of Horses

The breeding and trading in horses is regarded as a trade and consequently is a taxable activity. However, many farmers keep a horse or two as a hobby or an interest and there may be a very thin line in determining what constitutes a hobby or a trade, generally, it will be easy to tell the difference by virtue of circumstances, scale and involvement but occasionally professional guidance may be required to determine if the activity constitutes a trade.

Horse Breeding & Trading

Horse breeding or buying and selling horses is a taxable activity in the same way as any other form of livestock farming.

Horses Transferred to Training

When a horse is transferred to a racing stable, the winnings or indeed any sale proceeds are not taxable, but the costs are not tax allowable. In such situations, the farm accounts must reflect the removal of the horse from the accounts and there must be evidence of having incurred training fees. If the horse is later transferred back to the farm for breeding purposes, it will be added back in as trading stock at the same cost as it was transferred out for training. If a horse is purchased in training, and used for breeding purposes, it will be brought into trading stock at the value for which it was purchased.

Stallion Fees

Net profits from stud fees and gains on the disposal of stallions are liable to taxation. All relevant costs incurred are tax allowable but the cost of purchasing an actual stallion will be allowable over a four-year period. Stallion owners, who do not carry out a farming trade, will be considered to be carrying on an investment activity and their net income will be liable as a Case IV receipt. In other words, they are not carrying on a trade and will be limited in what expenses they can offset against any income earned

Value Added Tax

For VAT purposes, breeding horses is deemed to be a farming operation. While farmers are not required to register for VAT unless they are carrying on other VAT-able activities, they may elect to register. If you do not elect to register, you are deemed to be a 'flat-rate' farmer for VAT purposes and are entitled to apply a flat-rate addition of VAT (4.8% from 1 January 2024) to your sales proceeds when selling to VAT-registered customers, be they farmers or sales companies. If you elect to register for VAT (or are required to because you are importing horses) the VAT rates that apply are: 4.8% where the horse is sold to a flat-rate farmer or sold to a factory for the use in food products, 9% on the sale of racehorses or the supply of horses to other VAT registered entities.

Stamp Duty

Where the sole activity is the breeding of horses, the young-trained farmer exemption on farm transfers in not available.

Taxation of Private Forestry

All profits or gains, including grants and premiums, from the occupation of woodland in the State which is managed on a commercial basis and with a view to a profit are exempt from Income Tax and Corporation Tax but not PRSI and Universal Social Charge, Christmas trees also fall under the exemption, but other decorative trees, bushes or shrubs will generally not qualify. The following is the position as it relates to the various taxes: to which forestry may be liable.

Capital Gains Tax

Gains on the sale of standing trees are exempt from Capital Gains Tax in the case of an individual but not in the case of a limited company. The underlying land is liable to Capital Gains Tax but typically the underlying land will be of very little value due to the obligation to re-plant without the benefit of grant aid and may be worth considerably less than the acquisitions cost.

Stamp Duty

Sales of afforested land are subject to Stamp Duty on the land value only and not the standing crop. The rate of duty in all cases will be 7.5% as the land does qualify as farmland and therefore does not qualify for Consanguinity Relief (see page 283).

Capital Acquisitions Tax

Woodlands that are inherited or gifted are liable to Capital Acquisitions Tax but are eligible for Agricultural Relief. The condition that the beneficiary spends at least 50% of their normal working time farming the holding for the purposes of maintaining eligibility for Agricultural Relief does not apply in the case of forestry plantations. Furthermore, the '80% Agricultural Property Test' (see page 265) does not apply to forestry.

Vacant Homes Tax

Vacant Homes Tax is an annual tax that applies to residential properties in use as a dwelling for less than 30 days in a 12-month chargeable period. An exemption may be available in certain circumstances. Any liability to tax is in addition to a liability to Local Property Tax. The rate of the tax is being increased in 2024 from 3 times to 5 times the property's existing base Local Property Tax liability. This increase will apply from the next chargeable period, starting 1 November 2023.

Residential Zoned Land Tax

Residential Zoned Land Tax) is an annual tax. It is calculated at 3% of the market value of land within its scope. It will apply from 2024 onwards. Certain properties are excluded from the tax such as existing residential properties liable for Local Property Tax (LPT).The first liability date for tax will be deferred until 1 February 2025. Landowners will be afforded an opportunity to submit requests for a change in the zoning of their land to local authorities in respect of the mapping process being undertaken in 2024 and 2025.

Forming a Limited Company

The rate of tax payable by limited companies (Corporation Tax) is 12.5% but this rate only applies to profits retained within the company. Any money taken out of the company for personal use will be taxable at your normal personal rates, so incorporation best suits people with moderate personal drawings. Farmers, similar to their business counterparts are free to incorporate and all of the farm grant and subsidy schemes are open to farming companies. The decision to form a farming company is a complex one but, in many instances, the potential tax savings will be the overriding attraction. A married farmer earning a taxable profit of €90,000 with his wife working off the farm could in theory save in the region of €14,738 assuming he paid himself a gross salary of €51,000 per annum (see case study below). In practically all cases, only the farming activity and not the farm is transferred to the company. This means that the farmland and buildings will be rented or leased to the company and the stock and farm equipment will be sold into the company. Where the farmer and his spouse provide the use of land to the company that is in proportion to their shareholding, they are allowed, on a concessional basis, to apply a rent appropriate to their tax profile for their land and entitlements which gives him a large degree of flexibility in regard to his annual personal income.

CASE STUDY
Farmer Joe earns a taxable profit of €90,000 in 2024 Annual drawings from the farm are €39,000 which roughly equates with a gross salary before tax of €51,000. His wife is earning more than €42,000 and therefore there is no unused lower tax band.

	Sole Trader	Limited Company
Taxable Farm Profit	€90,000	€39,000
Wage from company		€51,000
Income Tax & Levies	€30,976	€11,634
Corporation Tax		€4,875
Total tax & Levies	€30,976	€16,509
Total saving		€14,467

Farmers Best Positioned to Incorporate
Incorporation will best suit farmers but is not exclusive to farmers who:
- Are currently paying tax at the 40% rate.
- Have moderate to low levels of debt, or;
- Are in a position to transfer debt into the company.
- Have moderate levels of personal drawings.
- Have used up most of their Farm Buildings Allowances.
- Are not participating in a Succession Farm Partnership.
- Have not drawn certain TAMS grants in the past 5 years.

Capital Acquisition Tax (CAT) Implications
In general CAT rules do not militate against incorporation. Land, buildings, entitlement etc., continue to qualify for Agricultural Relief (see page 265) for transfer purposes. Shares in a farming company will not quality for Agricultural Relief but may qualify for Business Property Relief (see page 269) where the entire farming operation is being transferred as a going concern.

Capital Gains Tax Implications
Farmers will continue to be eligible for Retirement Relief (see page 276) in the case of family transfers subject to the 25-year maximum letting rule. The transfer of shares in a farming company will also qualify providing the farmer is over 55 and has held the shares for 10 years or more.

Stamp Duty Implications
There are no stamp duty implications in transferring the farming operation to a company provided that no land passes. Young, trained farmers who have already availed of the Stamp Duty exemption and who incorporate the farm business will continue to satisfy the 5 year rule as they are regarded as continuing to farm the land but for the relief to apply in the case of a company, the individual must be the main

shareholder and be a working director of the company and must farm the land on behalf of the company.

VAT Implications

Similar rules apply to VAT registration as for sole traders. Accordingly, VAT registration is optional. Companies are entitled to the 'Flat Rate Refund' and are also eligible to VAT refunds on items of capital expenditure on buildings, fixed plant and land improvement.

Biss Farm Payment Implications

In order for payment under BISS to transfer over to the Limited Company, it will be necessary to register the herd number in the name of the company and also the entitlements. This can be done by sale or lease or by exercising the 'change of legal entity' provisions as set down by the Department of Agriculture.

It should be noted that where entitlements are sold to the company by farmers over 55 years, Capital Gains Tax will arise as Retirement Relief is not available unless the relevant area of land also transfers. It should be further noted that VAT will arise where the sale proceeds exceed the registration threshold of €40,000.

Nine Point To-Do List on Incorporation

Following incorporation, it will be necessary to:

- Register the herd number in company name.
- Register the Basic Payment Entitlements in the company name.
- Where it is intended to erect farm buildings it will be necessary to prepare a formal lease or license agreement of the farmyard (or site) to the company.
- Notify banks & finance companies of loans transferring to the company.
- Notify merchants, Co-ops etc., of the change of trading entity.
- Open a bank account in the name of the company.
- Cancel existing PAYE/PRSI registration and register company.
- Reassign existing land leases over to the company.
- Where required, transfer/acquire milk purchaser shares.

Advantages of Incorporation

- Potential for substantial tax savings resulting in opportunity to invest in the farm business.
- No PRSI and no Universal Social Charge on company profits.
- Suitable structure for involvement of family members.
- No audit requirement (turnover less than €12m).
- Can release a substantial amount of tax-free cash from sale of stock and machinery to company.
- Increased pension opportunities,
- May be a suitable vehicle to accommodate personal debt resolution in a tax efficient manner.
- A company may become involved in a registered partnership.

Disadvantages of Incorporation
- Access to retained profits for personal use may have an income tax cost.
- No tax savings if profits do not exceed personal drawings. Therefore, in years of low or nil profits, a liability to personal tax will still arise that could be greater than if the farmer had remained a sole trader.
- Farm Buildings Allowance cannot be claimed on buildings which are not owned by the company. So, you cannot carry existing available allowances into the company unless you are selling the buildings to the company, which would happen only in very rare circumstances.
- Where large debt exists, it may be necessary to transfer land into the company.
- Exiting or ceasing a limited company may have Capital Gains Tax implications where the company has accumulated some value.
- Future eligibility for Agricultural Relief (see page 287) may be threatened where the applicant's company share value has grown.
- Ceasing as a sole trader could have income tax consequences for farmers availing of income averaging.
- Disposals of land to unrelated parties may not be eligible for Retirement Relief if the land was not formally leased to the company.
- Increased accountancy charges.
- Selling land with farm buildings thereon into a company may have VAT implications if the buildings had been erected in the past five years and VAT was re-claimed in respect of the construction cost.
- Company formation within 5 years of claiming TAMS grants based on the increased partnership threshold or the young-trained farmer rate may result in a partial claw-back of grant aid received.

Incorporation demands expert professional advice not alone regarding taxation but also in regard to BISS, grant aid and herd number issues.

Taxation of BISS Payment Entitlements

On many farms the BISS payment will have a significant impact on tax liabilities. The annual payment is subject to income tax, PRSI and USC. Purchasing entitlements does not attract any tax relief but their value in the event of a transfer or sale may also be liable to capital taxes, and possibly VAT.

Capital Gains Tax on Sale of Entitlements

Gains made on the disposal of payment entitlements are subject to Capital Gains Tax. However, where a person is eligible to avail of Retirement Relief the sale proceeds will qualify for relief where sufficient land is disposed of at the same time and to the same person, that would support a claim to payment in respect of the number of entitlements disposed of. Where entitlements are sold with or without land, the gain may be liable to the 10% Entrepreneurial Rate of tax (see page 275).

Capital Gains Tax on Sale of Bought Entitlements
Where entitlements are purchased, the cost price can be offset against the sale proceeds to establish the taxable gain which will be liable at 33% or 10% subject to the conditions being satisfied.

Capital Acquisition Tax on Entitlements
Entitlements are subject to CAT arising on gifts or inheritances, but it is worth noting that "Agricultural Relief" applies to their value as they fall under the description of 'Agricultural Property' as defined.

Stamp Duty on Sale of Entitlements
The sale or transfer of entitlements is not liable to Stamp Duty.

VAT on Sale of Entitlements
If entitlements are sold without land, then VAT will be due at the standard rate on the sale, if the sale proceeds exceed the relevant threshold for registration (currently €40,000). A farmer who exceeds the threshold by virtue of selling entitlements will be permitted to register for VAT in respect of that single transaction. Non-VAT-registered farmers who purchase entitlements and suffer VAT will not be permitted to register in respect of the single transaction but will have the normal registration option open to them.

Taxation of Rental Properties

Apart from certain leases on farmland, rents received from rented property are subject to income tax, PRSI and Universal Social Charge. Relevant expenses incurred such as repairs, insurance, management charges etc., are allowable as a deduction against rental income. Expenditure on fixtures, fittings and equipment are deemed to be capital items and are allowable at 12.5% per annum.

Interest on Loans for Rented Property
Interest arising on borrowed moneys employed in the purchase, improvement or repair of rented residential or commercial properties by an individual, partnership or company will be allowed in full as a deduction for tax purposes against rental income. Interest arising on borrowings for non-residential property is also allowed in full. To be eligible to claim interest relief on loans for rented residential property, the property must be registered with the Private Residential Tenancies Board.

Registering a Rented Residential Property
Landlords of residential properties must register all tenancies with the Residential Tenancies Board (RTB). The RTB will use this information to maintain a publicly available register. This will not show the identity of the landlord or the tenants, or the amount of the rent. The RTB will exchange information with local authorities so that

they can enforce the regulations relating to standards and rent books. The RTB may exchange information with the Department of Social Protection. It may also supply registration details to the Revenue Commissioners on request. Landlords must be registered to use the RTB dispute resolution service (although tenants do not have to be registered to avail of this service). For information visit www.rtb.ie.

Rented Residential Relief
A new tax relief for landlords will be available against rental income from residential property for tax years 2024 to 2027 inclusive. The relief is available to individual landlords only for tenancies registered with the Residential Tenancies Board or for lettings of a residential property to a public authority. Landlords are also required to have tax clearance and to comply with their Local Property Tax. The relief will reduce the tax due on residential rental income by up to €600 in 2024, €800 in 2025, and €1,000 in 2026 and 2027. The relief is capped at the tax liability on the rental income and will be apportioned in the case of joint ownership of a property.

Tax Relief Check List

Have you claimed or considered the following:

- Family wages.
- Income Averaging.
- Stock relief.
- Dependent Relative Allowance.
- Medical expenses (including dependent relative).
- Tax allowable life assurance.
- Personal Pension payments.
- College Fees (subject to limits).
- The limited company option.
- A partnership with your spouse.
- Succession Farm Partnership tax relief.
- A wage to your spouse and/or children.
- Carbon Tax relief.

Capital Acquisitions Tax

Capital Acquisitions Tax (CAT) is the broader term covering gift tax and inheritance tax. Inheritance tax arises on the value of property passing to somebody on the death of another person. Gift tax arises on the value of gifts received from a living person.

Who is Taxable?
With the exception of gifts or inheritances between husbands and wives and for certain charitable or public purposes, all persons can be liable.

Rate of Tax
The rate of tax is currently 33%.

Small Gifts Exemption
The first €3,000 of the taxable value of a gift (not an inheritance) is exempt from tax. The exemption does not apply to an inheritance. The exemption is limited to one gift per disponer in a calendar year. In effect, a beneficiary can take €3,000 from the same disponer in different calendar years and these gifts will be exempt from CAT. A beneficiary can take gifts from several disponers in the same calendar year and the first €3,000 of each of those gifts will be exempt.

How Much can be Received Tax Free
The amount that can be received tax free will depend on the relationship to the donor. However, this tax free amount is not an annual allowance and any gifts or inheritances are aggregated with all gifts or inheritances received since 5   December 1991. Table 13.6 sets out the thresholds for the various categories in respect of gifts or inheritances received after the 9th. October 2019.

Table 13.6: Tax Free Amounts 2024 (Effective from 9th October 2019).

Relationship to the donor/testator	Tax free amount
Husband or Wife	All
Child or Favourite Nephew/Niece or Parent1 (Group A)	€335,000
Brother, Sister or Child of a Brother or Sister (Group B)	€32,500
Any Other Person (Group C)	€16,250

If a parent takes an absolute inheritance from a child, that parent has a Group A threshold. However, if in the previous five years that child had received a non-exempt gift or inheritance from either parent, the inheritance taken by the parent will be exempt if it is taken on the death of that child.

Agricultural Relief
Normally, tax is based on the market value of the property comprising the gift or inheritance and allowance is given for all liabilities and expenses that are properly payable out of the gift or inheritance. However ,a concession known as Agricultural Relief applies where the recipient is a 'farmer' as defined hereunder.

Definition of a Farmer (The 80% Farmer Test)

A farmer is defined as someone where:

(i) 80% of his or her gross property on receiving the gift or inheritance is "agricultural property". In this case 'gross property' means the value before considering any debts apart from mortgage debt on a principal private residence. People who cannot satisfy the 80% rule will still be eligible for the 90% reduction if the farm is being transferred as a going concern (i.e. is being actively farmed or short term let by the owner) and has been so for the past five years in the case of a gift or two years in the case of an inheritance. See Business Relief page 269.

(ii) The recipient must:

(a) be the holder of an agricultural qualification[1] similar to that required for the Stamp Duty exemption, (see page 284), or for a period of not less than 6 years commencing on the valuation date of the gift or inheritance spend not less than 50 per cent of that individual's normal working time farming agricultural property (including the agricultural property comprised in the gift or inheritance) on a commercial basis and with a view to the realisation of profits from that agricultural property, or

(b) lease the whole or substantially the whole (at least 75%) of the agricultural property, comprised in the gift or inheritance for a period of not less than 6 years commencing on the valuation date of the gift or inheritance to an individual who is a qualified or full-time farmer.

[1]If not already held, the necessary farming qualification must be achieved within the period of 4 years commencing on the date of the gift or inheritance.

Agricultural Property

For the purposes of agricultural relief "agricultural property" includes the gross value of farmland and woodland situate in any member state of the E.U., crops or trees growing on such land, farm buildings, farm houses and mansion houses (as are of a character appropriate to the property) livestock, bloodstock and farm machinery. The definition of "Agricultural Property" also includes the capital value of the farm payment entitlements. In calculating the gross value of agricultural assets, a deduction is allowed in respect of any mortgage associated with the construction or renovation of the farmer's principal private residence which did not qualify as agricultural property. Shares in a company deriving their value from agricultural property do not qualify for agricultural relief but may qualify for 'Business Relief' (see page 269).

To qualify for the relief the gift or inheritance must consist of agricultural property both at the date of the gift or inheritance and at the Valuation Date. The Valuation Date is the date at which the property is valued for tax purposes. In the case of a Gift, the Valuation Date is normally the date of the gift. In the case of an Inheritance, the Valuation Date is normally the earliest of the following dates:

• The date the subject matter of the inheritance can be retained for the benefit of the beneficiary.

• The date it is actually retained for the benefit of the beneficiary.

• The date it is transferred or paid over to the beneficiary.

Exceptionally, however, the relief is applicable to the whole or part of a gift or inheritance notwithstanding that, that whole or part did not strictly consist of agricultural property until after the date of the gift or inheritance. The following situations will qualify:

- Where an individual receives a gift or inheritance on condition that it is invested in whole or part in agricultural property and the condition is fully complied with inside two years after the date of the gift or inheritance; and
- Where, in the course of administration, agricultural property is appropriated to satisfy in whole or in part a benefit under a will or intestacy and that agricultural property was subject to the will or intestacy at the date of the inheritance.

Solar Panels

Land on which solar panels are installed is regarded as agricultural land for the purposes of the definition of agricultural property provided that the area of land occupied by the solar panels and ancillary equipment does not exceed half of the land comprised in the gift or the inheritance. Where such land is leased, it meets the active farmer requirement where all other conditions are met.

Normal Working Time

A 40-hour working week is taken as indicative of normal working time. So, a farmer who works 20 hours per week on the farm satisfies the requirement, even if he or she spends more than 20 hours per week in an off-farm employment. Revenue tend to adopt a flexible approach in this regard where a plausible case can be made.

Amount of Relief

Agricultural relief entitles a farmer to a reduction of 90% in respect of the market value of all eligible farm assets being gifted or inherited. The availability of agricultural relief will ensure a nil tax liability where the value of agricultural assets passing do not exceed €3.35m in vale, so it is vital that a prospective beneficiary can satisfy the 80% farmer test.

Measures to Secure Relief

A farmer who is considering willing or gifting his farm and cash reserves to his successor should establish that the successor will be eligible for Agricultural Relief after receiving the gift or inheritance. The successor may avoid a substantial tax liability if some or all the cash reserves are converted to agricultural assets prior to receiving the gift or inheritance. Alternatively, the person making the will or gift could direct that after his death (or granting the gift) such cash reserves be invested in whole or in part in qualifying farm assets within a two-year period. Qualifying assets includes expenditure on renovation or reconstruction of the farm dwelling.

Deductions

Given that the full market value of the agricultural property is reduced by 90% to arrive at the agricultural value, any liabilities, costs and expenses properly payable out of the property and any consideration paid for the property must be similarly scaled down before being deducted from the agricultural value.

Relationship Between Land and Farm Dwellings

It is agricultural land that determines whether the relief applies. A building, without the land, is not agricultural property. Therefore, a farmhouse transferred to a farmer on its own does not qualify for agricultural relief. On the other hand, if the farmland is then subsequently transferred to the same beneficiary, thereby 're-joining' the house and land, the farmhouse is treated as agricultural property in relation to any subsequent gift or inheritance taken by that beneficiary. If the land is gifted to the beneficiary and the donor separately retains the house, the house will not be 'agricultural property' on its own assuming it is later gifted to or inherited by the same beneficiary and although it may re-join the agricultural property and become, again, agricultural property, it was not agricultural property at the date of the gift/inheritance.

Farmers who intend to transfer the land but to retain ownership of their dwelling with the intention that the beneficiary of the land would eventually inherit the dwelling, may need to consider the future tax implications for their successor. Retaining a right of residence in the dwelling may be a better option.

Agricultural Relief Case Study

Joe & Kathleen Farmer are planning to transfer their jointly owned farm and farm dwelling worth €800,000 in total to their daughter Kate. Kate is living with her husband in a house which they built on a site on the farm. Their house which is in joint names is worth €300,000 but has a mortgage currently standing at €120,000. In addition, Kate and her husband have a rental property in Dublin worth €440,000 with a mortgage of €220,000. For the purposes of calculating Kate's entitlement to Agricultural Relief she is allowed her share of the mortgage to offset against her share of the family dwelling, but she is not allowed deduct the mortgage from the rental property value. Kate has a car worth €20,000 and a joint savings account with her husband of €30,000. For the purposes of the calculation, it is assumed that her parents' house qualifies as a farmhouse and as such is classed as an agricultural asset but their own house does not qualify as a farmhouse. The following is the calculation of her gross asset value if one includes the farm:

Farm and farmhouse	€ 800,000
Share of dwelling (value net of mortgage)	€ 90,000
Share of rental property (gross value)	€ 220,000
Savings ½ share	€ 15,000
Car	€ 20,000
Total assets	€1,145,000

Farm assets as a percentage of total assets is 69.86%. Accordingly, Kate does not meet the 80% requirement and the only realistic option open to her is to transfer sufficient assets to her husband to get her over the 80% limit.

Clawback of Relief

Relief will be withdrawn:

- Where land acquired is sold or compulsorily acquired within 6 years from the date of gift or inheritance and is not replaced within one year or six years in the case of compulsorily acquired lands. Acquiring replacement land from a spouse to whom the said land had previously been transferred, is not permitted. The extent of clawback is confined to the amount of proceeds not reinvested in qualifying assets within the reinvestment or replacement period.
- Where land is disposed of between 6 - 10 years after the date of gift or inheritance and which had qualified for agricultural (or business) relief, the relief granted will be clawed back in respect of any development value relating to the land at the time of gift or disposal.
- Where the recipient ceases to be an active farmer within 6 years.
- Where a farm is leased out and the farm dwelling thereon is rented out within the 6-year period, the relief applicable to the dwelling will be withdrawn if the dwelling accounts for 25% or more of the entire at the valuation date.

Business Property Relief

Where a beneficiary is ineligible for Agricultural Relief because of the 80% agricultural asset requirement, he/she may qualify for Business Property Relief which is similar in nature to Agricultural Relief in that it reduces the value of the business assets (including land but excluding the farm dwelling) being transferred to 10% but there is no 80% agricultural asset test as referred to above. However, in the context of farming assets, the relief is conditional on the transfer of the business as a going concern. This would exclude a situation where the business (farming) had ceased in the five years prior to the transfer (two years in the case of an inheritance) and the land had been leased. The relief is conditional upon the business (farming operation) continuing for a six-year period. Where the farming is being operated as a limited company, but the farmer owns the land, transferring the land without the company will not qualify the recipient for relief. It should be noted that a Circuit Court decision in May 2008 found that the letting of lands for grazing on conacre was a business.

Family Home Relief

There is an exemption from Capital Acquisitions Tax (CAT) in certain circumstances where a dwelling house is acquired by gift or inheritance. In the case of an inheritance the relief applies to an individual where...

He/she (the person inheriting) has no beneficial interest in any other residential property at the date of the inheritance.

It was occupied by the beneficiary as his or her only or main residence for the 3 years preceding the date of the inheritance or, where the dwelling house for which the exemption is claimed is replaced by another dwelling house as the beneficiary's only or main residence. The combined period of occupation must have been at least 3 years of the 4 years preceding the date of the inheritance. Similar to a disponer, a successor who is absent from his or her principal private residence because of physical or mental ill health is deemed to have lived in the dwelling house at that time.

- It was occupied as the 'only or main' residence (Principal Private Residence) of the person bequeathing the house at the date of his or her death. A person can have only one 'only or main residence'. An exception to the residency requirement is made where a disponer is absent from his or her only or main residence, such as residing in a nursing home, because of physical or mental ill health at the date of death.
- A successor cannot claim the dwelling house exemption if he or she has an interest in another dwelling house at the date of the inheritance. Such an interest includes both full ownership or part ownership (however small) and applies to dwelling houses situated either in the State or abroad. This is the position irrespective of whether the successor already owned or had an interest in another dwelling before the date of the inheritance or acquired the interest as part of the same inheritance.

The exemption also applies to residential properties that are gifted. There are a number of important conditions that apply to gifts which do not apply to inheritances as follows:
- The property gifted does not necessarily have to be a Principal Private Residence.
- The recipient must be a dependent relative of the donor, i.e. individuals who are incapacitated to such an extent that they are unable to maintain themselves by earning an income from working.
- If not incapacitated, the dependent relative must be aged 65 or over.

A dwelling house will cease to be exempt in the following circumstances,
- Where, within the period of 6 years beginning on the date of an inheritance it is sold or otherwise disposed of by a successor.
- A successor ceases to occupy the dwelling house as his or her only or main residence.

If a dwelling house ceases to be exempt, then tax is chargeable as if it had not qualified for the exemption at the date of the inheritance. However, a sale, disposal or cessation of occupation does not result in the withdrawal of the exemption in the following circumstances,
- Where the full proceeds from a sale are re-invested in a replacement dwelling house that will then be the only or main residence of the successor.
- The successor was 65 years of age or older on the date of the inheritance.
- The successor was required to reside somewhere other than the dwelling house because of his or her physical or mental infirmity.
- The successor was required by his or her employer to live somewhere else, whether in the State or abroad, in order to perform the duties of his or her employment.

For the purposes of the relief a "Relative" is defined as a lineal ancestor, lineal descendant, brother, sister, uncle, aunt, niece, or nephew of the disponer or the spouse or civil partner of the disponer.

Tip: Where the gift/inheritance will result in some level of liability, it is important to claim Family Home Relief, if available, as it grants 100% relief whereas Agricultural Relief will grant only 90% relief.

Favourite Nephew Relief

In certain circumstances a nephew or niece of the disponer who has worked on a full-time basis on the farm will be deemed to have a relationship to the disponer as that of a child in regard to the business assets. To be eligible the following conditions must be satisfied:

- The successor must be a child (including a step child or adopted child) of a brother or a sister.
- The successor must have worked 'substantially on a full time basis' for a period of five years prior to taking the gift or inheritance. Substantially on a full-time basis has been defined as to mean more than 15 hours per week where the farming is carried on exclusively by the disponer, his spouse and the successor. Otherwise, the lower limit is 24 hours per week.

Non-business assets such as the farm dwelling or cash will not fall under this relief and will be subject to the group B threshold, currently €32,500.

Other CAT Reliefs

Qualifying Expenses of Incapacitated Individuals
Gifts or inheritances taken exclusively for the purposes of discharging the expenses of an individual who is permanently incapacitated by reason of physical or mental infirmity are exempt from tax. Qualifying expenses are those that relate to medical care including the cost of maintenance in connection with such medical care.

Heritage Houses and Gardens Relief
Any house or garden in the State which appears to the Revenue Commissioners to be of national, scientific, historic, or artistic interest is exempt from Capital Acquisitions Tax. The following conditions for relief apply:
   Easonable access (as defined) must have been allowed to the public during the three years prior to the gift or inheritance.
   Reasonable access to the public must be allowed on an ongoing basis, and;
   The property must not be held for the purpose of trading.

Reasonable access means access to the house or garden must be available for a minimum of 60 days in any year, of which 40 days must be in the months of May to September inclusive (subject to reasonable temporary closure for necessary repairs, maintenance, or restoration).

Joint Deposit/Savings Accounts
Joint accounts not exceeding a value of €50,000 generally can be transferred into the sole name of the surviving account holder once the bank receives a certified copy of a death certificate and request to change the account to the surviving account holder's name. Where the balance in the account exceeds €50,000, it will not be possible for the surviving account holder to withdraw money until such time as he/she furnishes the financial institution with a certificate from the Revenue Commissioners certifying that there is no outstanding liability for inheritance tax. The origin of the joint deposit account will determine whether it is liable to Gift or Inheritance Tax. Apart from spouses, where the proceeds of the account are inherited on the death of the joint account holder, and those proceeds originated from the deceased, the survivor will be liable to inheritance tax.

General Points to Note

- If a person dies within two years of making a gift, it becomes an inheritance.
- There is no limit to the availability of Agricultural Relief or Business Relief, regardless of the number of gifts or inheritances one receives.
- People not qualifying for Agricultural Relief may qualify for Business Relief.
- In the unfortunate circumstances of a farm reverting back to the parent as an inheritance where the son or daughter dies, no tax is payable provided the farm was transferred to the son or daughter within the previous five years. If the five-year period has been exceeded, the same allowance is available as would be available to a son or daughter providing the parents had not received any gift or inheritance since 5 December 1991, in which case the value of all gifts or inheritances are aggregated.
- Agricultural Relief is not available where the property passing is shares in a company owning agricultural land, but Business Relief may apply.
- If somebody has the use of land rent-free from another person, the commercial rental value of the land is deemed to be a gift received by the person who is using the land and therefore may attract gift tax.
- All gifts and/or inheritances received since the 5th. December 1991 are aggregated when applying the individual's tax exemption threshold.
- Woodlands that are inherited or gifted are liable to CAT but are eligible for agricultural relief.

Inheritance & Gift Tax Insurance

In the case of larger holdings, the possibility of a significant capital tax liability exists. It is possible to make provision for such future liabilities by taking out a special type of insurance policy known as a Section 72 policy in the case of inheritances or Section 73 policies in the case of gifts. The proceeds from such policies will only be subject to CAT to the extent that they are not required to pay tax. However, where such policies exist, their necessity should be re-appraised by a tax consultant on a regular basis, as they can in certain situations render a beneficiary ineligible for Agricultural Relief. An important condition of the relief is that the policy must be payable on a date that is more than eight years after the date on which the policy is commenced. It should be noted that the premiums on such policies are not tax deductible for income tax purposes.

Separated Spouses

Transfers of assets between spouses whether by way of gift or inheritance are exempt from capital acquisitions tax. Separation does not affect this exemption, but divorce does. Transfers of assets pursuant to a court order in a Divorce Decree are exempt but transfers of assets after the granting of the Decree of Divorce that are not ordered by the court are not exempt.

Table 13.7: Capital Acquisitions Tax Pay and File Deadlines.

Valuation date	Pay & File by
On or before the 31st August	31st October in that tax year
From the 1st September to the 31st December	31st October in the following tax year

Tip: when a person is making a will that includes cash or investments, they could reduce the taxable value by directing that after their death such cash reserves be invested in whole or in part in qualifying farm assets which includes expenditure on renovation or reconstruction of the farm dwelling within a two-year period.

Capital Gains Tax

Where a farmer disposes of certain assets such as land, buildings, shares or entitlements he or she may be liable to capital gains tax.

Items Liable to Capital Gains Tax

Land and buildings (whether sold or transferred during the owner's lifetime).
Certain assets of the farming business including Payment Entitlements.
Company shares.

Rates of Tax
The current rate is 33% apart from gains attracting Entrepreneur Relief which re subject to 10% tax (see below).

Tax-Free Amounts
The tax-free amount in any year amounts to €1,270 for an individual. Where the asset is in joint names, they will each be entitled to the €1,270 exemption but it is not transferable from one spouse to the other.

Losses
Losses incurred on any disposals of assets in a given year can be offset against gains in the same year or gains in future years. Losses sustained by one spouse are transferable to the other spouse. Losses cannot be set against gains for earlier years except where those losses are made in the year of death in which case losses can be deducted from the gains of the previous three years. A loss on the disposal of development land can only be set against a gain on the disposal of development land.

Same Event Relief
Where a liability to Capital Gains Tax and Capital Acquisitions Tax arises on the same event, a tax credit for the Capital Gains Tax paid is available against the CAT due so that both taxes cannot arise on the same transaction. The tax credit granted will be clawed back where the beneficiary disposes of the asset within 2 years. A same event could be a father gifting his son or daughter an asset that creates a liability to Capital Gains Tax on the transfer and also a liability to Gift Tax on the value of the asset transferred.

Selling Part or All of the Family Farm
In the case of farmers under 55 years, where part or all of the family farm is sold, a liability to Capital Gains Tax may arise. Whether or not this will occur will depend on several factors, principally:

- Period of ownership.
- Sale proceeds.
- Valuation of farm at the time of acquisition.
- Amounts spent on capital improvements during the period of ownership.

The period of ownership is relevant as account is taken of inflation being a factor in the increased value of the property from the date of acquisition to 31 December 2002. To adjust the original cost or valuation of the farm to take account of inflation the original value is multiplied by the relevant indexation factor. (See Page 281).

Entrepreneur Relief

This relief is available to the individual owners including farmers of a trade or business (companies or sole traders) in respect of the disposal of all or a part of that trade or business which they have owned for at least 3 years. A Capital Gains Tax Rate of 10% will apply to the net chargeable gains arising on disposals of assets comprising the whole or a discrete part of a trade or business, subject to a lifetime limit of €1m on such gains. While the relief applies to shareholdings in unquoted companies such as farming companies, it will not be available to the actual company in respect of business asset disposals by such entities.

Rate of Tax

The effect of the relief is to reduce the rate of tax on a disposal of chargeable business assets from the standard rate of 33% to 10% for qualifying gains of up to €1m in a vendor's lifetime. The value of the relief can be worth up to €230,000 for an individual or €460,000 where relevant business assets are jointly held between spouses and both spouses satisfy all conditions.

Qualifying Conditions

The qualifying conditions are as follows:

- The disposal must relate to a "qualifying business" which will include the vast majority of active farmers whether trading as sole traders or companies.
- The disposal must comprise "chargeable business assets" which includes agricultural land which was used for the purpose of the business. He/she must have beneficially owned the chargeable business assets for a continuous period of three out of the five years before the date of disposal. This applies to both sole traders and sellers of shares.
- A disposal involving ordinary shares in a company will only qualify if the individual disposing holds 5% or more of the ordinary share capital in the company and is or has been a director or employee of the company who spent 50% or more of his/her working time in the service of that company for a continuous period of three out of five years immediately before the disposal of the shares in question.
- Personal assets, the use of which are provided to a company do not qualify. This includes land.

CASE STUDY
Farmer Joe, a married man in his early fifties, sold his 80-acre farm in late
December 2023. He originally purchased the farm in May 1990 for €240,000. Over
the period of ownership Joe spent €160,000 on new farm buildings. The following
calculation sets out how his liability to Capital Gains Tax is arrived at.

	€
Sales proceeds	980,000
Less: Cost as adjusted by indexation (see page 281)	346,080
Less: Enhancement cost	160,000
Gross Gain	473,920
Less: allowable costs	6,200
Net Gain	480,120
Less: Personal exemption	1,270
Taxable	478,850
Tax @ 33% - standard rate	158,020
or	
Tax @ 10% - Entrepreneur Relief rate	47,885

If Joe qualifies for Entrepreneur Relief, he saves €110,135.

Retirement Relief

This relief is available to farmers over 55 years and, even though it is called retirement
relief, it does not mean that the farmer has to retire to avail of it. The principal
condition of the relief is that the land was owned and farmed for the ten consecutive
years prior to transfer or, prior to entering into a letting/lease agreement subject to
certain conditions. In the case of lifetime sales or transfers, the ten-year ownership
requirement can be satisfied by either spouse in the case of joint ownership but the
ten-year worked requirement can only be satisfied by the individual spouses. Where
one spouse is deceased and the remaining spouse has inherited the land, the ten-year
owned and farmed rule for the remaining spouse will be met provided the deceased
spouse did own and farm the land for ten years.
There are two versions of Retirement Relief, as follows:

Family Transfers (S.599)

Assuming the conditions as set out hereunder are met, family transfers are free of Capital Gains Tax where the transferor is over 55. There are certain limits that apply as follows;

(i) In the case of transfers prior to the 31st December 2024, where the transferor is over 66, an upper limit of €3m in value will apply. Any excess over €3m will be subject to tax @ 33%.

(ii) In the case of transfers post 31st December 2024, the age limit rises to 70 years after which point the €3m. threshold applies.

(ii) In the case of all family transfers post 31st December 2024 where the transferor is between 55 and 70 years, an upper threshold of €10m will apply.

In the case of transfers to a child (son, daughter, favourite niece/nephew) where the land was rented or leased out prior to transfer, the maximum period in which the land can have been leased (or rented pre-31 December 2016) is 25 years unless they were a participant in the Early Farm Retirement Scheme. A child of a deceased child will qualify the transferor for this relief, It should be noted that the minimum 5 year lease requirement that applies since 31 December 2016 in respect of transfers/sales to unrelated parties does not apply in the case of a family transfer. The relief is clawed back where the child disposes of an asset within six years of the date of acquisition from his/her parent. The relief is withdrawn by way of an assessment on the child. In effect, the tax which would have been charged on the parent if the relief had not applied is charged on the child, in addition to any tax chargeable on the gain accruing on the child's disposal of the asset.

Transfer or Sale to Unrelated Parties (S598)

Providing the land was owned and farmed for 10 years prior to the date of transfer/sale or prior to first letting and the sale proceeds are less than €750,000, a farmer over 55 years and under 66 years (under 70 years from 1 January 2025) may dispose of part or all of his farm free of capital gains tax. Where the person disposing is over the upper age limit, the limit is reduced to €500,000. Where disposal proceeds exceed €750,000 (or €500,000) there is marginal relief which is based on the excess being subject to 50% tax. This applies up to the point whereby taxing the actual gain at 33% (or 10%) becomes more beneficial. In this context it is important to note that a subsequent disposal may result in a clawback of relief already gained because the €750,000/€500,000 is a lifetime limit.

Land which had been let under one or more than one conacre agreements in the previous 25 years shall not affect entitlement to retirement relief where a letting of the land for a period of not less than 5 consecutive years commences on or before 31 December 2016.

Retirement Relief - Shares in a Family Company

To qualify, the person disposing of the shares must have been a working director for a minimum period of 10 years during which he/she was a full-time working director for not less than 5 years.

Retirement Relief – Land and Buildings in Use by the Company
The relief also applies to land and buildings which the individual has owned for at least 10 years provided that such assets were used by the company throughout the transferor's period of ownership and were disposed of at the same time and to the same person as the shares in the company.

Entrepreneur v's Retirement Relief
Both reliefs' can be applied to the same transaction to establish which one works best providing the conditions for the relief's are met. The important point to note in respect of Retirement Relief is that the tax is calculated on the gross sale proceeds and not on the gain as in the case of Entrepreneur Relief. In this context it is important to note that a subsequent disposal may result in a clawback of Retirement Relief already gained as the €750,000/€500,000 is a lifetime limit and all disposals are aggregated. The following case study sets out a comparison of Entrepreneur Relief and Retirement Relief and which one yields the best outcome.

CASE STUDY: Retirement -v- Entrepreneur Relief

Joe Farmer who is 60 years of age disposes of land for €1.2m and satisfies all the conditions of both Entrepreneur Relief and Retirement Relief. Assuming a base cost of €400,000 which includes allowable deductions and his personal exemption, we will look at Joe's CGT liability under the following headings:

1. Normal CGT treatment with no relief
In the absence of any relief the taxable gain is €800,000 giving rise to a liability at 33% of €264,000.

2. Claiming Retirement relief.
Joe may claim Retirement Relief on €750,000 of the gross proceeds and marginal relief on the remainder. This will give rise to a liability of €225,000 so he saves €39.000 by claiming Retirement Relief.

3. Claiming Entrepreneur Relief
As Joe's gain is less than €1m his liability works out at 10% of €800,000, i.e., €80,000.

Conclusion
As Entrepreneur relief is greater than Retirement relief the lower CGT liability is due. The total value of Entrepreneur Relief in this case is a saving of €184,000 when compared to the normal CGT treatment.

Spouses - Period of Use and Ownership

The period of ownership of an asset by a spouse or civil partner of an individual is treated as if it were a period of ownership by the individual. Where a spouse or civil partner of the individual has died, the period of use of an asset by the deceased spouse or civil partner is treated as if it were a period of use of the asset by the individual. Where spouses own land jointly and one spouse cannot prove that they satisfy the period of use condition, it may be necessary to transfer their joint share back to the other spouse prior to sale in order to satisfy the conditions of the relief, assuming of course that the other spouse can satisfy the 10-year use rule.

Note: Where a spouse over 55 years is contemplating transferring land into joint names, they need to be aware that they will use up part or all of their Retirement Relief threshold depending on the value of the land transferred. However, by placing the land in joint ownership and where the land is subsequently farmed in partnership, each spouse will be entitled to make a gain of up to €1m at 10% tax.

Solar Panels

Where disposals of land with solar panels are made, the entitlement to Retirement Relief will not be affected by the fact that solar panels are installed on the land provided the area of the land on which the solar panels are installed does not exceed half the total area of the land concerned.

Transferring a Site to a Family Member

No liability to Capital Gains Tax will arise on the transfer of a site (one site only) to a son or daughter (or of their spouse or civil partner subject to the following conditions:

- It is for construction of the son or daughter's principal private residence.
- The market value of the site does not exceed €500,000.
- The total area of site transferred must not exceed 1 acre.
- The house is occupied for a minimum period of three years prior to sale.

Your child may have to bear a liability to Capital Gains Tax on the original transfer from the parent in two specific situations where they dispose of the land either:

- Without having built a house on that land, or;
- If they have built a house on the land, having not occupied that house as their only or main residence for a period of at least three years.

Farm Restructuring Relief

A relief from Capital Gains Tax is available to encourage farm restructuring whereby the proceeds of a sale of farmland are reinvested for the same purpose. The sale and purchase of the farmland must occur within 24 months of each other and the initial sale or purchase transaction must occur before the 31 December 2024. The relief will also apply to farmland swaps and whole farm replacement subject to certification by Teagasc for all transactions seeking relief. The following points should be noted:

- Where there is a sale and purchase of qualifying land(s) within the relevant time frame that satisfy Farm Restructuring, then Capital Gains Tax is only payable on the sale price to the extent to which it exceeds the purchase price. Where the sale price exceeds the purchase price, then the chargeable gain (i.e. the difference between sale and purchase price less allowable deductions) that accrues shall be reduced in the same proportion that the purchase price bears to the sale price.
- Where the sale takes place before the purchase, Capital Gains Tax will have to be paid in the normal manner. When a subsequent purchase takes place a claim for the relevant refund of tax paid can be made to the Revenue Commissioners, subject to both transactions meeting the eligibility criteria.
- Lands sold in joint names are eligible provided one of the joint owners is a farmer and lands subsequently purchased may be jointly owned provided one of the joint purchasers is the same farmer.
- The sale and purchase together must result in an overall reduction in the distance between parcels comprised in the farm, including land that has been leased for at least 2 years with a minimum of 5 years to run.
- The farmer availing of the relief must spend not less than 50% of his/her working time farming.
- The sale of an existing farm and the replacement of it by the purchase of another farm is considered Farm Restructuring for the purposes of the relief.
- It is not necessary that the land being disposed of was farmed by the person claiming the relief.
- Afforested land, peat lands and habitable dwellings do not qualify and the value of these should be deducted by the individual claiming relief when the relevant chargeable gain is being calculated.

Compulsory Purchase Order Compensation
All compensation under a CPO, including injurious affection, is subject to Capital Gains Tax. The proceeds will be entitled to indexation relief which takes account of the fact that inflation will have accounted for some of the increased value of the land since it was acquired. CPO proceeds resulting from road construction or widening are assessable to tax in the year in which the CPO proceeds are received. Subject to satisfying the conditions of the relief, CPO compensation is eligible for Entrepreneur Relief.

Section 604A Relief
Section 604A was introduced in the Finance Act 2012 and provides for a full Capital Gains Tax relief from any gain made in respect of the disposal of any property (land or buildings) purchased between 7 December 2011 and the 31st. December 2014 and held for at least four and no more than seven years. In other words, land purchased in 2014 and sold at a gain in 2020 may be exempt from Capital Gains Tax. Where the property is held for more than 7 years, relief is reduced in the same proportion that the period of 7 years bears to the period of ownership. So, relief on gains on land sold in 2024 which has been owned for 10 years will be reduced by 3/10ths.

Indexation Relief
Indexation relief which takes inflation into account as being a factor in any gain that arises. is still available but only to the extent that it applies to that period of the life of the asset up to and including 2002. See table 13.8.

Table 13.8: Capital Gains Tax Indexation Factors.

Year of Acquisition	Indexation Factor
1974/75	7.528
1975/76	6.080
1976/77	5.238
1977/78	4.490
1978/79	4.148
1979/80	3.742
1980/81	3.240
1981/82	2.678
1982/83	2.253
1983/84	2.003
1984/85	1.819
1985/86	1.713
1986/87	1.637
1987/88	1.583
1988/89	1.553
1989/90	1.503
1990/91	1.442
1991/92	1.406
1992/93	1.356
1993/94	1.331
1994/95	1.309
1995/96	1.272
1996/97	1.251
1997/98	1.232
1998/99	1.212
1999/00	1.193
2000/01	1.144
2001	1.087
2002	1.049
2003 onwards	1.000

Separated Spouses

Transfers of assets between spouses are exempt from capital gains tax. Transfers of assets between spouses who are separated are exempt from capital gains tax if they are made under a Separation Agreement or a court order. From the date that the separation is likely to be permanent, any transfer of assets between spouses is not exempt from capital gains tax. Similarly transfers of assets between spouses pursuant to a court order in a Divorce Decree are exempt but any transfer of assets subsequent to the granting of the Decree that are not ordered by the court are not. Separating couples should always seek specialist tax advice before entering into arrangements that have capital gains tax implications.

Payment Dates for Capital Gains Tax

Table 10.6: Capital Gains Tax Payment Deadlines.

Disposal	Tax due by:
On or before 30 November in the tax year -Initial Period	15th December in that tax year.
From 1 December to 31 December in the tax year -Later Period	31st January in the following tax year

Filing Date

Returns must be filed by the 31st October in the year following the year in which the gain was made. So, disposals giving rise to a gain in 2023 will need to be returned on or before the 31st October 2024.

Some General Points on Capital Gains Tax

- Where the land was acquired prior to 6 April 1974 the deemed cost is the market value that obtained on 6 April 1974. A farmer who owns land that was valued at £750 (€952) per acre on 6 April 1974 (which will have been a typical value for good land at that time) and now decides to sell, would only incur capital gains tax on sale proceeds in excess of €7,170 per acre. This is because of indexation relief. It should be noted that the indexation factors applicable to disposals from the tax year 2003 onwards remains fixed for disposals in all future years. See Table 13.8, page 281.
- Farmers of 55 years or over can dispose of lands up to €750,000 in value without incurring any Capital Gains Tax subject to certain conditions (see page 297). This limit is reduced to €500,000 for disposals by persons who are 66 or over (70 years from 1 January 2025) at the time of disposal.
- For the year 2024 in the case of family transfers by persons of age 66 or over, there is an overall limit of €3m. in the value than can be transferred free of tax. From 202! onwards, the threshold is increased €10m. but this threshold applies to all family transfers where the transferor is between 55 and 70 years.

- Capital Gains Tax does not arise in relation to assets owned at the time of death, regardless of who inherits such assets.
- There is no Capital Gains Tax on the sale of standing timber owned by an individual (but not a company) but the underlying land is liable.
- Lands leased for solar energy farming are regarded as agricultural property and are eligible for Retirement Relief subject to certain conditions (see page 279).

Stamp Duty

Stamp duty is a tax by any other name that arises on instruments i.e., written documents, conveying certain assets from one person to another.

Stamp Duty on Transfer of Farming Assets
Duty is payable on the value of the land only. The transfer of livestock, machinery and Basic Payment Entitlements are not subject to duty.

Rates of Duty on Various Transfers
The rate of duty will be determined by the persons circumstances at the time of purchase/transfer along with the nature of the property being transferred.
Consanguinity rate: Transfers of land between closely related persons will attract a rate of 1% subject to the condition that the individual to whom the land is conveyed or transferred must, from the date of execution of the transfer, farm the land for a period of not less than 6 years, or lease it for a period of not less than 6 years to an individual who will farm the land. This rate applies until 31 December 2028.

Young Trained Farmer Rate
Purchases by or transfers to young-trained farmers are exempt from duty subject to certain conditions as set out below. This rate applies until the 31st of December 2025.

Residential Dwelling Rate
Residential dwellings, apart from those farm dwellings qualifying for the Young Trained Farmer exemption, are liable to 1%.

Share Transfer Rate
Transfer or purchase of shares in a family farm company attract a rate of 1%.

Standard Rate
Purchases or transfers of land to unrelated parties will attract a rate of 7.5% where the purchaser or transferee is not a qualifying Young Trained Farmer.

Stamp Duty on Leases

Leases of agricultural land are currently subject to a rate of 1% of the first year's rent unless the lease satisfies the following conditions in which case the duty will be zero;

- The term of a lease must be for a period of not less than 6 years and not more than 35 years.
- The land must be used exclusively for commercial farming carried on by the lessee.
- the lease may be to an individual, to a partnership or to a company whose main shareholder and working director farms the land on behalf of the company.
- The lessee (be it an individual, partners or a main shareholder and working director) must also have an agricultural qualification or farm the land for not less than 50% of his or her normal working time.

Leases at Less Than Market Value Rent

Where the rent payable is considered by Revenue to be less than the market rent, they will calculate the gift element of the lease over the entire term and charge the appropriate rate of stamp duty that would apply between nonrelatives, currently 7.5%.

Stamp Duty on Residential Property

The rate of duty on residential property is 1% where sale proceeds do not exceed €1m. Over that the rate is 2%. Where property is acquired by way of inheritance, no stamp duty is payable. In the case of a farm transfer which includes the dwelling, the dwelling is valued separately and a rate of 1% will apply.

Stamp Duty Relief on Farm Restructuring

Stamp Duty Relief for farm restructuring allows for a 1% rate of stamp duty (as opposed to the general rate of 7.5%) where the sale and purchase or exchange transactions qualify for a "Farm Restructuring Certificate" for the purposes of Capital Gains Tax Relief. The 1% rate will apply to purchases or exchanges of land that are executed on or after 1 January 2018 and on or before 31 December 2025. Where there is a purchase and sale of land within 24 months of each other that satisfy the conditions of consolidation, then stamp duty will only be paid to the extent that the value of the land that is purchased exceeds the value of the land that is sold. In addition, both the purchase and sale must occur before the 31 December 2025.

Special Relief for 'Young Trained Farmers'

A zero rate of stamp duty applies to farmers who are under 35 years of age and who have satisfactorily attended a course as set down by the Revenue Commissioners. The relief applies to sales and gifts where no power of revocation exists and runs until 31 December 2025. The exemption is subject to the following conditions:

- The transferee must be under 35.
- The transferee must hold a relevant agricultural qualification at the time of transfer to claim the exemption or they may acquire the qualification within 3 years (4 years for transfers executed prior to May 15th 2023) and claim a rebate of the stamp duty paid.

- Only agricultural land will qualify along with such farmhouses and buildings on the land that are of a character appropriate to the land. It should be noted that land occupied as commercial woodland is not eligible.
- The land which is the subject of the transfer must be retained for five years or, if disposed of, it must be replaced by a similar value of land. Where the required agricultural qualification is acquired after the date of execution of the deed of transfer, the five-year period commences on the date on which the claim for a refund is made.

The transfer cannot be subject to a revocation clause, but a transferor can retain certain rights such as rights of residence, support and maintenance.

- The transferee must devote at least 50% of their normal working hours to farming. A certificate is required from Teagasc at the time of signing the conveyance confirming that a farm business plan has been prepared.

A lifetime ceiling of €100,000 applies to the cash value (tax saved) of aid received under the Stamp Duty, Stock Relief (100% scheme) and Succession Farm Partnership Schemes. The current cash value of a family transfer that would otherwise qualify for consanguinity relief is 1% of the value of the land being transferred. The current cash value of a purchase from an unrelated party is 7.5% of the value of the purchase. The stamp duty exemption is available in startup situations and also subsequent transfers or purchases. In other words, it is possible to make multiple applications for the exemption subject to the €100,000 limit.

0% Working Time Rule

In considering whether the normal working time requirement is fulfilled, it can be accepted that "normal working time" (including on-farm and off-farm working time) approximates to 40 hours per week. This will enable farmers with off-farm employment to qualify for the relief provided they spend a minimum of 20 hours working per week, averaged over a year, on the farm. If a farmer can show that his or her "normal working time" is somewhat less than 40 hours a week, then the 50% requirement will be applied to the actual hours worked – subject to being able to show that the farm is farmed on a commercial basis and with a view to the realisation of profits. It is expected that in most situations it should be clear from the evidence provided and the level of farming activity being carried on that the normal working time requirement is satisfied. If there is any doubt, Revenue will consider all information (including farming records) provided by a farmer in relation to his or her normal working time and farming activities and give a ruling.

Business Plan

The young-trained farmer must submit a business plan to Teagasc before the execution of the deed transferring the land. Where the relevant agricultural qualification s acquired after the date of execution of the deed of transfer, the business plan must be submitted before a refund is claimed. The business plan should be implemented within the period of nine months after the stamp duty return claiming the relief has been filed,

Refunds of Stamp Duty - Young Trained Farmers

Where the education requirements have not been met at the time of transfer, stamp duty will be payable, however, a refund may arise where:

- The deed of transfer was executed and stamped and all the conditions for granting the relief are met.
- The minimum education requirements have been met within a three-year period of the date of signing of the transfer.
- A business plan must be submitted before a refund is applied for. The plan should be implemented within the period of nine months after the refund has been claimed.

Separated Spouses

Transfers of property between spouses are exempt from stamp duty. Transfers of property between spouses who are separated or divorced are exempt from stamp duty if they are made pursuant to a court order.

Stamp Duty - Points to Note

- No stamp duty arises on inheritances.
- No stamp duty arises in transfers between husbands and wives or to former spouses under an order of the Family Law or Family Law Divorce Acts.
- No stamp duty arises on the sale of commercial timber but the underlying land is liable at the standard rate.
- The zero rate for young trained farmers continues until the 31 December 2025.
- The 1% Consanguinity rate for transfers between closely related persons runs out on 31st December 2028.
- Leases of farmland are not liable to duty subject to certain conditions.

Self Employed PRSI

In most cases, self-employed people between the ages of 16 years and 66 years with earnings of €5,000 or more per annum are liable for Class S PRSI. The rate of PRSI is 4% subject to no upper limit but to a lower payment limit of €500.

Benefits from Paying PRSI (Class S)

PRSI Class S provides cover for:

Widow's and Widower's (Contributory) Pension.
Guardian's (Contributory) Payment.
Old Age (Contributory) Pension.
Invalidity Pension.
Maternity Benefit.
Paternity Benefit.
Adoptive Benefit.
Bereavement Grant.
Treatment Benefit Scheme (incl. Dental, optical and aural).
Job Seekers Benefit.

People Excluded from Paying

The following are examples of people who are excluded from paying PRSI Class S:

'Prescribed Relatives' (that is, spouse son/daughter, parent, brother/sister etc.) who help out a self-employed person in the running of the business but who are not partners in the business.
People getting Unemployment Assistance, Pre-Retirement Allowance or Farm Assist on a continuous basis.
People insured as employees whose only income is unearned income such as share dividend payments or rent.
Occupational pensioners, whose only income is unearned.

Income Liable to Self Employed (Class S) PRSI

Income liable to PRSI i.e. Reckonable Income is income from the following sources:

Income from a trade/profession such as farming (less Capital Allowances).
Interest, annuities and income from foreign property such as, investments.
Rent from any premises in Ireland. In the case of rents that qualify for the exemption relating to certain farm lands, the exempted amount is not liable to PRSI.
Income from which tax has been deducted at source such as, annuities, bank interest or building society interest, maintenance payments and other miscellaneous sources of income not included in the above.
Income from share dividends.
Forest Premium.

PRSI for Those Working with their Spouse

Spouses who receive a wage for helping out in the running of the farm but who are not in partnership are not covered under Class S PRSI. However, where the farm is run as a partnership between both spouses, both are liable to Class S PRSI provided they each earn a minimum of €5,000 per annum. Where the farm is run as a limited company or farm partnership and a spouse is an employee of that partnership or company, they are covered under Class A PRSI.

Income Not Liable to PRSI

The following types of income are excluded and do not have to be taken into account when calculating the PRSI contribution:

- Any non-cash income that is, benefits-in-kind.
- Any sums received by way of benefit, pension, allowance or supplement from the Department of Social Protection.
- Any sums received for Training courses or schemes such as, Community Employment.
- Any payments from income continuance plans or permanent health insurance plans payable in the event of being unable to work due to ill health where the scheme has been approved by Revenue.
- Rents attracting the income tax exemption applicable to qualifying leases of farmland.

Contributions

All reckonable income is subject to a PRSI contribution equal to 4% or €500 whichever is the greater.

Voluntary Contributions

If you cease farming or if your income falls below the €5,000 limit and you are under age 66, you may apply to become a Voluntary Contributor paying a special rate of €500 per annum. Voluntary Contributions ensure that your entitlements remain intact. To be eligible to make voluntary contributions you must:

- Have at least 520 PRSI contributions paid under compulsory insurance in either employment or self-employment.
- Apply to make your voluntary contribution within 60 months (5 years) of the end of the last completed tax year (contribution year) during which you last paid compulsory insurance, or you were last awarded a credited contribution.
- Agree to pay voluntary contributions in respect of all years immediately following the year of your last compulsory contribution.

PRSI for those Exempted from Making a Tax Return

Where a self-employed individual on low income is notified by the Inspector of Taxes that he or she is not required to make a tax return, they are obliged to apply to Social Welfare to become contributors to PRSI which will safeguard their eventual entitlements. This type of contributor is described as a 'no net liability contributor' and the total annual contribution is currently €300. This amount can be paid quarterly, half yearly or annually. For people who are in arrears, there is no time limit in operation in which to bring their contributions up to date. It will of course mean paying all arrears applying to any contribution years missed out since 1988/89 which can in certain circumstances attract an interest charge.

Contact
For more information on PRSI for the self-employed, contact your local Social Welfare Office or Self Employment Section, Social Welfare Services Office, Cork Road, Waterford. Tel: Waterford (051) 356000

Value Added Tax

Farmers, including farming companies, are not obliged to register for VAT irrespective of their turnover. Farmers receive what is known as a 'flat rate refund' of VAT amounting to 5% on the sale of farm produce. However, where a farmer operates a contracting business or other type of service he will be required to register if the turnover from that source exceeds €40,000 per annum.

VAT Claims by Unregistered Farmers
Claiming VAT refunds on expenditure incurred on the erection of farm buildings, land drainage & reclamation, hedgerows, underpasses and fixed plant items are made online through eRepayments. You will need the details of your claim including the invoice number, the supplier details and the amount of VAT being claimed. You do not have to include supporting documentation for your claim, unless requested to do so but all invoices should be kept for six years as these may be required by Revenue for inspection. Each claim must be greater than €125, and a separate claim must be made for each calendar year. Claims can be lodged up to four years after the expenditure being incurred.

Clawbacks or Exposure to VAT
Claiming back VAT whether as a registered or unregistered farmer can have consequences if you sell your farm or if you simply cease farming or indeed cease being registered. There are a number of situations where VAT can be clawed back or where a disposal may be liable to VAT as follows:

(1) Where a farmer claims a VAT refund through the VAT 58 process, a claw back arises if the farmer ceases to farm or ceases to use the buildings or land in respect of which the claim was made for farming purposes within twelve months of the VAT having been incurred. While it might be unusual for a farmer to cease farming or to dispose of his holding within twelve months of doing a development, it can happen and in recent times it occasionally happens where a farmer decides to sell his farmyard to his limited company. In any event, it is something to bear in mind where a farm is being disposed of or where a farmer ceases to farm.

(2) A situation where a disposal could become vatable is where the land or farm buildings were developed within five years prior to the sale, VAT may be due on the sale even though the farmer may or may not be a VAT-registered person. This may cause a difficulty with the sale as the buyer, more than likely, will not be able to recover the VAT paid.

(3) A claw back of VAT reclaimed on a farm development can arise where a VAT registered farmer disposes of land containing the development in question

between year 5 and year 20 following the claim unless the purchaser is agreeable to apply VAT on the sale which would be unlikely.

(4) Where a registered farmer decides to de-register, they will be liable to repay the net benefit, if any, as compared to if they had not been registered in the three years prior to ceasing.

Vat on Sale of Basic Payment Entitlements

Where the proceeds exceed €40,000, the transaction is liable to VAT @23%. The seller must register for VAT but may do so solely in relation to this single transaction. The purchaser of the entitlements is not entitled to reclaim the VAT, unless of course he is registered for VAT in relation to his main farming business.

Universal Social Charge (USC)

The Universal Social Charge is applied to income after deduction of normal expenses including capital allowances. People over 70 years earning less than €60,000 per annum and people on medical cards under 70 earning less than €60,000 per annum will pay a maximum rate of 2.5%. The following persons and sources of income are exempted from the charge:

- All Department of Social Protection Payments.
- Income subject to DIRT.
- Legally enforceable maintenance payments made.
- People with an income of €13,000 or less.

Table 13.9: Rates of Universal Social Charge.

Income after capital allowances	Rate of levy	Amount €	Cumulative €
€0 - €12,012	0.5%	€60.06	€60.06
€12,013 - €25,760	2%	€274.94	€335.00
€25,761 - €70,044	4.%	€1,771.32	€2,106.32
€70,045 - €100.000	8%	€2,396.48	€4,502.80
Over €100.000 (self-employed)	11%	+11% of excess	+11% of excess

The following sources of income are chargeable to the Universal Social Charge:

Income from farm or other profits (after deduction of Capital Allowances).
Rent from any property in Ireland (before deduction of any Land Leasing exemption or designated area relief's).
Income from share dividends from companies based in Ireland.
Forest Premium.
Income from a Personal Pension Scheme.
Legally enforceable maintenance payments received.

INDEX

A
Accident Reporting, **163, 183**
Adversarial System, **121**
Adverse Possession, **128, 172**
Agri-Climate Rural Environment Scheme
(ACRES), **37, 48, 86, 91, 140, 218**
Afforestation, **119, 154**
Afforestation Grant and Premium Scheme, **162**
Agricultural College Open Days, **135**
Agricultural Contractor Charges, **12, 105**
Agricultural Relief, **168, 184, 235, 258**
Agricultural Vehicles, **120, 126**
Altering a Will, **194**
AMRF's, **254**
Animal Fodder Requirements, **111**
Areas of Natural Constraint (ANC), **39**
ARF's, **254**
Ash Dieback, **159**
Averaging of Farm Profits, **235, 245**

B
Basic Payment Scheme, **39**
Beef Data and Genomics Programme (BDGP), **50**
Bereavement Leave, **176**
Basic Income Support for Sustainability (BISS),
8, 37, 60, 104, 140, 174, 192, 218, 235, 261
Boundaries, **48, 120, 127**
Burning of Waste, **120, 128**
Business Property Relief, **168, 235, 260, 269**

C
CAP Reform, **8, 37**
Capital Allowances, **133, 166, 235, 245, 287, 291**
Capital Acquisitions Tax, **16, 185, 197, 235, 254,
264, 271**
Capital Gains Tax **16, 21, 168, 184, 236, 258,
273, 280**
Carbon Tax Relief, **235, 248, 264**
Care Needs Assessment, **231**
Carer's Benefit, **203, 212, 225**

Carer's Allowance, **22, 203, 214, 225**
Carer's Support Grant, **203, 216**
Caveat, **194**
Challenging a Will, **16, 194, 201**
Child Benefit, **22, 203, 216**
Child Minding Income Relief, **243**
Civil Court System, **12, 120**
Complementary Income Support for Young
Farmers Scheme (CIS-YF), **39**
Compulsory Disposal of Livestock, **235, 247**
Compulsory Purchase Order Compensation, **280**
Continuous Cover Forestry, **156, 160**
Contractor Charges, **12, 105**
Contribution Towards Care, **231**
Contributory State Pension, **203, 239**
Conversion Factors, **8, 23**
Converting to Organic, **137**
Court Award Limits, **121**
Complementary Redistributive Income Support
for Sustainability (CRISS), **8, 37, 43**
Crop Diversification, **43**
Crop Storage Requirements, **113**
Cross Border Directive, **203, 226**

D
Dairy Beef Welfare, **64**
Dairy Equipment Scheme, **37, 53**
Dental Benefit, **222**
Deposit Interest Retention Tax, **239**
Discretionary Trusts, **194, 198**
Dismissal Notice, **177**
Domestic Animals, **123**
Domiciliary Care Allowance, **203, 212**
Drugs Payment Scheme, **203, 223**

E
Earned Income Credit, **18, 239, 241, 256**
ECO Schemes, **140**
Eligible Land, **41, 47, 53**
Employers Obligation **14, 163, 176**

INDEX

Employing a Carer, **244**
Entitlements Under a Will, **16, 194, 199**
Entrepreneur Relief, **236, 274**
Exempt Structures, **117**
Exempted Trees, **125**

F

Fair Deal Scheme, **187, 231**
Family Home Relief, **235, 269, 271**
Farm Planning, **8, 28, 69**
Farm Partnerships, **50, 164, 221, 247**
Farm Labour, **14, 163, 174**
Farm Wages **163, 174**
Farm Relief Services **14, 163, 179**
Farm Safety, **14, 37, 52, 58, 60, 68, 163, 180**
Farm Assist, **22, 203, 215, 217, 219, 224, 287**
Farm Restructuring Relief, **236, 279**
Farming Losses, **237**
Favourite Nephew Relief, **235, 271**
Feedstuffs, Relative Value of, **112**
Felling License, **119, 125**
Finished Beef from the Dairy Herd Budget, **78**
Fodder Beet Production Cost, **111**
Forest Premium Rates, **156**
Forest Roads, **154, 159**
Forestry Programme, **154**
Forestry, **154**

G

Gift Tax, **14, 184, 190, 264, 272, 274**
GLAS, **41, 86, 91, 218**
GP Visit Cards, **203, 225**
Grant of Probate, **68, 194, 196, 199**
Grazing Grass Production Cost, **110**
Greening, **41**
Guideline Farm Wages, **163, 174**

H

Hay Production Cost, **109**
Health Expenses, **243**

Hearing Aids, **221, 223**
Hedgerow Cutting, **120, 125, 129, 149**
Heritage Houses and Gardens Relief, **271**
Hill Sheep Budget, **90**
Holidays, **175**
Home Carers Credit, **240**
Horses Transferred to Training, **257**
Horses, Taxation of, **235, 257**
Household Benefits Package, **203, 213, 217, 227**
Housing Aid for Older Persons Scheme, **203, 228**
Housing Adaptation Grant, **203, 228**

I

Imputed Distribution, **254**
Income Tax Credits, **18**
Income Tax Rates and Bands, **20**
Income Tax, **8, 14, 16, 162, 172, 184, 192, 208, 217, 235, 239, 245, 258, 273, 288**
Income Averaging, **133, 193, 208, 245, 256, 262**
Incorporation, **164, 167, 259**
Indexation Relief, **280**
Inheritance Tax Insurance, **14, 184, 191**
Inheritance Rights, **194, 200**
Inheritance Tax, **191, 195, 254, 264, 272**
Inspections, **41, 137,**
Interest on Late Payment of Tax, **237**
Invalidity Pension, **287**

J

Joint Assessment, **238**

K

Kale Production Cost, **111**

L

Land Availability Rule, **40**
Land Leasing, **41, 291**
Leasing of Land, **173**
Legal Aid Board, **121**
Life Assurance, Tax Allowable, **244, 264**

INDEX

Limited Companies, **163, 167, 173, 248, 259**
Limited Company, **16, 59, 164, 167, 186, 235, 246, 249, 255, 258, 269, 287, 290**
Lost Wills, **194, 197**
Low Emission Slurry Spreading Equipment Scheme, **37, 56**

M

Maize Production, **110**
Malting Barley Budget, **93**
Manure, Value of, **105, 108**
Medical Cards, **203, 223, 291**
Medical Cards over 70s, **227**
Medical Expenses, **232, 243, 264**
Mid-Season Lamb Budget, **89**
Mobility Aids Grant Scheme, **203, 228**
Motor Expenses Tax Relief, **235, 248, 249**
Motor Vehicles Tax Allowance, **250**

N

National Reserve, **37, 40, 156, 165**
Native Woodland Conservation scheme, **154, 160**
Nitrates Derogation, **14, 65, 136, 148, 150**
Noxious Weeds, **120, 128**
Nursing Homes Support Scheme, **203, 231**

O

Oil Seed Rape Budget, **99, 104**
One Parent Family Credit, **240**
Optical Benefit, **222**
Organic Capital Investment Scheme, **37, 53, 140**
Organic Farming Scheme, **8, 37, 52, 56, 136, 140**
Organic Farming, **14, 136**
Organic Certification Bodies, **137**
Outpatient, **223**

P

Partnership Law, **164**
Partnerships, **48, 50, 163, 221, 247**
Peas Budget, **101, 104**

Permanent Health Insurance, **243, 288**
Personal Tax Credit, **8, 16, 235, 240, 256**
Personal Pensions, **235, 253**
Pig and Poultry Investment Scheme, **53**
Planning Permission, **53, 70, 113, 117, 151**
Planning Charges, **119**
Plant & Machinery Allowance, **250**
Pollution, Measures to Prevent, **14, 136, 146**
Potatoes Main Crop Budget, **103**
Private Forestry, Taxation of, **235, 258**
Proprietary Estoppel, **194, 202**
Protection of Water Regulations, **14, 136, 142**
Protein Aid Scheme, **45**
PRSI for Self-Employed, **16, 204, 211, 216, 286, 290**
PRSI Class S, **221, 236, 287**
PRSI Voluntary Contributions, **204, 217, 288**
Public Liability, **12, 120**
Public Roads, **120, 124**

Q

Qualified Adult Allowance, **22, 188, 206, 239, 256**

R

Rape Production cost, **111**
Redundancy, **177**
Registered Farm Partnership, **50, 53, 165, 247**
Relative Value of Feedstuffs, **112**
Rent a Room Relief, **242**
Rental Properties, Taxation of, **235, 263**
Restructuring Relief, **236, 279**
Revoking a Will, **194**
Right(s) of Way, **47, 120, 127**
Risk Assessment, **182**
Rural Social Scheme, **203, 220**

S

Same Event Relief, **274**
Sample Will, **198**

INDEX

SCEP, **66**
Section 117, **201**
Section 604A Relief, **236, 280**
Seniors Alert Scheme, **203, 230**
Separate Assessment, **238**
Share Farming, **163, 169**
Share Milking, **164**
Sheep Improvement Scheme, **64**
Silage, Settled Storage Requirement, **113**
Silage, Grass Production Cost, **109**
Single Suckling Budget, **79**
Single Assessment, **238**
Site, Transferring, **279**
Slurry Storage Requirements, **146**
Slurries, Value of, **105, 108**
Sound Mind, **194**
Spreading Periods, **142**
Spring Milk Production Budget, **72**
Spring Barley Budget, **92**
Spring Wheat Budget, **69, 96**
Spring Oats Budget, **69, 98**
Spring Oil Seed Rape Budget, **100**
Squatters Rights, **120, 128, 172**
Stallion Fees, **257**
Stamp Duty, **16, 168, 173, 184, 192, 236, 247, 258, 263, 266, 283**
Stamp Duty On Leases, **173, 284**
Stamp Duty – Young, Trained Farmers, **168, 192, 247, 260, 283**
State Pension, Contributory, **203, 239**
Stock Relief, **135, 167, 192, 235, 246, 264, 285**
Straw Incorporation Measure, **37, 45**
Stubble Turnips Production Cost, **111**
Student Maintenance Grant, **134**
Succession Planning, **64, 174, 186, 189,**
Succession Farm Partnership, **166, 235, 245, 260, 264, 285**
Succession Farm Partnership Tax Relief, **264**
Suckler Carbon Efficiency Programme, **37, 50,**
56

Summer Grazing Budget, **84**
Support for Sustainability, **8, 37, 42, 60, 65, 150, 156,**
Surcharge on Late Submissions, **237**

T
TAMS, **8, 37, 52, 140, 151, 165, 260,**
Teagasc Course Charge, **12, 130, 134**
Third Level Education Fees, **242**
Three Year Cap, **232**
Tillage Capital Investment Scheme, **37, 53, 59**
Towing – Licensing Rules, **120, 127**
Trading Structures, **164**
Treatment Benefit Scheme, **203, 221, 287**
Tree Preservation Order, **124**
Trees – Overhanging, **124**
Trespassers, **120**

U
Unfair Dismissal, **178**
Universal Social Charge, **16, 162, 168, 219, 236, 239, 255, 258, 291**

V
Value Added Tax, **16, 236, 258, 290**
Voluntary Contributions, PRSI, **204, 217, 288**

W
Water Regulations, **14, 136, 142**
Widowed Parent Grant, **203, 212**
Widow's Contributory Pension, **203, 211**
Wills, **16, 194**

NOTES

NOTES

NOTES

NOTES

NOTES

NOTES

NOTES

NOTES

 **FDC GROUP**

SUPPORTING IRISH FARMERS

FDC Agri-Consultants guide you through Department of Ag schemes. Our team of experts understands the complexities of government regulations and can help you navigate the process from start to finish. Whether you're looking to apply for a grant or need assistance with compliance, we're here to help.

FARM TRANSFERS
ACRES PLANS AND ASSESSMENTS
BEEF DATA GENOMICS
COMPLIANCE REPORTS
CARBON NAVIGATOR & NITRATES DEROGATIONS
YOUNG FARMERS SCHEME / NATIONAL RESERVE
BASIC INCOME SUPPORT FOR SUSTAINABILITY (BISS)

Talk To Our Experts
At Your Local Branch Today!

SCAN ME

Scan the QR
code for an
office near you.
www.fdc.ie